Reclaiming Accountability

Reclaiming Accountability

Transparency, Executive Power,
and the U.S. Constitution

HEIDI KITROSSER

THE UNIVERSITY OF CHICAGO PRESS   CHICAGO AND LONDON

HEIDI KITROSSER is professor of law at the University of Minnesota.

The University of Chicago Press, Chicago 60637
The University of Chicago Press, Ltd., London
© 2015 by The University of Chicago
All rights reserved. Published 2015.
Printed in the United States of America

24 23 22 21 20 19 18 17 16 15   1 2 3 4 5

ISBN-13: 978-0-226-19163-8 (cloth)
ISBN-13: 978-0-226-19177-5 (e-book)
DOI: 10.7208/chicago/9780226191775.001.0001

Library of Congress Cataloging-in-Publication Data

Kitrosser, Heidi, author.
  Reclaiming accountability : transparency, executive power, and the U.S. Constitution /
Heidi Kitrosser.
        pages ; cm
  Includes bibliographical references and index.
  ISBN 978-0-226-19163-8 (cloth : alk. paper) — ISBN 978-0-226-19177-5 (e-book)
  1. Executive power—United States. 2. Government accountability—United States.
3. Executive privilege (Government information)—United States. 4. Transparency in
government—United States. 5. Executive power—United States. 6. Constitutional law—
United States. I. Title.
  KF5050.K58 2015
  342.73'066—dc23

                                    2014016928

Curiosity is insubordination in its purest form.

VLADIMIR NABOKOV

Contents

CHAPTER ONE

The Constitutional Law of Government Secrecy

Transparency and Accountability

Americans long have treated government accountability as a birthright. This spirit is manifest in calls by today's Tea Partiers to "take our country back" and in earlier cries to the same effect by opponents of the George W. Bush administration. It is embodied in Senator Howard Baker's repeated demand throughout the Watergate hearings that Nixon administration officials reveal what the president knew and when he knew it. It is present when federal courts "review the legality of the President's official conduct" or "direct appropriate process to the President himself."[1] And it sounds throughout writings from the founding era, both in Anti-Federalist warnings that the new Constitution created a monarchy and in Federalist responses that the president had only narrow powers and would be overseen by the people and their representatives.

But like any old and dearly held ideal, accountability frequently is tossed about in a rhetorically effective but substantively empty way. The philosopher John Stuart Mill once observed that "however true [an opinion] may be, if it is not fully, frequently, and fearlessly discussed, it will be held as a dead dogma, not a living truth."[2] And so it is with invocations of accountability. We Americans frequently say that those in government "work for us" and must "answer to us," but too often we fail to grapple with the conditions that must be in place before we can meaningfully assess what our government is up to and can hold it accountable for the same.

This is perhaps truest with respect to matters of secrecy and transparency in government. Accountability, at bottom, demands that one actor have the ability "to demand an explanation or justification of another actor for its actions and to reward or punish that second actor on the basis of its performance or its explanation."[3] To have this ability, the first actor must be able to access information necessary to assess the second actor. More so, the first actor must be able meaningfully to respond to this information, whether at the ballot box, in the courts, by taking steps to make the information available more widely, or otherwise. Yet while Americans routinely voice support for transparency and accountability in the abstract, we too often tolerate, even embrace, secrecy with few questions asked when secret keepers utter the words "national security" or invoke principles of executive discretion.

To be sure, secrecy in government is neither categorically unjustified nor intrinsically antithetical to accountability. The government plainly needs to keep some information secret. And there are ways to reconcile secrecy with accountability. This book's concern is not secrecy per se, but rather, unchecked secrecy. Secrecy is unchecked, for instance, where the executive branch keeps the very fact of a program's existence from the other branches and the people. It also is unchecked where no other actors—whether the judiciary, members of Congress, or members of the public or press—can access information about a program beyond what the executive branch chooses to tell them. Insufficient checking breeds unnecessary, even counterproductive, secrecy. It also is deeply antithetical to accountability.

Secrecy and Executive Power

Excessive secrecy is partly a product of the executive branch's very nature. This is not to suggest that secrecy is never abused by Congress or the courts. It is, and such abuses merit attention in their own rights. But the problem is most severe and most intransigent in the executive branch. Unlike Congress, which acts predominantly through publicly recorded legislation and through partly public oversight, and the judiciary, which wields power mainly through the force of written public opinions, the executive branch's major tasks are not intrinsically transparent. The executive's most basic job, after all, is to execute the laws passed by Congress. While the Constitution prescribes a legislative process that is fairly open and dialogic, it does not and feasibly could not lay out detailed processes by which infinite pieces of legislation are to be executed. Absent congressionally mandated procedures to foster transparency in law execution, laws can be implemented largely in the dark. Furthermore, as the government's "doer" branch, the executive has unique access to its human and technological resources. Unlike Congress, which can draft legislation but lacks the tools to implement it, and the judiciary, which announces but lacks the means to execute legal rulings, the president is uniquely equipped for self-propelled action. Such actions—whether unauthorized or even barred by statutes—can take place in secret because interbranch assistance is not required.[4]

The executive's innate advantages, both generally and for secret keeping, are dramatically compounded by the rise of what Arthur Schlesinger Jr. famously called "the imperial presidency." As Schlesinger and others have explained, multiple cultural, historical, and technological phenomena have expanded the power of the executive branch relative to countervailing forces. Among other things, the human and technological resources at the executive's disposal have increased exponentially.[5] The executive not only has more capacity to instigate activities unilaterally than ever before, but it has more resources at its disposal to keep those activities secret. Not least among these resources is an enormous classification system, one that did not exist outside of the military until 1951.[6]

In speaking of the imperial presidency and the presidency generally, it is important to understand that these terms encompass much more than the president himself. They effectively include all actors within the vast and sprawling U.S. bureaucracy who can claim to act for the president. These individuals range from White House staffers in close contact with the president, to personnel throughout the Executive Office of the President, to employees deep within the bureaucracy who take orders from political appointees who answer ultimately to the president, to the millions of persons with some form of authority to classify information based on presidential classification orders.[7] The very reach of "the presidency" exacerbates its imperialism, including its expansive capacity to keep secrets. Indeed, power exercised in the president's name can, paradoxically, obscure the very fact of personal knowledge or involvement by the president. Consider the controversy involving the removal of U.S. attorneys during the administration of George W. Bush. Though U.S. attorneys by statute serve at the president's pleasure, the removal and replacement of several of them in the middle of President Bush's second term caused no end of mystery as to who made what decisions and why, prompting one columnist to joke that "magical pixies" had done the job.[8]

Similarly, much of the Iran-Contra controversy during the Reagan administration involved Congress's efforts to determine who did what when and on what authority, and whether the president knew what was going on. Indeed, John Poindexter, national security advisor to President Reagan, claimed that he limited what he told the president so as to give him "future deniability."[9]

How Constitutional Arguments Advance Government Secrecy

Increasingly, constitutional arguments are among the forces that foster executive secrecy, justifying and staving off checks on the same. For example, both the Obama and George W. Bush administrations have repeatedly invoked the "state secrets" doctrine to urge courts to dismiss lawsuits alleging illegal government activities. When Congress considered legislation in 2008 to limit the state secrets privilege, the Bush administration deemed it an unconstitutional interference with the president's discretion to keep secrets. While the Obama administration declined to comment on the state secrets legislation when it was reintroduced in 2009, it has claimed a constitutional prerogative to disregard statutory transparency directives in other contexts. Both the Obama and Bush administrations claimed such a prerogative with respect to statutes requiring them to notify the congressional intelligence committees of certain programs. Furthermore, while resisting inquiries into alleged executive branch wrongdoing, both administrations have aggressively pursued those who leaked information about such activities. Each has suggested that leakers warrant little if any protection under the First Amendment in light of the president's broad constitutional discretion to protect national security. Outside of the national security realm, presidents of both parties repeatedly have argued that the president has a constitutional prerogative to prevent executive branch employees from testifying to Congress without White House preclearance or from disseminating information to the public without such prior review.[10]

This book refers to constitutional arguments against checking the president's capacities, including secret-keeping capacities, as "presidentialist" arguments. Such arguments can undermine accountability by facilitating largely unchecked information control. The term "information control" denotes both government secrecy and government efforts to manipulate the information that the public sees or that select groups (for example, congressional committees) receive. Constitutionalizing information control tends to stunt accountability both directly and at a meta-level. The latter occurs when presidentialism undermines meaningful debate about law, policy, and case-by-case decisions regarding government secrecy. The invocation or even potential invocation of presidentialist arguments too often shuts down, rather than stimulates, debate over the arguments' merits or the costs and benefits of secrecy in a given case. This stunting effect is reflected in public discourse and in congressional and judicial behavior. The effect is attributable partly to the nature of presidentialist secrecy arguments. Citing the president's unique structural capacities and political visibility, presidentialists demand full or near-complete presidential discretion to determine when and if secrecy is warranted in a given case. Thus, presidentialism lends itself to tautologies to the effect that secrecy is necessary because the president says so, and that interbranch checks on the president's judgment at best are ineffectual (because only the president has the expertise and can safely access all information necessary to make the judgment) and at worst dangerous (because the other branches might make poor decisions given their lack of expertise or might leak the information that the president says must remain secret).

Of course, the other branches, the public, and the media could push back against such tautologies, and they do so at times. Yet presidentialist secrecy arguments often short-circuit, rather than generate, discussion among these actors. In public discourse, the stunting effect is attributable partly to a perception on the part of the public and the press of their relative ignorance. Hence, they may accept even specious constitutional assertions as debating trump cards.

Apart from sheepishness by nonexperts to challenge executive assertions on constitutional law, the executive branch has powerful means to shape public and interbranch perceptions of its own power's legal scope. For one thing, the executive branch has a formidable legal infrastructure in the Department of Justice, particularly its Office of Legal Counsel (OLC). As the office that advises the president on the legality of his actions, the OLC is enormously influential. Because many executive power issues never reach the courts, or do so only long after the president has acted, the OLC's legal opinions often are determinative.[11] And while the OLC need not always act with a pro-executive bent, its position within the executive branch and presidential appointment of its head and of the attorney general (AG) incline it in that direction structurally.[12] The OLC and the Department of Justice advance the cause of presidentialism in important ways. First, the attorney general—or other executive branch offi-cers, speaking under the AG's direction or that of the OLC—at times has reached out to the public directly to advocate presidentialism.[13] Second, the OLC's opinions constitute a body of in-depth legal analysis, struc-turally tilted toward the executive, without any real peer in Congress or the judiciary. Administrations can point to OLC opinions to argue that their own assertions of power are not new or that they follow naturally from precedent.[14] Third, since at least the Reagan administration—when the West Publishing Company began, at the administration's request, to include presidential signing statements in legislative histories—signing statements, too, have been treated by administrations as vehicles for pres-identialist precedent.[15]

Furthermore, members of Congress often bow with little debate to ac-tual or potential presidentialist arguments against disclosing information. There are at least three reasons for this phenomenon. First, it often is not in the political interests of individual congresspersons to be fully in-formed as to what is going on in the executive branch. Where the choice is between knowing enough to be held responsible should things go awry versus retaining ignorance and preserving the flexibility to align with or distance one's self from presidential actions as events develop, igno-rance can be bliss. This is particularly, though not exclusively, true in the realm of national security. From this perspective, presidentialist argu-ments for secrecy are a godsend, enabling congresspersons to claim that they would like to know more but that their hands are tied by the Con-stitution.[16] Second, founding assurances that Congress will demand infor-mation from the president as a means to oversee and check him were grounded in the assumption that the interests of individual congressper-sons would be aligned with that of their respective institutions, the House of Representatives and the Senate. Hence, while the president might fight to keep secrets, members of Congress would surely fight back to protect their institutions' oversight functions.[17] What the founders did not antic-ipate, however, was the rise of partisan politics and presidents as party leaders in the United States. Congresspersons who share a party affilia-tion with the president frequently vote to defend the interests of "their" president and party rather than the constitutional prerogatives of their institutions.[18] Third, the mere possibility that the White House will make a presidentialist secrecy claim can deter congresspersons from demand-ing information in the first place. While information disputes between the White House and Congress rarely result in judicial review, they can delay inquiries so dramatically as to make information requests futile. For instance, the chair of the House Government Reform Committee noted his reluctance to subpoena the Bush administration for documents related to Hurricane Katrina, explaining that a subpoena "would be tied up in court by the administration until the Committee's writ had expired."[19]

Federal courts, too, can be quite willing to forgo direct factual or legal analyses of presidentialist secrecy claims in the name of deferring to the constitutional prerogatives of the executive. In 2004, for example, the U.S. Supreme Court held that Vice President Richard Cheney could evade a broad discovery order without formally raising an executive privilege claim, as requiring him to invoke the privilege with particularity would itself unduly burden executive power.[20] And in the realm of national security, it is increasingly common for courts to dismiss entire cases on the basis of executive branch assertions that litigation would reveal important state secrets, without the courts examining the evidence to assess the accuracy of the executive's claims. Such cases, too, are underscored by an implicit and sometimes explicit notion that the president alone has the constitutional prerogative to determine what information is too dangerous to reveal.[21]

Despite the relative independence of federal courts from politics, courts' frequent willingness to defer to claims of executive prerogative without serious inquiry can be traced to at least three factors. First, federal judges are appointed by the president and confirmed by the Senate. To the extent that a president deems it a priority to maintain or broaden the scope of his powers, he can take this into account in selecting a nominee.[22] And as presidentialist views increasingly enter the legal and political mainstream and prove consistent with the political incentives of many in Congress, such views may positively help, and at minimum not hurt, nominees in attaining Senate confirmation. Second, federal judges are not immune to the lure of what Schlesinger called the "presidential mystique." The mystique is a cultural feature of the imperial presidency. It amounts to a belief that the president alone has the knowledge, expertise, resources, and other tools to discern what is best for the nation.[23] From this perspective, it is pointless at best and damaging at worst to require presidents or other high-level officials to explain in detail, even in camera to a judge, why secrecy is required. While the mystique has particular purchase in the realm of national security, the scope of that realm and its porous boundaries make the reach of the mystique long indeed.[24] Third, courts have strong institutional incentives to avoid decisions that could undermine their legitimacy either by straying far beyond the bounds of public opinion or by risking the executive branch's refusal to cooperate. There thus is an institutional basis for judicial attraction to constitutional doctrines that foreclose serious probing of executive branch secrecy claims. The strength of that attraction correlates with the degree to which presidentialist secrecy arguments are considered legitimate in mainstream legal and political circles.

As the discussion thus far reflects, there is a cyclical relationship between presidential imperialism and presidentialist argument. Most fundamentally, presidents and their partisans long have sought, unsurprisingly, to push to the limits the capacities intrinsic in the presidency's role and structure—its relative "secrecy . . . and dispatch."[25] They also have sought to characterize these capacities as "rights." Hence, for many presidentialists, the president's *capacity* to keep secrets means that he must have a constitutional *right* to keep secrets.[26] To the extent that presidentialist arguments succeed, they facilitate greater secrecy and greater unilateral exercise of presidential capacities. Such expanded use of presidential capacities is exacerbated yet further by other building blocks of presidential imperialism, including government growth, broadened international commitments, technological change, and a deepened cultural belief in the president as the symbolic and practical font of all national triumphs and tragedies.[27] As presidential capacities and their discretionary uses of the same broaden, so such discretion is increasingly normalized in the eyes of the public and the other branches. These developments make presidentialist arguments seem more intuitive. Such arguments thus become more viable politically.

Another important aspect of this cycle is the use of "evolving history"—often called "historical gloss"—arguments.[28] Some presidentialists argue that a power exercised by previous presidents becomes a constitutional right by virtue of its past assertion. This can occur even when earlier presidents exercised such powers fully or partly in secret so that the other branches or the public lacked meaningful opportunities to object. From an evolving history perspective, past unilateral uses of the president's capacities—including secrecy itself as well as acts enabled by secrecy—can create constitutional rights to exercise such capacities free from statutory or judicial abridgement.[29] These arguments get a boost from the executive's formidable legal infrastructure, which bootstraps from past presidential actions to support later actions. Such bootstrapping tends to be a "one-way ratchet in favor of expanding the power of the presidency." Legal scholar William Marshall observes, for example, that some presidentialists invoke President Lincoln's suspension of habeas corpus to support broad presidential powers in times of war or emergency. Yet, as Marshall explains, "[t]he fact is that every President but Lincoln did *not* suspend habeas corpus. But it is a President's action in using power, rather than forsaking its use, that has the precedential significance. In this manner, every extraordinary use of power by one President expands the availability of executive branch power for use by future Presidents."[30]

The cycle is also perpetuated and catalyzed by presidentialism's shadow effect. By shadow effect, I mean the effect that a legal theory or doctrine has even when it is not explicitly invoked in a particular case. A shadow effect of executive privilege, for example, is the fact that congresspersons may forgo seeking information in the first place, or may give up after an initial refusal, because they suspect that their continued insistence will result in nothing more than a years-long court battle. A more subtle shadow effect enabled candidate Barack Obama to criticize the Bush administration for invoking claims of a presidentialist prerogative to bypass statutory limits on electronic surveillance and torture, while leaving room for President Obama to deride proposed investigations into such actions as "backward-looking" and potential "witch hunt[s]."[31] President Obama could credibly state the latter without directly defending presidentialism because the constant repetition by others of presidentialist arguments to support the programs had done the work for him. Through their very ubiquity, the arguments created a public sense that the legal questions are so hopelessly contested as to boil down to petty political differences. The arguments thus cast a shadow in which the president could stand.[32] Congresspersons of both parties also have benefited from presidentialism's shadow effect. The shadow effect of arguments against congressional disclosure requirements, for example, removes much of the political onus from congressional intelligence committee members to push back (and to take the political risks of so doing) against presidential refusals to disclose information to which the committees are statutorily entitled.[33]

Presidentialism Meets Substantive Accountability

For all of its influence, presidentialism badly misreads the Constitution. Yet before presidentialism can effectively be countered, it must first be understood. This book's agenda thus is partly descriptive. The book endeavors, first, simply to describe presidentialism and its major component parts—"supremacy" and "unitary executive theory"—in a clear and accessible manner. Second, the book details how supremacy and unitary executive theory manifest themselves as arguments for a broad presidential power to control information. In these two descriptive aspects, the book aims to be of use to readers ranging from nonlawyers to constitutional experts. For the former, the book explains concepts that readers likely hear bandied about in political and legal debates but that are rarely explained in any depth. For the latter, the book builds on concepts that may already be familiar in isolation—such as executive privilege, state secrets doctrine, unitary executive theory, and the clash between government secrecy and the First Amendment—to craft a comprehensive study of the relationship between constitutional theories of presidential power and government secrecy.

The book's descriptive elements lay the groundwork for its own constitutional arguments, which constitute its third and fourth pieces. One argument is that the Constitution situates the presidency within what I call a "substantive accountability framework." This framework entails substantial congressional and judicial leeway to impose and enforce external and internal checks on presidential power to foster transparency and accountability. The second argument, closely related to the first, is that supremacy and unitary executive theory misread the Constitution.

Presidentialism and Its Connection to Government Secrecy

Presidentialism is comprised of two main categories of constitutional argument. The first is "presidential supremacy." Supremacists deem the president to have broad legal prerogatives to make decisions that he deems necessary to protect the country or his ability to execute the law, even in the face of contrary statutory or judicial directives. To supremacists, laws constraining the president's ability to collect intelligence through the wiretapping or interrogation methods of his choosing, or to keep secrets as he deems necessary to protect national security or candor in his deliberations, tend to stray from the constitutional design.

Supremacy encompasses, but is not limited to, the school of thought sometimes called "exclusivity." Exclusivity is the view that statutes that unduly restrict the president's discretion in either his commander-in-chief or executive capacity are unconstitutional.[34] Exclusivity impacts transparency in a number of ways. Most obviously, exclusivity can be used to justify presidential circumvention of statutory openness requirements. It undermines transparency even more fundamentally when it is used to justify secret law. Secret law is made when the president not only circumvents a statute, but does so in secret, pursuant to a secret policy or legal rationale. In such cases the president effectively amends public law without the knowledge of the public or the other branches and without going through the relatively transparent, deliberative processes mandated by Article I, § 7, of the Constitution.[35]

Supremacist secrecy claims also include nonexclusivist arguments to the effect that Congress and the courts cannot second-guess presidential judgments as to the need for secrecy. For example, an executive privilege argument is a claim by the president or another high-level executive branch officer of a constitutional right to withhold requested information from Congress, the courts, or persons or agencies empowered by statute to receive information. Some executive privilege claims are exclusivist, in that they object to—or justify circumventing—legislation demanding some degree of public or interbranch transparency. But executive privilege claims can also take the form of nonexclusivist objections to congressional information requests made through House or Senate rules or judicial information requests made under inherent judicial power.[36]

A second presidentialist approach is called unitary executive theory, or "unity" for short. To unity's supporters, the question is not, as with supremacists, how much power Congress or the courts must cede to the executive branch. Rather, the question is, of whatever executive power legitimately exists in the United States, does the president have discretionary control over all of it? To unity proponents, the answer must be yes. This means that the president must have the prerogative to fire at will or act in place of administrators charged with promulgating or enforcing regulations. For example, should Congress delegate power to an agency to pass and enforce clean air regulations, the president must have full control of the process and its players. Absent such control, presidential energy and accountability are hopelessly diffused.[37]

Modern manifestations of unity include presidentially mandated review of agency testimony and reports by the Office of Management and Budget, which sits within the Executive Office of the President. Such review presents opportunities for politically motivated information control. Unity also is manifest in arguments against statutory restrictions on the president's ability freely to hire and fire agency personnel throughout the administrative state who perform discretionary executive acts. Such arguments are directed toward broadening political supervision and control within agencies. Such broadening, in turn, creates opportunities for intra-agency political control over the information that agency scientists and other experts convey to the public and the other branches.[38]

The Trouble with Presidentialism

Both unitary executive theory and presidential supremacy theories are mistaken on a number of fronts. For example, presidential supremacists correctly observe that the president structurally is equipped to act with qualities of secrecy and vigor, and that the founders extolled these presidential capacities. Yet supremacists fatally overplay their hand by conflating these capacities with a right to exercise them largely free from interbranch limits and checks. Unitary executive theorists, too, overread the relevant evidence. For instance, unity proponents emphasize that the founders decided not to annex an advisory council to the president or to establish a multiheaded presidency, opting instead for "unity" at the head of the executive branch. From a unitary president they extrapolate to a unitary executive branch in which the president has a legal discretion not simply to oversee, but to personally make all discretionary executive decisions. They do this despite the facts that a unitary executive branch head is a very different thing from a unitary executive branch, and the founders expressed varied, conflicting, and often downright confused views on the degree of control that the Constitution provides the president over executive decisions and officers.

The most fundamental failing of presidentialist approaches—which connects in myriad ways to their more specific flaws of historical, textual, and structural analysis—is their troubled relationship to accountability. Neither supremacy nor unitary executive theory simply ignores accountability. To the contrary, each—especially the latter—claims accountability as an advantage. Each approach relies in part on the founding decision to establish a single president rather than a multimember executive body, and each cites the advantages that the founders linked to a unitary president. As noted, these advantages include the president's capacity for energy, encompassing qualities of secrecy, vigor and dispatch. The founders also touted the greater responsibility, or accountability, of a single person. Supremacists and unity theorists thus seek to bolster their respective conclusions that the founders adopted a supremacist or unity model

by explaining that they did so in part to foster accountability. Supremacists and unity theorists also independently cite accountability as a functional advantage of their respective theories, apart from its tie to their respective readings of history, text, and constitutional structure. For each
theory, the core functional points are similar: The president alone is politically responsible to the entire national electorate. He is also uniquely
visible. Apart from the president's direct responsibility to the public,
Congress can hold him accountable politically, including through impeachment and the power of the purse. To vest power in the president—
whether all discretionary executive power, from a unitary perspective, or
the bulk of national security related decision making, from a supremacist
perspective—is to vest it in the nation's most politically responsive, visible, and accountable being.

Incredibly, presidentialists overlook the extent to which their own
theories enable and excuse accountability-defeating information control.
To draw an example from the realm of supremacy, consider a defense of
the Terrorist Surveillance Program (TSP)—through which the Bush administration secretly violated the Foreign Intelligence Surveillance Act
(FISA) for four years—by former Bush administration official John Yoo.
Yoo explained that "Congress could easily eliminate the surveillance program ... simply by cutting off all funds for it. It could also link approval
of administration policies in related areas to agreement on changes to
the ... program. Congress could refuse to confirm cabinet members, sub-
cabinet members, or military intelligence officers unless it prevails" with
respect to the program.[39] Yet these assurances assume that the program
is transparent. This assumption runs smack into the reality of the TSP's
several-years-long secrecy, and defenses of a presidential discretion to determine when information—including the fact of an entire program like
the TSP—cannot be disclosed. Similarly, Yoo's suggestion that Congress
"could hold extensive hearings that bring to light [programs like the TSP]
and that require ... officials to appear and be held to account,"[40] flies in
the face of executive privilege and related supremacist assertions of a
presidential discretion to determine when information may not be shared
with Congress.

Eric Posner and Adrian Vermeule make a similar move in discussing
executive accountability. Their emphasis is not on what the Constitution
requires, but rather on what types of checks do and do not cultivate accountability as a practical matter. They conclude that the executive is relatively unconstrained by legal checks but that this is not a problem because

the executive is constrained by political checks including voting, whistleblowing, media reporting, and monitoring by engaged and educated elites.[41] Yet their analysis overlooks the dependence of political checks on legal safeguards. It overlooks, for instance, the extent to which the First Amendment—both through its shadow effect and through its occasional active invoking—provides a zone of legal safety within which the media and whistleblowers operate. It also ignores the extent to which information access statutes facilitate news gathering that aids media coverage and other public monitoring and that can trigger the use of other legal tools including congressional oversight.[42]

Presidentialists' oversimplified approach to accountability manifests itself not only in functional reasoning but in textual, structural, and historical analyses. For example, unity proponents rely partly, as noted, on the founding decision against annexing an advisory council to the president. In so doing, unity proponents cite founding fears that the president would hide behind his council, blaming it for his own poor decisions and thus defeating accountability. From this, unity proponents leap to the conclusion that the founders wanted the president to have full control over all discretionary executive decisions and executive officers. Yet this conclusion massively oversimplifies the nature of the council debate. Council opponents focused on features specific to the proposed council, including its small size and its ability to collude with the president in relative secrecy. Notably, they also feared that the president and his council would seek to appoint executive branch officers who "possess[ed] the necessary insignificance and pliancy to render them the obsequious instruments of [the president's] pleasure."[43] At minimum, the council debate, centering as it did on the specific features of the proposed council, simply did not address whether the executive branch must in all respects be unitary. If anything, the accountability-related concerns articulated in the debate suggest that the founders feared full presidential control over executive branch decision making and officers. Unfettered control could, among other things, foster secretive collusions between the president and those in his thrall.

Reclaiming Accountability: The Constitution's Substantive Accountability Framework

If presidentialists get the Constitution wrong, who gets it right? Roughly speaking, those who champion robust roles for Congress and the courts in

setting and enforcing statutory checks—checks both internal and external to the executive branch—on presidential power, in overseeing executive behavior, and in carefully scrutinizing executive refusals to provide
requested information, get matters basically right. In a sense, this point
is very simple—it could be summed up in the phrase "checks and balances." Yet the point requires thorough unpacking for at least two reasons.
First, while the concept of checks and balances on presidential power is
simple and well tread at its most basic level, it—like its parent concept
of accountability—has gone somewhat stale from lack of sustained inquiry. Like accountability itself, it must be "fully, frequently, and fearlessly
discussed" to avoid becoming but a "dead dogma."[44] Second, the point
of full discussion is not simply to relearn old lessons, but to refine them
as warranted by experience and reflection. This book does just that with
"old" concepts of accountability, transparency, and checks and balances as
they relate to the president's constitutional powers. Specifically, it develops an analytical framework that reconciles the Constitution's structural
and historical promise of a presidency that will bear traits of "energy,"
including the ability to operate in secret, with its promise of presidential
accountability.

This book explains that the Constitution situates the presidency within
a "substantive accountability framework." As a matter of terminology, this
book refers both to the framework itself and to the "substantive accountability approach" as an interpretive view consistent with the framework.
As the framework's name suggests, substantive accountability—that is,
the ability of the people or another branch to "demand an explanation
or justification" of the president or his subordinates "for [their] actions
and to reward or punish [them] on the basis of [their] performance or
its explanation"[45]—is at the framework's core, and thus at the heart of
the constitutional scheme for the presidency. Substantive accountability
demands two sets of conditions. First, the public and the other branches
must have means to respond to presidential misdeeds. Second, and most
fundamentally, the public and the other branches must have mechanisms
to discover and assess such misdeeds in the first place. Substantive accountability permits, even demands, flexibility for political and legal
actors to experiment with measures that enable the people and the other
branches to discover and respond to executive wrongdoing.

Substantive accountability encompasses, but goes well beyond, the
mechanisms of *formal accountability*. The latter concept fixates on one or
two mechanisms by which the public or the other branches can formally

respond to executive behavior—such as the ballot box or impeachment—but concerns itself little with whether those mechanisms are rendered ineffective by information control. Formal accountability thus includes some avenues for response to presidential behavior. Yet it says little about the ability of the people and the other branches to learn of this behavior, beyond what the president wishes for them to know, in the first place.

The Constitution's substantive accountability framework consists of two constitutional principles and three mechanisms to effectuate those principles. The first principle is substantive accountability itself. The second is substantive accountability's corollary principle of "contained energy." The concept of contained energy embodies the twofold notion that the presidency is endowed with energetic capacities, including a secret-keeping capacity, and that this energy must be contained by accountability-generating mechanisms.

The first mechanism through which substantive accountability and its corollary are effectuated is macro-transparency. Macro-transparency is the constitutional phenomenon whereby the laws that the executive executes are the products of a transparent and deliberative process. While those laws may license the executive to implement them in secret—in short, to engage in micro-secrecy—the fact that the laws themselves are publicly known and produced through a relatively transparent process keeps their execution within reach of the people and the other branches. Macro-transparency keeps laws' execution, in short, tethered to opportunities for checking. This mixture of a macro-transparency directive with the potential for micro-secrecy is echoed in other constitutional relationships aside from that of lawmaking and law execution. It is echoed, for instance, in the relationship between a ratifying Senate and fund controlling legislature with a treaty negotiating and implementing president.

The second mechanism by which the Constitution protects substantive accountability is by providing for the creation and use of accountability tools. Because laws may be executed abusively or incompetently or even circumvented, and because these risks are heightened by executive energy—particularly secret-keeping capacity—Congress has substantial leeway to create tools that enable its members or others to investigate, bring to light, and respond to executive misconduct. Some of these tools are directly granted to Congress in the Constitution, such as the impeachment power. Some are implicit in Congress's power to "make all Laws which shall be necessary and proper for carrying into Execution" Congress's own enumerated powers and those of the executive branch.[46]

Oversight tools created through the latter power must themselves surmount the checks intrinsic in the macro-transparent legislative process—
including their presentation to the president with an opportunity for his
veto—to come into being. The Constitution grants other accountability
tools directly to the people and the press through First Amendment rights
to report on and criticize government. Other tools are internal to the executive branch. One internal tool is the intrinsic possibility that officers
may report on others' misconduct. This possibility is bolstered by protections that such officers may claim under the First Amendment. It is bolstered also by Congress's leeway to structure the executive branch to facilitate internal checking through whistleblower protections or otherwise.

The final piece of the substantive accountability framework is extraordinary prerogative. Extraordinary prerogative is a highly circumscribed
presidential leeway to depart from statutory law. Presidential energy and
historic rationales for the same suggest that the president must have discretion to act unilaterally to preserve the nation when—but only when—
there is no time for Congress first to enact or amend statutes to avert
catastrophe. The limited nature of this exception is as crucial as its substance. Without such limits the exception would swallow the constitutional rule that lawmaking is a deliberative, collaborative, and macro-
transparent process. Any deviations from statutory limits must be timed
to coincide not only with an emergency but also with the period in that
emergency before new legislation can reasonably be sought through the
ordinary lawmaking process. Accountability tools are the means through
which the limits of extraordinary prerogative are enforced. For example,
absent meaningful First Amendment protection for internal executive
branch whistleblowers and the press, congressional power to demand information about executive branch activities, and judicial power to scrutinize executive efforts to block lawsuits through state secrets claims, the
president could too easily hide legal transgressions.

The Chapters That Follow

The chapter that follows this one gets to the very root of things by exploring the methodology and politics of constitutional interpretation and their
relationship to presidential power. It identifies key methodological flaws
underlying presidentialism and details the methodologies underlying the
substantive accountability approach. Chapter 3 elaborates on the justifi-

cations for the substantive accountability framework. It also details the framework's content as it relates to external checks on presidential power. Chapter 4 outlines and refutes the major justifications for supremacy. Supremacy is substantive accountability's antithesis with respect to external checks on presidential power. Chapter 5 details how supremacy manifests itself in defenses or assertions of government secrecy against external checks on presidential power. The chapter focuses, through a range of examples spanning administrations and political parties, on executive privilege, state secrets privilege, justifications for executive branch programs that amount to secret law, and arguments that persons who leak or publish classified information warrant little if any First Amendment protection from prosecution. Chapter 6 analyzes judicial precedent relating to executive and state secrets privileges, the phenomenon of secret law, and First Amendment protections for leaks and publications of classified information. Chapter 7 revisits the task of describing and justifying the substantive accountability framework, this time insofar as the framework relates to internal checks on presidential power. The chapter also discusses relevant judicial precedent. Chapter 8 demonstrates through examples how unity—which is substantive accountability's antithesis with respect to internal checks on presidential power—can undermine substantive accountability and how disunity can further it. Chapter 9 concludes with thoughts on how substantive accountability advocates can move forward from here.

Putting This Project in Perspective

Much has been said by scholars, journalists, and others about government secrecy and presidential power. This book references many of these works, disagreeing with some and building on others. Still, it is easy for one to get lost in the thicket of existing literature. This section thus explicitly situates the book within, and explains its core contributions to, the literature.

The book focuses on one aspect of the many issues raised by secrecy, accountability, and presidential power. Specifically, it focuses on the role of U.S. constitutional law. This choice of emphasis is by no means premised on the notion that secrecy, accountability, and presidential power are solely matters of formalistic legal argument. To the contrary, this book acknowledges the vast influence of other forces, including political and cultural factors. Yet it demonstrates that constitutional arguments frequently accompany and bolster these other forces, whether as direct tools wielded by political actors or as shadow factors that influence public opinion and indirectly shape the range of viable judicial and political options. This book thus illustrates constitutional analysis's substantial supporting role in government secrecy and in disputes over the same. Furthermore, the book directly engages the substance of the relevant constitutional debates.

In explicating and engaging the relevant constitutional debates, this book adds to the existing literature in several respects. In its descriptive aspects, the book identifies the intellectual and practical connections between manifestations of presidential supremacy that typically are studied in isolation from one another. Indeed, this book coins the term "presidential supremacy" as an umbrella under which executive privilege, state secrets privilege, the phenomenon of secret law, and classified speech prosecutions fall. This grouping illuminates the concepts' shared intellectual foundations, their combined practical effects, and their related historical and political trajectories. This book also breaks new descriptive ground in revealing the theoretical and practical connections between unitary executive theory and government information control.

In its critiques of supremacy and unitary executive theory, the book makes two further contributions to the existing literature. First, the book elaborates on the historical and textual flaws of each theory and relates those flaws to each theory's misconstruals of executive accountability and energy. Second, it demonstrates the connection between each theory's interpretive and methodological failings and presidentialism's early constitutional politics.

In its affirmative constitutional arguments—comprised of its explication and defense of the substantive accountability framework—the book builds on existing defenses of constitutional checks and balances in two major respects. First, it introduces the concept of substantive accountability. It demonstrates the concept's constitutional centrality as evidenced by text, structure, and history. It also details the ways in which substantive accountability does, and the ways in which it should, manifest itself in constitutional doctrine. Second, it introduces the concept of contained executive energy. A corollary of substantive accountability, contained energy also is very significant in its own right. The concept incorporates the notion that the presidency is equipped with energetic capacities, including a presidential capacity to keep secrets. Yet of equal importance, it embod-

ies the understanding that that energy does not amount to a legal prerogative to exercise it free from checking. The latter point—the notion
of containment—follows from the same textual, historical, and structural
factors that evidence executive energy itself.

Finally, the project's intersecting thematic threads are executive transparency, accountability, and constitutional law. The book's many pieces
thus come together as a study in what I call the constitutional law of government secrecy. Among the book's aims is to introduce this topic as a
field in its own right among scholars, constitutional lawyers, journalists
who cover presidential power and government secrecy, and all who seek
to understand the relationships between constitutional law, government
secrecy, and accountability in the United States.

CHAPTER TWO

The Tools and Politics of Constitutional Meaning

Constitutional Politics

A s the examples in chapter 1 reflect, constitutional debate is not just for courts. This is as it should be. Even if one starts from the conventional premise that the judiciary, as between the three federal branches, gets the final word on matters of constitutional interpretation,[1] there remains substantial room for popular and political deliberation and influence. For one thing, many constitutional questions—particularly those involving the tug-of-war between the legislative and executive branches—never reach courts. When courts do decide such questions, the decisions often leave much space for interpretation as to the meaning of the doctrine crafted and its applicability to different facts. Furthermore, a judicial ruling to the effect that a political branch or branches constitutionally *may* do something does not dictate that the branch or branches *must* take that action. For example, a holding that the president has a broad prerogative to invoke executive privilege does not mean that the president *must* invoke the privilege in all cases in which he has such discretion. This leaves room for others to urge the president to use his discretion narrowly to support constitutional checks and balances, or conversely to invoke executive privilege to preserve the strength of the presidency. Members of the political branches and the public also play crucial roles in litigation itself—urging courts as parties or amici to develop particular rules or standards, to interpret and apply past doctrine in certain ways, or to overrule earlier case law. Furthermore, the judicial nomination and confirmation processes themselves are political events, informed by public and party views on the parameters of reasonable constitutional argument.

That the public and the political branches have important roles to play in deliberating on the Constitution's meaning is a notion old as the Constitution itself. The meaning of the Constitution drafted in Philadelphia, and whether it should be ratified, were sources of ongoing, high-profile public debates in the late 1780s.[2] As historian Pauline Maier writes in her majestic study of the ratification process, ratification debates "raged in newspapers, taverns, coffeehouses, and over dinner tables. . . . People who never left their home towns and were little known except to their neighbors, studied the document, knew it well, and on some memorable occasions made their views known."[3] After ratification, matters of constitutional interpretation were major issues in election campaigns and political branch decisions. Legal scholar Larry Kramer explains that "[t]he great controversies of the 1790s [were] *constitutional* controversies . . . The issues before the country in those years were *constitutional* issues: strict versus broad construction, federal versus state power, the existence or not of federal common law, the meaning of freedom of the press."[4] These controversies played out in political forums ranging from election campaigns to the halls of Congress.[5]

The present moment is a complicated but potentially transformative one for constitutional politics—that is, for the state of constitutional argument and its resonance in public and political branch debates. On the one hand, for some time now "we the people" have been relatively estranged from the notion that it is our role, or within layperson abilities, to deliberate on constitutional meaning. As Kramer writes, "[s]ometime in the past generation or so . . . Americans came to believe that the meaning of their Constitution is something beyond their compass, something that should be left to others."[6] On the other hand, we may be on the cusp of a renaissance in constitutional politics. This can be attributed partly to a very deliberate conservative movement to popularize and politicize notions of judicial restraint and originalist interpretive methodology, one that goes back to the Nixon administration and gained new life during Ronald Reagan's second term. The movement's outgrowths and effects range from the public debates over constitutional methodology during Robert Bork's 1987 nomination to the Supreme Court, to rallying cries heard today from the Tea Party and others, calling for narrow readings of the Commerce Clause and expansive readings of the Tenth Amendment. The movement also has sparked responses from progressives, who increasingly seek to reshape the debate on their terms. Progressive moves include the 2001 creation of the American Constitution Society as a counterpart to the conservative Federalist Society.[7] In a 2007 interview, legal scholar Barry Friedman nicely summed up both the achievements of the conservative constitutional movement and the task ahead for progressive constitutional leaders: "It's unclear to me that the left understands what it is to re-imagine a constitutional agenda and sell it to the American people. . . . That's what the right did. They lived for a long time in the diaspora. They found issues and ways to market them, with a single-mindedness of purpose and vision that has served them well."[8]

While the very fact of public constitutional discourse and politics—or what legal scholar Reva Siegel calls a "constitutional culture"[9]—holds promise, the content of much that has occurred has yet to live up to this promise. For example, concepts like executive privilege and exclusivity sometimes are held up like talismans to preempt rather than engage debate. Other times, such concepts need not even be named for their shadows to skew or end discourse. Such shortcomings are attributable partly to factors specific to the realm of presidential power. But they also are partly a product of this historical moment. In this moment, constitutional politics is a real phenomenon, and it may be a growing one. At the same time, our intellectual infrastructure for public constitutional debate remains lacking, for reasons that include atrophy, a sound-bite culture, and a historical strain of anti-intellectualism in American politics. Furthermore, as Friedman's statement suggests, the public debate has not been evenly joined for much of the past few decades. Rather, it has been dominated by a conservative movement that has devoted tremendous resources to constitutional politics. Their opponents too often have failed to engage their efforts, ceding—and missing chances to enrich—important aspects of constitutional culture.

Still, the game remains well worth the candle. As the successes of the conservative legal movement reflect, the United States continues to possess a politically resonant constitutional culture. For those of us who perceive substantive inadequacies in that culture, the only solution is to engage it. As legal scholar Jack Balkin writes, such engagement, or "democratic constitutionalism[,] is not simply a fact of life" in the development of American constitutional law, "it is a responsibility."[10] This book attempts to honor that responsibility. It does so by unpacking presidentialist arguments and their implications in an effort to make them accessible to an audience ranging from nonlawyers to constitutional experts. It seeks also to lay bare the role of politics in presidentialism's rise. It is important to understand the political aspect of presidentialism's intellectual history for several reasons. For one thing, presidentialists often deem their positions to follow inescapably from the text, structure, and history of the Constitution. It is instructive to understand the extent to which such positions have not simply been unearthed through disinterested fact finding but, like some competing ideas, have ascended through concerted campaigns. Furthermore, while presidentialism's political appeal today extends to both major political parties, its underlying methodology has stayed fairly constant. That methodology's groundwork was developed in the 1970s and 1980s as part of a partisan political movement. As we shall see, presidentialism's major interpretive fallacies today stem from features linked to that movement.

The remainder of this chapter explores major aspects of interpretive methodology as they relate to presidential power, and the politics of the same. It begins with brief intellectual histories of originalism and presidentialism. Those histories lay the groundwork for the section that follows them, "Presidentialism's Two Foundational Mistakes." That section outlines two core flaws in presidentialism and explains that the flaws flow organically from the aims of the movement in which both originalism and presidentialism first arose. The subsequent section explains and criticizes presidentialism's use of the methodology of "evolving history." The final section of this chapter explains the methodology underlying the substantive accountability approach.

Originalism's Original Politics and Their Continued Salience

Among the most important developments in constitutional law and politics over the past several decades is the rise of originalism. Originalism "as a distinct theory of constitutional interpretation" was first espoused by prominent conservative legal scholars in the 1970s as a corrective to the perceived activism of the Warren Court and to a lesser degree of the Burger Court.[11] At the 1971 Senate hearing on his nomination to the Supreme Court, then judge William Rehnquist promised not to "disregard the intent of the framers of the Constitution and change it to achieve a result that [he] thought might be desirable for society."[12] And Robert Bork argued, in an influential law journal article, that the framers' intended applications of constitutional text should govern in cases where those intentions are knowable. This plea was part of Bork's larger call to judges to apply "neutral principles" in constitutional cases, an approach that Bork contrasted with the "value-choosing role of the Warren court."[13]

In the Reagan administration, advancing originalism was part of a larger project to reset the parameters of constitutional analysis in politics and courts for the long term. An important piece of this project was the hiring of young movement conservatives into the Reagan Justice Department, "both for the short-term purpose of ensuring control over the permanent bureaucracy and in order to credentialize a generation of future senior movement lawyers."[14] Indeed, the department hired all three founders of the fledgling Federalist Society and participated in public exchanges with the group to enhance the latter's profile as an incubator for conservative ideas and leaders. The department, particularly during the term of Reagan's second attorney general, Edwin Meese, became a think-tank of sorts for developing conservative legal ideas and a forum for conveying those ideas to the wider legal community and the public at large. Of the ideas developed and conveyed, none was more central than originalism.[15]

Like other proponents of originalism, the Reagan Justice Department deemed it the only principled means of constitutional interpretation. For example, in a 1985 speech to the American Bar Association (ABA), his first major speech promoting originalism, Attorney General Meese argued that "[a] jurisprudence seriously aimed at the explication of original intention would produce defensible principles of government that would not be tainted by ideological predilection."[16] Meese was even more explicit in characterizing originalism as the sole alternative to an interpretive Wild West in his remarks for the Federalist Society's first annual lawyers' convention in 1987. There, he distinguished originalism from the view of "certain judges, politicians, and academics today ... [that] the United States Constitution [is] a document virtually without legally significant, discernible meaning."[17] To these nonoriginalists, the Constitution "merely provides a starting point for philosophical adventurism."[18]

The promise of originalism in these early appeals was entwined with what I call the "determinism premise."[19] By the determinism premise, I mean the notion that originalism is sufficient, on its own, to resolve the bulk of most constitutional questions. That is, originalism yields "thick" answers, meaning answers that leave little room for judicial discretion in resolving particular disputes. Indeed, the notion that originalism would leave little room for discretion is implicit in Meese's promise, in his 1985 speech to the ABA that his department would "endeavor to resurrect the original meaning of constitutional provisions and statutes as the *only reliable guide for judgment.*"[20] In his 1987 remarks to the Federalist Society, Meese again painted a picture of originalism as providing answers thick enough to keep discretion at bay. He posed the rhetorical question: "How, then, do we know when a judge is acting properly in declaring an executive or legislative act unconstitutional?" "The answer," he said, "is found by looking at the relevant written constitutional provision and checking to see if it is being enforced according to its plain words as originally understood."[21] Similarly, in his 1971 article championing framers' intent as a tool in the tool kit of neutral principles, Bork warned of the dangers of judicial reliance on thin, underdeterminate principles. He deemed it "easy enough to meet the requirement of neutral application by stating a principle so narrowly that no embarrassment need arise in applying it to all cases it subsumes. . . . But that solves very little. It certainly does not protect the judge from the intrusion of his own values."[22]

Among academics and some jurists, originalism has undergone much rethinking since these early days. The best-known change is the shift among many originalists from an emphasis on the actual intentions and understandings of the Constitution's framers and ratifiers to the "original public meaning" of the constitutional text. Original public meaning refers to the meaning that "the words and phrases of the [constitutional] text . . . would have had at the time they were adopted as law, within the political and linguistic community that adopted the text as law."[23] While intent- or understanding-based originalists seek to discern the views of actual founders, public meaning originalists search for "objective" meaning, or the meaning that a reasonable founding-era reader *would* have assigned to the text in light of the linguistic and other relevant context of the time.[24] Intent- or understanding-based originalism sometimes is called "old" originalism while public meaning originalism sometimes is called "new" originalism.[25] For ease of reference, this book adopts these labels.

The consensus—albeit not unanimous—among legal scholars is that new originalism is both easier to justify intellectually and less determinate than old originalism. On the former point, scholars observe that the founders ratified the Constitution's text, not their subjective intentions. They also argue that it is prohibitively difficult, and hence subject to manipulation through cherry picking, to settle on a definitive set of founding-era understandings.[26] On the latter point, some scholars argue that new originalists confronted with broad or vague constitutional language cannot simply ask how the founders would have expected the language to apply. In theory, they must acknowledge that the text's original meaning "runs out" where it does not provide precise answers that can be applied mechanically. At that point, interpreters must turn to tools beyond original meaning.[27]

Later in this chapter, I quibble with the notion that new originalism is less prone to deterministic overreach than is old originalism. For the moment, however, it is important simply to know that the current academic consensus detaches new originalism from the determinism premise. This conventional academic wisdom, however, is reflected little if at all in public discourse about originalism. In the public discursive realm, time has stood still. There, originalism's image as a uniquely principled and determinate tool of constitutional analysis remains largely intact.[28] The persistence of this perception stems partly from static assumptions to the effect that originalism means old originalism.

Rush Limbaugh captures the ongoing view of a neutral, determinate originalism in a December 2005 edition of the *Limbaugh Letter*, where he writes that "[t]he only antidote to [liberal] judicial activism is the conservative judicial philosophy known as Originalism." Elaborating, he quotes Supreme Court Justice Clarence Thomas to the effect that "'[t]he Constitution means what the delegates of the Philadelphia Convention and of the state ratifying conventions understood it to mean; not what we judges think it should mean.'"[29] Legal scholar Jamal Greene recounts another popular depiction of originalism to the same effect:

> In 2005, Mark Levin, an alumnus of the Reagan Justice Department under Edwin Meese and, of greater moment, an extremely popular radio talk show host, authored a book called *Men in Black: How the Supreme Court Is Destroying America*. ... [In it,] Levin set about showing that all judges are either originalists or "activists." Rush Limbaugh wrote the introduction, Meese the afterword. The book spent nine weeks on the *New York Times* best-seller list, reaching as high as third. At the time of publication, Levin's radio show was ranked number one in the evening-commute time slot—in New York City.[30]

Polling data confirms originalism's popular currency and its public image as a near-mechanically applied tool of determinism and restraint. "A series of polls conducted annually by Quinnipiac University from 2003 to 2008 consistently found that roughly 4 in 10 Americans agreed that '[i]n making decisions, the Supreme Court should *only* consider the original intentions of the authors of the Constitution' as opposed to 'consider[ing] changing times and current realities in applying the principles of the Constitution.'"[31] Analysis of data from the Quinnipiac polls and from two

other sets of polls by Jamal Greene, Nathanial Persily, and Stephen Ansolabehere shed light on the nature of originalism's popular appeal. Greene
et al. identify three traits that they consider predictive of originalism: a desire to limit judicial discretion, identification with conservative or Republican political ideologies, and a set of cultural values that include moral
traditionalism.[32] While Greene and colleagues acknowledge that further
research is needed to determine cause and effect, these predictive traits
suggest that an important part of originalism's popular appeal is the assumption that it drastically narrows judges' discretion by tying them to
the mast of thick meanings as discerned through founding-era intentions.
This point is straightforward with respect to the first trait, a desire to limit
judicial discretion.[33] With respect to the third trait, possession of certain
cultural values including moral traditionalism, the point is nearly as obvious. If the popular view of originalism is that it ties judges to precise historical expectations that yield determinate meanings—precluding judges,
for example, from discerning rights to abortion or gay marriage in the
Constitution—it follows that originalist judges are unlikely to block legislation that reflects traditional moral beliefs.[34] Finally, while the point is a
bit weaker with respect to the second trait—identification with conservative or Republican ideologies—two additional pieces of information
bolster the connection between that trait and the view that originalism
is determinate and discretion-minimizing. First, originalism proponents
ranging from Rush Limbaugh to Edwin Meese have expended significant resources linking conservatism, originalism, and judicial restraint to
one another in the public imagination. It thus seems likely that for many,
the concepts of conservatism and originalism are intertwined with determinism and judicial restraint.[35] Second, policy goals associated with social
conservatism—for example, allowing prayer in schools, outlawing abortion, and prohibiting gay marriage—sound in moral traditionalism. Indeed, among the predispositions that Greene, Persily, and Ansolabehere
count as conservative or Republican in nature are opposition to the 1973
Supreme Court decision in *Roe v. Wade* establishing a constitutional right
to abortion, opposition to gay marriage, and support for school prayer.
Thus, conservatism or republicanism as measured by these scholars is
partly a function of moral traditionalism, which is well served by a historically bound, determinate approach to constitutional interpretation.[36]
Overall, Greene et al. read their results to "gesture at a political market for judicial constraint [through originalism], or at least the appearance of it."[37]

Some of originalism's most high-profile advocates—with access to large audiences in both the scholarly community and the public at large—portray originalism as deeply determinate in their public writings and speeches. For example, in a 2002 column in the religious periodical *First Things,* Justice Scalia explained that his adherence to originalism makes it impossible for him to read his own moral preferences into the Constitution. Invoking the example of the death penalty, Scalia wrote that "[f]or me ... the constitutionality of the death penalty is not a difficult, soul-wrenching question. It was clearly permitted when the Eighth Amendment was adopted.... And so it is clearly permitted today."[38] Referencing this column, one commentator joked that Justice Scalia "can make all the speeches he wants without compromising his neutrality, simply by acting as the constitutional Ouija board he was meant to be."[39]

Justice Thomas, too, frequently conjures a vision of originalism as a determinate antidote to judicial activism. Recall the passage, cited earlier, in which Justice Thomas states that "[t]he Constitution means what the delegates of the Philadelphia Convention and of the state ratifying conventions understood it to mean; not what we judges think it should mean."[40] Elsewhere, Justice Thomas elaborates that "[s]trict adherence to [the originalist] approach is essential if we are to fulfill our constitutionally assigned role of giving full effect to the mandate of the Framers without infusing the constitutional fabric with our own political views."[41]

Presidentialism's Early Politics

Like originalism, presidentialism's rise is deeply tied to the modern conservative movement. Prior to the 1970s, conservatives typically lamented and progressives supported strong presidents. Both groups had associated strong presidencies with ambitious domestic programs in the model of the New Deal and, through World War II, with using American military power as a protective and value-exporting force around the world.[42] Yet by the 1970s, conservatives began to embrace robust presidential powers in the belief that Republicans would have better luck taking the presidency than the Congress.[43] They reasoned that conservative presidents might curtail the regulatory activities of the administrative state through top-down White House control.[44] Furthermore, conservatives by this point increasingly defined themselves as cold war hardliners and painted progressives as soft on national security and communism.[45] They questioned whether Congress had much business overseeing, let alone curtailing, the president's national security initiatives.

These parallel tracks of conservative thought—on domestic regulatory affairs and national security—manifested themselves, respectively, in unitary executive theory and presidential supremacy. Unitary executive theory's development was closely tied to the Reagan administration and the Meese Justice Department. Of course, President Reagan was not the first to seek tighter control over the administrative state. Since at least the Taft administration, presidents had sought to centralize and control the budgetary process.[46] The Nixon administration moved such efforts beyond the budget, seeking to stymie bureaucratic regulatory initiatives more broadly.[47] And a number of presidents, including Andrew Jackson and Andrew Johnson, insisted that they have a constitutional prerogative to remove executive officers at will.[48] Still, it was not until the Reagan administration that these earlier efforts were harnessed into a detailed theory of the unitary executive, one that the administration "very open[ly] and public[ly] embraced" in political and judicial forums.[49] In keeping with its originalism project, the Meese Justice Department deemed unitary executive theory faithful to the "framers' original intent."[50] Citing a popular movie of the time, Attorney General Meese told the Federal Bar Association that unitary executive theory takes us "'Back to the Future,'" to "a proper sense of how the Framers of the Constitution intended the federal systems to work."[51] Conservative legal and political groups made similar appeals.[52] While aspects of the theory have been elaborated and refined since the 1980s, these early efforts fleshed out its basic constitutional justifications.

As for presidential supremacy, its roots stretch at least to the early cold war years, when the modern national security state was in its embryonic stage and executive secrecy became institutionalized in a number of ways, including through the classification system's birth in 1951.[53] Yet as with unitary executive theory, it was not until the 1980s that supremacy was widely articulated as a coherent set of legal arguments and part of a larger legal and political movement. To many conservatives in the mid- to late 1970s, Congress's increased assertiveness in the wake of Watergate and Vietnam—including the passage of the War Powers Resolution, the Pike and Church Committee investigations in the House and Senate, and the passage of the Foreign Intelligence Surveillance Act (FISA)—was disastrous.[54] These events planted the seeds of a conservative backlash against restrictions on presidential power, one that boasts

Dick Cheney as its best-known embodiment. Cheney had served as Gerald Ford's chief of staff, and "left the Ford White House ... with the abiding belief that post-Nixon reforms unduly hobbled the commander in chief." David Gergen, who had worked with Cheney in the Ford White House, attributed Cheney's later "zealous reassertion of the power of the presidency" during the George W. Bush administration to that earlier experience.[55]

Still, it was not until a second backlash in the 1980s—this one triggered by perceived congressional overreaching in the Iran-Contra hearings—that conservatives began to articulate a detailed theory of supremacy. Indeed, supremacy's major public debut took the form of the report of a minority of congresspersons (hereinafter "Minority Report") who dissented from the Report of the Congressional Committees Investigating the Iran-Contra affair in 1987. The Minority Report was joined by Senators James McClure and Orrin Hatch and by Representatives Dick Cheney, William S. Broomfield, Henry J. Hyde, Jim Courter, Bill McCollum, and Michael DeWine.[56] Years later, as vice president, Dick Cheney would point to the Minority Report—written partly by David Addington, then a committee staff member and later chief of staff to Vice President Cheney—as reflecting his views on presidential power.[57] The Minority Report argues that some of the statutory directives that President Reagan and his subordinates were said to have violated in the Iran-Contra affair were unconstitutional infringements that the president was free to ignore.[58] Similar supremacist arguments were also articulated at the time in law reviews and books.[59]

Like unitary executive theory, supremacy was and is frequently justified in originalist terms. Much supremacist work adopts a "fettered presidency" narrative. The narrative posits that Congress, for the bulk of American history, respected supremacy and thus passed few statutory constraints in the realms of foreign affairs or national security. It was only in the twentieth century, for a period between the two World Wars and then again—with a vengeance—from the 1970s through today, that Congress broke this pattern. From this perspective, we are left today with a "fettered presidency" that stands in sorry contrast to the constitutional plan that Congress acknowledged and respected for nearly two centuries. Indeed, *The Fettered Presidency* is the title of a 1989 book published by the American Enterprise Institute. Many of the book's essays follow this historical narrative.[60] And while the Meese Justice Department did not champion supremacy as wholeheartedly as it did unitary executive theory, it embraced aspects of the former and invoked originalism to justify the same.[61]

While presidentialism's rise was closely tied to the conservative legal movement of the 1970s and 1980s, it has gained enormous traction across the political spectrum over the past several decades. As explained in chapter 1, a number of political and structural factors make it very difficult to reverse or contain expansions of the president's constitutional powers in popular, political, and judicial conceptions. It is not surprising, then, that presidentialist advancements in one realm and among one set of partisans tend to spread over time to other settings. This is not to say that the views of particular groups and individuals do not ebb and flow over time. It is hardly shocking, for example, when politicians become more amenable to presidentialism when their party is in the White House and vice versa. In the aggregate, however, forces militate toward presidentialism's staying power, even expansion, once it gains a foothold in a given area.[62]

Presidentialism's Two Foundational Mistakes

Overreach, or an overly deterministic reading of original constitutional meanings, was a key flaw of modern originalism from the beginning. In their desire to present originalism as the only principled means of constitutional interpretation and the antidote to judicial activism, originalists promised far more determinism than the Constitution's text and history could deliver. And while many academic commentators take the view that new originalism is both more reliable and less determinate than old originalism, new originalism itself is capable of generating strained, unjustifiably thick readings of constitutional meaning.

Such strained interpretations are facilitated partly by the malleable means through which new originalists discern public meaning. Recall that new originalists eschew actual founding-era intentions or understandings. Instead, they seek to locate the text's "objective" original meaning, or the meaning that a reasonable founding-era reader *would* have assigned to the text in light of the linguistic and other relevant context of the time. This approach implicitly—and sometimes explicitly—demands a hypothetical original reader through whom to channel original meaning. Yet the array of potential hypothetical readers and their hypothetical reading materials is broad. For example, while Justice Scalia emphasizes the hypothetical reader's ordinariness, explaining that the original meaning is that which would have "been known to ordinary citizens in the founding generation,"[63] Gary Lawson and Guy Seidman emphasize the hypothetical reader's extraordinariness. They characterize this person as

> highly intelligent and educated and capable of making and recognizing subtle connections and inferences. This person is committed to the enterprise of reason, which can provide a common framework for discussion and argumentation. This person is familiar with the peculiar language and conceptual structure of the law.[64]

Other public meaning originalists offer further variants. For example, Vassan Kesavan and Michael Paulsen refer to a "hypothetical, objective, reasonably well-informed reader ... within the political and linguistic community in which [the relevant constitutional words and phrases] were adopted."[65] And Randy Barnett refers simply to the meaning "that a reasonable listener would place on the words used in the constitutional provision at the time of its enactment."[66]

Presidentialist works span the realms of old and new originalism alike. For example, some supremacist works from the 1980s use the language of framers' intent,[67] while some more recent works refer interchangeably to framers' understanding, ratifiers' understanding, and original meaning.[68] Yet all of these works suffer, through slightly different mechanisms, from deterministic overreach. For example, each category just described includes works that rely partly on statements of a few founders including Alexander Hamilton, James Madison, and Thomas Jefferson. The same works also speculate about the intentions of founding generation members by drawing on philosophies that influenced them.[69] Each work reaches thick, supremacist conclusions through strained interpretations of the primary materials and by overlooking contrary indications from the relevant framing, ratification, and intellectual histories. From a new originalist perspective, these conclusions can be deemed original public meanings. In the realm of old originalism, the same interpretations can be said to follow from the fact that particular framers did, or their ratifier contemporaries would have, reached those conclusions. In each case, the result is the same—a series of overreaching claims as to the depth and breadth of the presidential powers locked in by the Constitution.[70]

Subsequent chapters detail the problem of originalist overreach as it relates to supremacy and unitary executive theory. For now, consider one example from the realm of supremacy. Supremacists commonly argue that the original meaning of the term "executive power" locks in many of the prerogatives enjoyed by the British Crown. They reach this conclusion despite the disagreement and confusion that reigned among the founders as to the term's meaning and the emphatic public denial by many that the term extended beyond the power to implement the laws created by the legislature. Supremacists rely largely on a few philosophical works by which educated founders were influenced, engage in their own interpretation of those works, and conclude that the works clearly associate the executive power with the king's prerogatives. Yet as will be discussed in chapter 4, the texts do not establish that the founding-era definition of executive power clearly encompassed the prerogatives held by the Crown. At the very most, they suggest that seventeenth- and eighteenth-century British and French thinkers who influenced the founders believed that the one charged to execute the law is also the one to whom the prerogatives enjoyed by the Crown should attach for functional reasons. In seeking to lock in a robust definition of executive power, presidentialists make a mistake much like that made by those who equate original expected applications of vague constitutional terms with the terms' semantic meanings. That is, they take assumptions by influential thinkers about the privileges that typically attach to the person who executes the law, and conflate those assumptions with the original linguistic meaning of "executive power." More important, they ignore evidence from the drafting and ratification debates to the effect that confusion and disagreement imbued actual understandings of executive power and that the only point of consensus was on the executive's power to carry out legislation.[71]

Worse still, originalist overreach combines with presidentialism's other core mistake—its siphoning of substance from the concept of accountability. Supremacists and unitarians alike deem accountability an important constitutional value and claim that their respective theories bolster it. To support this, each group invariably cites founding-era statements to the effect that a single president is more accountable than any multi-member body or entities. When a single person acts, there is no question of who to blame, and the president is subject to the judgment of the entire nation at the ballot box. Yet this view ignores accountability's substantive preconditions—including a degree of transparency as to actual, not merely formal chains of decision-making responsibility—and the extent to which supremacy and unity can undermine such preconditions. It assumes instead that a one-time presidential reelection opportunity, combined with formal presidential authority over a massive range of decisions—including decisions that legitimately may, from a supremacist perspective, remain unknown to voters—is both necessary and sufficient to ensure accountability.

This formal accountability-based approach is misguided not only as a matter of functional reasoning, but as a matter of historical and textual analysis. Indeed, the functional mistake is facilitated partly through over-reading of text and history. For example, supremacists frequently cite to founding statements extolling presidential energy and accountability to support the points that the president must control all national security re-lated decision making—including decisions to keep information secret—and that such control ensures presidential accountability. Yet they reach this conclusion only by ignoring the larger historical context, including founding statements that assume the necessity of checks and balances on presidential energy and power. Presidentialism's two core errors—its overly deterministic originalism and its substituting of formal for substan-tive accountability—thus exacerbate one another.[72]

Presidentialism and Evolving History

Evolving History as Methodology

Presidentialists sometimes supplement their analyses with arguments from "evolving history." In an evolving history argument, presidentialists typically cite to past presidential actions that resemble the challenged act and claim that Congress acquiesced in those past activities.[73] Unitarians occasionally cite to evolving history as additional support for unity, al-though they rely predominantly on text, structure, and originalist history.[74] When supremacists cite to evolving history, on the other hand, they tend to weave it more centrally into their arguments.

Supremacists often fail to articulate the reasoning behind their uses of evolving history. That is, they often do not explain why the bare fact that past presidents engaged in certain actions buttresses the constitu-tionality of similar actions taken by subsequent presidents. Still, at least two justifications logically can be inferred and sometimes are invoked ex-plicitly. The first justification is that a pattern of presidential supremacy in American history necessarily reflects the presidency's structural advan-tages as crafted by the founders. Presidential supremacy over time thus reveals (or confirms) the true and intended nature of the constitutional presidency and its relationship to the other branches.[75] The second justification is that a history of presidential supremacy and congressional acquiescence reflects an implicit interpretive consensus in favor of supremacy by both branches.[76]

A Critique

It is not intrinsically mistaken to use evolving history, or history's "gloss" as Justice Frankfurter famously called it,[77] as a tool in constitutional interpretation. Yet even the most compelling evidence from evolving history does not automatically make an action constitutional. To determine the light that evolving history sheds on an interpretive question, one must look at the history cited and the relationship between that history and the constitutional provisions at issue. From such a vantage point, supremacist reasoning from evolving history does not fare well.

Consider the first type of supremacist argument from evolving history: that past acts of supremacy and legislative acquiescence arise naturally from the president's and Congress's respective capacities and therefore reflect the proper constitutional order. Such an argument assumes that the president's energetic capacities constitute legal prerogatives. It also assumes away substantive accountability by treating the president's capacities as properly uncontained by macro-transparency or other accountability mechanisms. Without these assumptions, there is no reason for supremacy's constitutional correctness to follow from the fact that supremacist acts have occurred repeatedly. Instead, a history of presidential circumvention of legislation—or of other forms of supremacy—could mean any number of things, including that constitutional boundaries have been insufficiently policed.[78]

The second rationale—that evolving history reflects an interpretive consensus within the political branches—should be credited only where the facts show a long-standing pattern of presidential activity explicitly and actively assented to by Congress. To derive an interpretive consensus from anything less overlooks the reality of the president's energetic capacities and treats substantive accountability as dispensable. The president's structural advantages make it possible for him, under certain circumstances, to act in contravention of statutes or otherwise in a supremacist manner. Such acts may be facilitated by the president's capacity for secrecy, or they may take place in the open and be enabled by his sheer capacity for unilateral action. In such cases, Congress at minimum would

have to gather a majority of each house to counter the president's unilateral actions legislatively, and even then it may face a presidential veto.
Congress's disadvantage is greater still where the president acts in full
or partial secrecy or where the president's actions already flout statutory
authority. Given these structural realities, it makes little sense to deem a
history of supremacist action without effective congressional response a
mark of studied interbranch interpretive consensus.[79]

The Substantive Accountability Framework:
Underlying Methodology

Despite this book's criticisms of some originalist applications, it does accept what legal scholar Lawrence Solum identifies as originalism's two
core premises. These premises include the notions that each constitutional
provision's meaning "is fixed at the time [that] provision is framed and
ratified" and that "constitutional actors ... ought to be constrained by
the original meaning when they engage in constitutional practice."[80] Indeed, as Jamal Greene has explained: "To assign some other meaning to a
text—some contemporary meaning wholly unmoored from the original,
for example—is to disclaim fidelity to it. If, by fortuity, the word 'Senator'
comes in a later age to mean 'sandwich,' each state is not thereby entitled
to two free lunches."[81]

Yet to agree that constitutional meaning does not shift over time is not
to agree on the tools by which that meaning should be discerned or on
how to apply those tools. It is on these latter points that this book parts
ways from the originalism reflected in much presidentialist discourse. Specifically, this book takes issue with presidentialist tendencies to overread
original meaning. Presidentialists strain to derive thick and determinate
bundles of presidential power from constitutional language, particularly
from Article II's Vesting Clause. They do so despite substantial evidence
that the founding-era meaning of executive power at best was confused
and contested beyond the bare power to carry out the laws of the legislature. What is more, the thick meanings that presidentialists glean from the
Constitution run afoul of constitutional principles themselves derivable
from text, structure, and history.

The first step in this book's methodology entails looking, quite simply,
for evidence of the original meaning of the relevant constitutional provisions. In so doing, however, it remains mindful of the risk of overreading

original meaning, and the related risk of running afoul of constitutional principles. The book operates within two self-imposed guidelines to guard against these risks. First, it considers evidence both of "objective" public meaning and of the actual understandings of framers and ratifiers. Given the shortcomings of both old and new originalism, consideration of each is necessary to check the other. For example, among the well-known criticisms of old originalism is that it lends itself to cherry picking, enabling modern interpreters to rely on quirky or out-of-context historical statements to reach desired results.[82] There also is a risk that interpreters will rely on evidence of intentions not well publicized at the time of the founding, thus elevating secret or near-secret subjective intentions to the status of constitutional law.[83] For these and other reliability and legitimacy concerns, it is important for modern interpreters (a) to seek out the meaning of the textual provisions ratified in the Constitution, rather than relying solely on subjective intentions as to how those provisions would apply; and (b) to look not only to actual understandings of the text's meaning by framers and ratifiers, but also to any evidence of constitutional terms' meanings during the relevant period more broadly. Such public meaning evidence includes any evidence of common usage and other relevant information that sheds light on how a reasonable person of the time would have understood the terms at issue.[84]

Yet there is as much if not more risk of error or manipulation in objective public meaning analysis as in analysis based on actual understandings of framers and ratifiers.[85] As such, one must pay as careful attention to the latter as to the former. The latter can serve as a literal reality check against out-of-whack objective meanings. Perhaps the most straightforward risk of objective public meaning analysis is that it will run afoul of actual understandings of the time. The risk, to be clear, is not that public meaning may contradict founding expectations as to how a provision would apply. Rather, the concern is that it will contradict founding-era understandings of a provision's semantic meaning.[86] A closely related risk is that public meaning interpreters will deem objectively correct a meaning that was expressed by a small segment of founders, but that for the most part was heavily contested or the subject of widespread confusion and contradiction. Indeed, legal historians and scholars of English emphasize the strongly contested nature of many provisions' meanings at the time of the founding. They note that the meanings of constitutionally important words and phrases, including the very word "constitution," were deeply in flux during the framing and ratification periods.[87] They stress the problems that this reality poses for interpretive approaches directed toward pinpointing single, objectively correct original meanings.[88]

Second, the book pays careful attention not only to specific constitutional words and clauses, but to relevant constitutional principles and goals as discerned by the larger historical context, the drafting and ratification debates, and constitutional structure. A conflict between a particular interpretation of original meaning and constitutional goals and principles should raise a red flag that one may be overreading what the text demands. Worse, it suggests that one may, ironically, be undermining constitutional principles in one's zeal to derive thick constitutional directives.

Beyond helping to impose discipline in the search for original meaning, constitutional principles are important interpretive tools in their own right. Where original meaning locks in only a thin directive and leaves substantial room for future innovations to build on that base, one must look toward constitutional principles as boundaries within which political or judicial innovations may occur. The principles—and guidance as to means that might further or undermine them—can be gleaned partly from constitutional structure and the historical context surrounding the development and ratification of the relevant provisions. Other points of guidance include judicial precedent and evolving history in the political branches. Evolving history in particular can shed the light of experience on means that may further or, alternatively, that may undermine constitutional principles. Note the distinction between the latter point and a theory of evolving history that presumes historical patterns to be constitutional simply because they took place.[89]

For simplicity's sake, I use the term "interpretation" to cover both the search for textual meaning and the policing of loose, principle-based boundaries where precise answers are unavailable. The latter exercise overlaps with what scholars sometimes refer to as "construction." To these scholars, interpretation occurs when locked-in original meaning is discerned—when courts determine, for example, the original linguistic content of the term "the executive power." Yet once the text "runs out," that is, once it ceases to tell us precisely what to do—either because it encodes a thin standard or principle subject to multiple applications, or because it establishes a thin rule and beyond that is silent—guidance can be found in tools of construction.[90] Beyond this difference in nomenclature, my principle-based approach to the second phase of interpretation (that is, to the "construction" phase) largely tracks that of Jack Balkin.

Indeed, Balkin refers to the method of "text and principle" as an aspect of his approach to originalism.[91] As he observes, courts, political actors, and the public all can and do participate in interpretation's second phase as means to build on the framework established by the Constitution's original meanings. They do so by debating the content and application of the relevant principles and by resolving their disputes through new laws, institutions, and doctrines.

CHAPTER THREE

Substantive Accountability and External Checking

This chapter details the substantive accountability framework and its constitutional basis, focusing on the framework's relationship to external checks on presidential power. The chapter begins by explaining that constitutional text and structure provide for macro-transparency and accountability tools. These elements, in turn, reflect commitments to substantive accountability and its corollary principle contained energy. Historical evidence confirms these commitments. The chapter then notes that structure and history also support the inclusion of extraordinary prerogative within the substantive accountability framework. Finally, the chapter elaborates on the nature and breadth of the accountability tools that the Constitution enables. Specifically, it discusses Congress's constitutional leeway to create statutory accountability tools, the extent to which Congress and the courts possess inherent accountability tools to oversee the executive, and the extent to which the First Amendment protects classified information leaks and publications.

Contained Energy, Macro-Transparency and Accountability Tools

Legislating and Executing the Law: Textually Locked-In Features and Underlying Principles

Perhaps the most well-known rules locked in by Articles I and II of the Constitution are that statutes are passed through the legislative process and implemented by the executive. Indeed, the core original meaning of executive power—the one aspect of it that was undisputed during the founding period—is the power to "carry[] the will of the Legislature into effect."[1] The Constitution does not specify how it is that laws are to be executed. Nor could it feasibly lay out detailed procedures for executing infinite, highly varied pieces of legislation. In contrast, the Constitution locks in an intricate set of requirements for the process of legislating. Article I, Section 7, mandates that a majority of the House of Representatives and of the Senate approve a bill. Once each chamber approves a bill, it must be shared with the president who concurs and signs the legislation or who, if he disagrees, not only must return the legislation to the chamber in which it originated but must do so "with his Objections." The relevant chamber must then "enter the Objections at large on their Journal." The president's objections ultimately must be shared with both congressional chambers, and the bill becomes law only if two-thirds of each chamber approves it. "[In] all such Cases the Votes of both Houses shall be determined by yeas and Nays, and the Names of the Persons voting for and against the Bill shall be entered on the Journal of each House respectively."[2]

The substantive policy domain within which the legislature may operate is largely set out in Article I, Section 8. Among other things, Article I, Section 8, permits the legislature to regulate foreign and interstate commerce, to raise funds through taxation and borrowing, to spend in furtherance of the "general welfare," to "make Rules concerning Captures on Land and Water," "to raise and support Armies," "to provide and maintain a Navy," and "to make Rules for the Government and Regulation of land and naval Forces." The legislature also is empowered to "make all Laws . . . necessary and proper" to effectuating its enumerated powers and those of the executive and judicial branches.[3] Thus, while the Constitution does not itself lay out a process by which the law is to be executed, it explicitly authorizes Congress to craft such processes under the Necessary and Proper Clause. More broadly, it is plain from the text of Articles I and II that legislation is a prerequisite to most if not all effective executive action. It is for Congress, after all, to create and fund—or not to create and fund—federal offices, agencies, and the armed forces.[4]

When one looks closely at this well-known arrangement and its players, what is striking is the careful balance that it reflects between government's energetic traits, including secrecy, and its accountability-protective features, including transparency. The arrangement appears structured to contain energy and to ensure substantive accountability through rather ingenious means—that is, through the negative correlation between the relative energy of each branch or function and the relative legal discretion attached to the same. While the legislative function is an awesome one that precedes virtually all government activity, it is made relatively safe for liberty by the transparency and deliberativeness that the Constitution builds into it. Law execution, on the other hand, is largely free from constitutionally required transparency and procedural mechanisms. Yet the potential for abuse is mitigated by the fact that executive activity is subject to legislative direction and restriction, including any statutory transparency requirements. The executive, in short, benefits from substantial energetic capacities. Those capacities are containable through legislation. And legislation itself is produced through a nonenergetic but relatively safe and transparent process.

The executive's energy, including its capacity for secret keeping, is evidenced both structurally and historically. Indeed, the founders who championed constitutional ratification, most famously Alexander Hamilton, boasted that the president is uniquely structured to be energetic, that is, to operate with "[d]ecision, activity, secrecy, and dispatch."[5] Energy results partly because the executive branch is headed by a single president, and energy "will generally characterize the proceedings of one man in a much more eminent degree than the proceedings of any greater number."[6] Furthermore, as we have seen, the executive is largely unburdened by constitutionally mandated procedures for law execution. As the government's "doer" branch, the executive also has unparalleled access to its human and technological resources, and is uniquely equipped to act spontaneously and unilaterally.

Congress and the legislative process, on the other hand, are rife with transparency-generating features and procedural requirements. As we saw just above, Article I, Section 7, dictates a relatively open, dialogic legislative process. Further enhancing Congress's relative transparency, Article I, Section 5, Clause 3, requires "[e]ach House [to] keep a Journal of its Proceedings, and from time to time publish the same." Although the clause allows Congress to exempt "such [p]arts as may in their Judgment require Secrecy," this allowance notably is framed as an exception to a general openness norm.[7] This is supplemented by the constitutional protection of legislators against punishment for "Speech or Debate," which suggests an expectation of open legislative dialogue.[8]

History also makes clear founding expectations of legislative openness. The Continental Congress had operated in relative transparency for at least a decade by the time of the framing. As political scientist Daniel Hoffman notes, "In principle, any information laid before Congress was a matter of public record unless placed under specific injunction of secrecy; and the votes and official acts of Congress were likewise, unless entered in a separate secret journal reserved for matters of delicate nature."[9] Expectations of legislative openness also were reflected in the framing and ratification discussions over Article I, Section 5, Clause 3. As Hoffman explains, both proponents and opponents of the provision agreed that secrecy should be "limited to the most highly sensitive military and diplomatic affairs; they differed only as to whether the Constitution made this sufficiently clear."[10]

The founders had additional reasons to believe that legislative proceedings would facilitate information flow. At the time of the founding, the legislature's powers of inquiry and investigation were well established. These powers included the right to call public and private witnesses alike, to demand testimony and documents from them, and to enforce these calls through legislatively issued contempt orders and punishments, including imprisonment. As James Landis wrote in 1926, "[a] legislative committee of inquiry vested with power to summon witnesses and compel the production of records and papers is an institution rivaling most legislative institutions in the antiquity of its origins."[11] By the late sixteenth century, Parliament had asserted its right to use the contempt power to compel testimony from monarchs and officers in service of its legislative functions. The Glorious Revolution of 1688 marked the triumph of such assertions over claims of monarchical prerogative.[12] The American colonists, too, treated it as a given that colonial legislatures were entitled to demand information—even from royal governors and other Crown officials—and to enforce those demands through contempt proceedings and imprisonment. "[M]any of the early American state constitutions explicitly gave state legislatures broad contempt powers. . . . [M]ore importantly— . . . even those states that did not explicitly mention contempt in their constitutions understood their legislatures to have broad contempt powers, even as against state executives."[13]

None of this is to say, of course, that founding expectations as to legislative powers—apart from those locked in by original meaning— themselves are determinative as to the powers' meaning or scope. Such expectations do, however, help to confirm that the constitutional design is geared partly toward fostering transparency through legislative operations. More so, while the constitutional text does not speak explicitly to the expectations just cited—namely, that legislative information will generally be public and that the legislature will possess investigative and oversight powers—the text strongly implies both points. The secrecy allowance of Article I, Section 5, is framed as an exception to a general rule of congressional journal keeping. And Congress's power to make all laws "necessary and proper" to effectuating its own enumerated powers and those of the other branches easily encompasses powers of oversight and investigation.[14] The latter implication is further bolstered by the constitutional power of "each House [to] determine the Rules of its Proceedings."[15]

The familiar system of legislative lawmaking and executive implementation thus embodies contained energy. The government's doer, its executive, has substantial energetic capacities, including the capacity to operate in secret. Yet potential executive abuses are structurally mitigated by the executive's dependence on the legislative process for resources and legal authority. The legislative process, in turn, lacks energy, laden as it is with transparency and accountability generating features. Because the executive is dependent on the legislature to create and fund programs, and is subject to statutory conditions and restrictions on the same and to oversight, executive energy remains tethered to the protective features of the legislative process.

Perhaps the most important feature of contained executive energy is the relationship that it entails between "macro-transparency" and "micro-secrecy." As we have seen, the legislative process is built to be relatively transparent and deliberative, and its products—legislation—are intrinsically public. The Constitution thus embodies a "macro-transparency" directive insofar as it requires transparency in the macro-policymaking, or legislative process. At the same time, the executive is structurally capable of operating in secret. The legislature may permit and even facilitate "micro-secrecy," whereby the president may implement legislation in secret. The secret implementation of macro-policy directives by the executive can have obvious benefits for national security and for energy and efficiency more generally. Yet the openness of the process through which governing macro-directives are formulated guards against the threats to liberty and wisdom that secrecy breeds.[16]

Furthermore, the legislative process can generate accountability tools, including information-sharing requirements and oversight mechanisms. Hence, the legislative process not only is protective in its own right, it can generate further means to contain, and protect against abuses of, presidential secrecy and energy.

At the heart of contained energy and its component parts is the principle of substantive accountability. The system of contained energy is unlikely to have been generated by accident, as in the "infinite monkey theorem" that monkeys typing at random for an infinite amount of time will produce a Shakespearean play.[17] Rather, the system reflects a goal of enabling regular and adaptable checks against abuses of executive energy and secrecy. It reflects, in short, a commitment to substantive accountability.

Beyond Legislation and Law Execution

Contained energy and macro-transparency—and the underlying principle of substantive accountability—characterize not only the legislative and law execution processes, but other aspects of separated powers as well. For example, while the Constitution's text assumes presidential initiative in negotiating treaties, which is consistent with presidential energy, Article II requires two-thirds Senate approval before a treaty may be enacted. Similarly, while the president nominates judges and executive officers, the Senate must consent to their appointments.[18] Thus, presidential secrecy and energy—whether in negotiating treaties or choosing potential nominees—ultimately are subject to oversight in a deliberative and transparent forum. Furthermore, as we shall see in chapter 4, the original meaning of the Commander-in-Chief Clause parallels that of the executive power or Vesting Clause. In both cases, the president oversees the execution of legislative plans, subject to legislative direction and restriction. Like the relationship between executive and legislature, then, that between commander-in-chief and legislature is characterized by contained energy, macro-transparency, and the possible use of statutory accountability tools.

Congress's relative legal control over the executive also is exemplified by its power to punish the same for official acts, and the absence of a reverse power on the president's part. Constitutional text provides the two houses of Congress with ultimate oversight of the president and other officers through impeachment and conviction. In contrast, members of Congress are not subject to impeachment.[19] Furthermore, under Article I, Section 6, of the Constitution, congresspersons "shall in all Cases, except Treason, Felony and Breach of the Peace, be privileged from Arrest during their Attendance at the Session of their respective Houses, and in going to and returning from the same; and for any Speech or Debate in either House, they shall not be questioned in any other Place."[20] The president enjoys no such textual privileges. The president thus may be brought and questioned before a public forum—whether in an impeachment or judicial context—as another means to contain his energy and ensure that secretive abuses can be forced to the surface and examined.

Substantive Accountability as Constitutional Principle

The Constitution's structure thus reflects an important principle and its corollary. The principle is substantive accountability, meaning not simply that the people have sporadic opportunities to vote, but that they have multiple opportunities to discover information relevant to their votes. Congress and the courts too, are positioned to demand and discover information about secretive executive activities and to check those activities. There is an obvious cyclical relationship between the discovery and checking powers of Congress, the courts, and the people, as actions by the other branches can lead to press and public discoveries.[21] The First Amendment—discussed in more detail below—adds to this structural picture whereby government and its secrets are kept in check through the ever-present risk of public or interbranch discovery. Contained energy is an important corollary of substantive accountability. While the president has energetic capacities, including the capacity to keep secrets, those capacities are tethered to mechanisms designed to ensure safety, including accountability tools and macro-transparency.

Commitments to substantive accountability and contained energy were evident throughout the founding period. As supremacists frequently point out, Alexander Hamilton and other Federalists celebrated presidential energy, including qualities of "[d]ecision, activity, secrecy, and dispatch."[22] Yet in the same breaths in which they extolled the energy and secret-keeping capacity of the single-headed presidency, many Federalists championed its substantive accountability. For example, in the same essay containing his just-cited statement on presidential energy, Alexander Hamilton assured Americans contemplating ratification that the very quality facilitating energy—unity—would also create visibility and accountability. It is "far more safe," Hamilton explained, that "there should be a single object for the jealousy and watchfulness of the people."[23] Unity gives "the people . . . the opportunity of discovering with facility and clearness the misconduct of the persons they trust, in order either to their removal from office or to their actual punishment in cases which admit of it."[24]

William Davie made a very similar point in the North Carolina ratification debate, explaining that "the public were never at a loss [as to where to fix blame for a crime] when there was but one man."[25] Other examples abound. For instance, during the Massachusetts ratification debates, a commentator wrote in the *Independent Chronicle* that while "secrecy and dispatch" will flourish under a unitary president, it is also the case that "even treason in an individual, can be nipped in the bud."[26] Similarly, a commentator wrote in the *Virginia Independent Chronicle* that "secrecy and dispatch" will attach to the unitary presidential office, and also championed the fact that "[t]he *United States* are the *scrutinizing spectators* of [the president's] conduct, and he will, always, be the distinguished object of *political jealousy.*"[27]

Ratification proponents tied substantive accountability to energy containment mechanisms. Tench Coxe wrote, for example, that the president's "person is not so much protected as that of a member of the House of Representatives; for he may be proceeded against like any other man in the ordinary course of law."[28] Americanus I wrote that the president's "power is limited in such a manner as to preclude every apprehension of influence and superiority. Should he, however, at any time be impelled by ambition, or blinded by passion, and boldly attempt to pass the bounds prescribed to his power, he is liable to be impeached and removed from office."[29] James Monroe wrote: "There should be no constitutional restraint, no equivocation of office, to shield a traitor from the justice of an injured people. No circumstance to blunt or turn aside the keen edge of their resentment."[30] And James Wilson assured the Pennsylvania ratifying convention that "not a *single privilege* is annexed to [the president's] character; far from being *above the laws,* he is amenable to them in his *private character* as a *citizen,* and in his public character by impeachment."[31]

The president's dependence on congressional or Senate action in most matters was deemed an important means to facilitate substantive accountability and contain presidential energy and secrecy. For example, Alexander Hamilton extolled the requirement that the president obtain Senate consent for treaty ratifications. In addition to the advantages of the "numbers and characters of those who are to make [treaties,]" Hamilton predicted that any misbehavior by the executive surely would be reported by the Senate to the people: "[T]he usual propensity of human nature will warrant us in concluding that there would be commonly no defect of inclination in the body to divert the public resentment from themselves by a ready sacrifice of the authors of their mismanagement and disgrace."[32]

The narrative that these statements comprise—that the Constitution would both facilitate presidential energy and enable the people, Congress, and the courts to detect and prevent abuses of the same—makes perfect sense in light of the era's historical backdrop. As supremacists point out, the founders' most immediate preframing experiences involved weak state and national executives. By the end of the "critical" period just prior to the Constitution's drafting, there was significant support for strengthening the national executive.[33] But the critical period hardly existed in a vacuum, and the founders did not forget their earlier hard-won lessons about the dangers of executive power. They were informed not only by the critical period but by the painful break with King George III, colonial resentment of royal governors, and the fight in seventeenth-century England against royal prerogative culminating in the Glorious Revolution of 1688.[34]

Given the historical backdrop, the founders faced the difficult task of reconciling executive energy with fears of tyranny. As Forest McDonald writes:

> Many of the delegates to the Philadelphia convention remained wary of executive power, and even those who believed the establishment of an energetic executive was imperative understood that it was necessary to proceed cautiously. Not only was care necessary lest members of the convention be offended, it was doubly necessary to avoid arousing the fears of the voters who would be called upon to ratify any constitution the delegates could agree upon.[35]

Original principles concerning executive energy thus are far more complex than those identified by supremacists. Supremacists routinely focus on founding celebrations of presidential "[d]ecision, activity, secrecy, and dispatch,"[36] while ignoring the substantive accountability mechanisms that the founders assured one another would keep presidential energy, including secrecy, under the control of the people and their representatives. Supremacists do offer rote assurances of presidential accountability. Yet the accountability to which they refer is the formal accountability embodied primarily in the opportunity to elect, and a single opportunity to reelect, a president. As we have seen, however, the accountability reflected in constitutional structure and history is rich and substantive, with myriad avenues for multiple players to discover information and respond to the same. Constitutional structure and history thus support neither unchecked exertions of presidential energy nor mere formal accountability. Rather, they reflect substantive accountability and contained energy.[37]

Extraordinary (vs. Ordinary) Prerogative

Thus far, we have seen that the substantive accountability principle and its corollary, contained energy, include the component parts of macro-transparency and accountability tools. A third component can be inferred from structure and principle. That is, the concept of "extraordinary prerogative," whereby the executive has some, but very carefully limited, room to depart from statutory restrictions.

Extraordinary prerogative can be inferred from the structural reality that the executive alone is equipped to act unilaterally and at a moment's notice should an unanticipated emergency arrive before Congress physically can act. It can also be inferred from founding-era connections made between presidential energy and unanticipated emergencies, particularly the notion that the president, as commander-in-chief, has a prerogative to act unilaterally to "repel sudden attacks."[38]

The limited—indeed, extraordinary—nature of this exception is as crucial as its substance. One way to look at it is that the "prerogative" part of extraordinary prerogative stems from the notion of presidential energy, whereas the "extraordinary" part is essential to containing that energy and protecting substantive accountability. Without such limitation the exception would swallow the rules of macro-transparency and legislative (as opposed to executive) lawmaking. Any deviations from statutory limits thus must be timed to coincide not only with an emergency but with the period in that emergency before new legislation can reasonably be sought through the ordinary lawmaking process.

These limits can only be enforced through constitutional and statutory accountability tools. For example, absent some degree of First Amendment protection for internal executive branch whistleblowers and the press, congressional power to demand information about executive branch activities, and judicial power to scrutinize executive efforts to block lawsuits through state secrets claims, the president too easily could hide transgressions.

The notion of extraordinary prerogative owes a debt to John Locke's concept of executive prerogative, with which the founding generation was familiar. The basic idea of Lockean prerogative is that an executive may at times be warranted in acting without or even against legal authority to address emergencies. However, whether the actions are warranted are for the people to judge. Furthermore, where an executive acts in the absence of, or against legislation in response to unforeseeable events, he is expected to do so only until "the [legislature] can conveniently be assembled to provide" appropriate legislation.[39]

Political and legal theorists have applied derivations of Lockean prerogative to the U.S. Constitution. A key contribution of these derivations is the notion that the people or their representatives must have an opportunity to review and deliberate on an act of prerogative shortly after the fact in order to ratify or punish it. Some argue, for example, that the president may exceed the Constitution in an emergency but that he must then throw himself on the judgment of Congress or the people.[40] Some members of the founding and early postfounding generations took this view.[41] Others have argued that subsequent ratification can retroactively make such actions constitutional.[42] Under either variant, accountability mechanisms are crucial to prevent the president from cloaking or misrepresenting his actions so that they cannot meaningfully be judged.

Extraordinary prerogative contrasts sharply with the exclusivist strain of supremacy. To exclusivists, the president may override those statutes that unduly restrict his discretion to protect the nation or to execute the law, and in so doing he is not constrained by temporal or transparency requirements. Indeed, exclusivity has been raised at points to justify yearslong, secretive statutory violations. It also is raised at times to prevent legislative restraints from coming into being in the first place.[43] The exclusivity championed by many supremacists, then, is best described as an "ordinary prerogative," whereby the president regularly may override statutory limits and may do so in secret and without temporal limits. The concept of an ordinary prerogative runs deeply counter to the constitutional structure and its underlying principle of substantive accountability.

Accountability Tools: An Elaboration

The final element of the substantive accountability framework—that is, the final means by which executive energy is contained—is the large, varied, and flexible category of accountability tools. Accountability tools range from congressional oversight procedures to statutory information-sharing requirements to constitutional and statutory whistleblower protections. As a general matter, the propriety of, even need for, accountability tools follows very naturally from constitutional structure and the principle of substantive accountability. The relationship between the executive and commander-in-chief powers and the legislative power logically entails a legislative discretion to impose requirements on the executive branch. More pointedly, it suggests that for the constitutional system to work as a practical matter, the legislature must provide means by which the executive can be overseen by Congress, the people, and the judiciary. Such means are essential to detecting executive transgressions of macro-transparent legislative limits. They can also include avenues for judicial redress when the executive strays from these limits. Beyond the basic textual framework of Articles I and II, these points flow from the principle of substantive accountability and from its corollary element of contained executive energy.

Substantive accountability also should infuse understandings of the First Amendment's speech and press protections. The following subsections focus in greater detail on each of three major types of accountability tools: those created by statute, those exercised by Congress through nonstatutory procedures or by the courts in managing litigation, and those that flow from the First Amendment.

Statutory Accountability Tools

Statutory accountability tools run the gamut from statutes requiring public access to information, to those mandating disclosures to particular congressional committees, to those laying out the procedural steps by which congressional committees or special investigative bodies can obtain information from the executive. Other examples include statutes, such as whistleblower protection laws, that encourage, require, or provide protections for executive branch employees to disclose information to Congress or other bodies. The contention of this subsection is that such laws are in no way barred or limited by the Vesting or Commander-in-Chief Clause.

The most basic affirmative justification for this position stems from the structural directive of macro-transparency and the textual directive of legislative lawmaking. Furthermore, as chapter 4—which counters supremacist arguments for ordinary prerogative—will demonstrate, there is no textual commander-in-chief or executive power–based prerogative to surmount legislative directives. Statutory circumvention can be justified only through structural and historical inference, and only when the conditions of extraordinary prerogative are met.

Even if one does not buy arguments against ordinary prerogative as a general matter, the arguments carry special weight in the context of statutory accountability mechanisms. As we have seen, constitutional structure reconciles the need for both substantive accountability and secrecy through means to contain and check executive energy. At the core of these means is the tethering of the executive's secret-keeping capacity to avenues for congressional, judicial, public, or press discovery. Elsewhere, I have used the concepts of "shallow secrecy" and "deep secrecy" to help elucidate this point.[44] A shallow secret is a secret, the very existence of which is known. A deep secret is a secret whose existence is unknown. If the president were to operate a program that violated statutory directives and kept Congress and the public in the dark about this fact, the program would be a deep secret vis-à-vis Congress and the people. Adding to the depth of the secret in this scenario would be the existence of public, statutory directives contrary to the program. On the other hand, if the program were authorized by statute and the statute allowed it to be implemented in secret, then the program's day-to-day execution would be a shallow secret. In the latter case, Congress could create and use tools—such as information-sharing statutes whereby information is funneled to a select group of congresspersons who can decide by vote to inform a broader group should illegality surface—to help oversee the program and ensure that it is not transformed into a different, deeply secret, program. Of course, these examples do not exhaust the nuances of deep and shallow secrecy. Indeed, most secrets are neither completely deep nor completely shallow. Rather, there are varying degrees of shallowness and depth, depending on factors such as the number and identities of those who are aware of a given secret.[45] I invoke the concepts of depth and shallowness solely to help illuminate the basic constitutional directive that presidential secrecy be tethered to mechanisms that can control it and reel it back when necessary. One way to understand this directive is that it seeks to keep presidential secrets from becoming so deep as to slip from the grasp of constitutional checking mechanisms, including Congress's lawmaking and spending powers, judicial review, and the forces of free speech and a free press. The ultimate goal is to prevent such secrets from defeating substantive accountability.

The integrity of this scheme requires that legislative accountability mechanisms—again, ranging from public information statutes to whistleblower protection laws to interbranch information-sharing directives—constitute the final word on the matters that they address (as a matter of separation of powers, that is, not precluding objections on unrelated grounds). Three factors make this so. First, the basic directives of legislative lawmaking and macro-transparency dictate as much. Second, the legislative process constitutes a transparent, deliberative forum within which macro-transparent secrecy policy—authorizing and laying out rules and limits on micro-secrecy—can be formulated. The president's role in that process—specifically, the requirement that legislation be presented to him and his power to veto it, subject to a two-thirds override by each congressional chamber[46]—not only enhances the process's deliberativeness generally, it helps to ensure that legitimate secrecy needs will be raised and considered.

Third, apart from the benefits of the legislative process itself, any access rights created through this process can actively support macro-transparency and substantive accountability by facilitating day-to-day oversight of the executive. For example, individuals can vindicate congressional openness policies by seeking specific pieces of information through open government laws, and congressional subcommittees can check compliance with macro-transparent laws through statutorily authorized investigations. The ability to rely on statutory access rights—without regular limits and delays caused by executive privilege claims and the like—is particularly important because executive branch secrets often exist in layers, with some secrets buried under other secrets. Access laws thus not only can illuminate information directly but can strip away layers that keep some secrets deep rather than shallow. For the latter to happen, one must be able to make multiple inquiries and receive answers within reasonable periods of time so that leads can be followed to their logical conclusions. Perhaps the most famous example of such layer stripping is the revelation of the Watergate tapes' existence. It was only through its capacity to question former presidential aide Alexander Butterfield that the Senate Select Committee on Presidential Campaign Activities discovered the tapes' existence in the first place. Once the tapes became a shallow rather than a deep secret, further legal and political maneuvering could take place in an effort to discover their contents.[47]

Finally, it is worth considering the extent to which supremacy, particularly exclusivity, stymies meaningful policy debates and innovations regarding congressional oversight and its limits.[48] At present there is no general, or "framework" statute that outlines procedures for handling executive privilege disputes that arise in the context of congressional oversight. The result is a process defined largely by internal House and Senate procedures and the politics of the moment rather than the policy merits of a given dispute. Under this system, oversight of important programs may be thwarted by partisan loyalists in Congress, while an inquiry focused on salacious personal gossip may move full steam ahead in a period of divided government. These problems are compounded by the obfuscating effect of constitutional executive privilege claims. A president who is well positioned politically to ward off a meritorious inquiry can frame his stance as a matter of constitutional principle that transcends the particular controversy, and partisan loyalists in Congress can make the same argument in support of the president. Conversely, a congressional committee that is well positioned politically to investigate can elide questions as to whether their investigation is good public policy by emphasizing instead that they have the constitutional right to pursue it.[49]

Were there a consensus that statutory directives on executive privilege are final and cannot be overridden by the executive as a legal matter, public and political attentions might turn to whether statutory recognition of executive privilege is desirable as a policy matter and, if so, how executive privilege disputes should be handled. Once we shift our focus accordingly, we can draw from important ideas that already abound, in addition to seeking out new ones. For example, William Marshall has argued that Congress's current internal rules make it insufficiently costly, politically, to initiate investigations.[50] Legal scholars Daryl Levinson and Richard Pildes suggest procedural innovations to counter the debilitating impact of interbranch party unity on congressional oversight and on other forms of interbranch challenge.[51] And the Brennan Center for Justice in 2009 released a comprehensive proposal for a statute that would establish procedures to resolve executive privilege disputes.[52]

Exclusivist claims of a right to override statutory openness demands thus are wrong constitutionally and misguided as a matter of policy. Ironically, by emphasizing the illegality of statutory openness directives, the executive branch bypasses an opportunity to influence legislative debates on the policy wisdom of particular procedures for resolving executive privilege disputes. Given the tremendous power of the veto and the bully pulpit, the president likely would be an important player, if not the key player, in any such debate. This fact should also remind us that it is oversimplified to deem statutory directives forms of unilateral "congressional control." To the contrary, the statutory process builds in presidential participation just as it builds in a degree of dialogue and transparency generally. These ingredients give the process democratic legitimacy, and suit it well to serve as a means to channel and contain presidential energy.

Nonstatutory Information Disputes

It is less obvious who must prevail in information access disputes in the absence of legislation mandating disclosure. Such disputes can arise in one of two ways. First, they can arise when a congressional body, such as a committee or subcommittee, seeks information pursuant solely to its internal rules. In such cases, the executive might rely explicitly or implicitly on executive privilege to refuse the request. Second, such disputes can arise where courts demand information in the course of litigation, for instance, by issuing a subpoena pursuant to a litigant's discovery request. In such cases, the executive might refuse disclosure on the basis either of executive privilege or the state secrets privilege.

CONGRESSIONAL-EXECUTIVE DISPUTES.   In nonstatutory access disputes between Congress and the executive, congressional proponents cannot rest on general rules of macro-transparency and legislative lawmaking. Nor can they rely on the related notion that the legislative process and its fruits foster contained energy and substantive accountability. They can, however, rightfully argue that the Constitution's text empowers each chamber to "determine the Rules of its Proceedings"[53] and that those proceedings necessarily include oversight and the ability to demand information. More so, congressional oversight clearly comports with structure and constitutional principles.

It is not difficult, in short, to demonstrate that Congress has oversight powers. Indeed, there is little if any serious dispute on that point. The harder and more contested questions are what Article II–based limits, if any, constrain those powers and whether the final word in a given dispute belongs to Congress, the executive, or the courts.[54] These questions turn on structural and historical principles of substantive accountability. A plausible case could be made on that basis against any such limits. The better case, however, is for some degree of judicial checking before a nonstatutory contempt finding can be enforced. Judicial review should entail a balancing test that examines the weight of the executive's secrecy need against that of the congressional interest in obtaining the information. Importantly, the review should contain a presumption favoring disclosure. While the mechanics of a presumption will vary case-by-case, it generally would require that the executive spell out with some specificity why secrecy is necessary in a given case, provide in camera disclosures of the requested material for court review, and minimize the amount of withheld information wherever possible through redactions or otherwise.

There are several reasons for requiring some judicial check before a contempt of Congress finding is enforced. First, any impairment of congressional oversight functions is mitigated by Congress's ability—in cooperation with the executive in light of the latter's veto power—to use the legislative process to create statutory rules and procedures to obtain information, to find executive officials in contempt, and to enforce those findings. Unquestionably, Congress's ability to impose statutory criminal contempt sanctions is limited by executive branch refusals to prosecute such cases.[55] Congress can also provide, however, for civil contempt sanctions. Furthermore, courts can and should deem cases ripe for declaratory rulings sought by members of Congress once a chamber has voted to hold an executive official in contempt. Additionally, Congress can legislate the same congressionally enforceable sanction—arrest by the sergeant at arms and imprisonment in the capitol jail—that it has, in the (admittedly distant) past imposed pursuant to its internal rules.[56] Second, the crafting of statutory mechanisms to obtain information and to address executive branch objections best serves constitutional values of contained energy and substantive accountability, as detailed above. Incentivizing the creation and use of such provisions thus is desirable from the perspective of constitutional values. Third, another reason to impose some judicial review on Congress when it relies on its nonstatutory powers is that in such cases, the president may have a valid basis to rely on his own executive or commander-in-chief powers. Depending on the facts, the president may be able credibly to argue that he seeks to keep secrets to further a particular statutory policy.

As for the content of the judicial review, a pro-disclosure presumption is warranted by two factors. First, even outside of the statutory context, if the president's capacities are to be contained in part through oversight, then executive efforts to resist interbranch information requests must be approached skeptically. After all, as legal scholar Josh Chafetz points out, "in order for [Congress's] oversight power to be effective in rooting out executive branch malevolence and incompetence, Congress must have access to precisely that information that the executive does not wish to turn over."[57] Second, the executive begins with a strong practical advantage in information disputes. It is the executive, after all, who possesses the sought-after information. It thus benefits from delays and other maneuvers that perpetuate the status quo. The deck is also stacked in its favor as it is structurally well positioned to prevent potential information requesters from knowing what information it possesses in the first place. It is well positioned, in other words, to benefit from and maintain deep secrecy.

DISPUTES ARISING IN LITIGATION. Courts also encounter executive privilege or state secrets claims that arise in litigation. For example, an agency head might refuse to disclose information sought through discovery by a plaintiff suing her agency. She might explicitly or implicitly invoke executive privilege, arguing that disclosure could reveal high-level White House discussions and inhibit the candor of such discussions in the future. Alternatively her refusal might be grounded in the state secrets privilege, whereby she might claim that disclosure would endanger national security. In some cases, of course, the information at issue might be requested pursuant to statutory disclosure rights. In those cases, as discussed above, Article II–based objections should not prevail. The question that this subsection raises, however, is how courts should handle executive privilege or state secrets based refusals against discovery requests not grounded in statutory directives.

In such cases, judicial approaches should mirror those prescribed for nonstatutory disputes between Congress and the executive. That is, courts should perform a balancing test with a pro-disclosure presumption. Litigation and discovery are powerful mechanisms to advance substantive accountability and contain executive energy. These mechanisms are important where cases are brought against the executive to vindicate common law or constitutional rights. They carry additional significance where statutory violations are alleged. In such cases, discovery helps to support macro-transparency by policing executive statutory compliance. Litigation and discovery thus make unique contributions to substantive accountability, warranting a pro-disclosure presumption. Furthermore, a pro-disclosure presumption is independently warranted for the same reasons that it is called for in congressional-executive disputes.

Disclosures of Classified Information: The First Amendment, Whistleblowers, and the Press

Public disclosures of inside information that the president wishes to keep secret also can constitute essential accountability tools. Such communications reflect the close relationship and interdependence between external and internal checks on executive power.[58] Inside information comes from sources that are, by definition, internal to the executive branch. On the other hand, the judiciary plays an important role in crafting and applying First Amendment protections. And much of such information's checking power, as well as executive punishments for disclosure, come after the information is disseminated beyond the executive branch. Chapters 7 and 8 address internal checking measures—such as limits on the president's hiring and firing powers—that are among the structural conditions that can facilitate such communications. In this chapter and chapters 5 and 6, I focus on the external check of the First Amendment, especially as it is and as it ought to be interpreted and applied by courts. The chapter considers First Amendment protections with respect to two categories of communications in particular—leaks and publications of classified information. Specifically, it considers the protections that should apply to those prosecuted for leaks and publications.

The first subsection explains why, from the perspectives of text, structure and principle, information from government insiders about national security and public policy presumptively merits strong constitutional protection against criminal prosecution. Following that, it observes that classification status does not undermine the rationale for strongly protecting such speech from prosecution. The second subsection considers the doctrinal standards that courts should apply to assess prosecutions for, respectively, leaks of classified information by government insiders and publications of classified information by third-party publishers.

THE BASIC CASE FOR ROBUST PROTECTIONS. The First Amendment provides, in pertinent part, that "Congress shall make no law . . . abridging the freedom of speech, or of the press." Given the vagueness of the phrase "freedom of speech," commentators and courts long have sought to discern its underlying principles and apply them to concrete cases.[59] Notwithstanding the occasional exception,[60] even self-described originalists generally do not target the Free Speech or Free Press Clause as vessels for thick founding-era expectations as to how the clauses should apply. Indeed, the view—which is prominent and long-standing though by no means undisputed—that the clauses originally were meant predominantly to protect against prior restraints,[61] has had no directly restrictive impact on modern free speech doctrine or commentary.[62] Instead, arguments about free speech long have centered on debates over the thin principle or principles underlying the clause and how to apply the same.

The quest to identify free speech principles has captured the attention of countless scholars over many decades and engendered much disagreement. Nonetheless, there is at least one point of virtual unanimity: Whatever else the freedom of speech may encompass, it undoubtedly includes a right to convey information and opinion about government.[63] This point also encompasses—sometimes implicitly and sometimes explicitly— the notion that such communications are means to oversee and check government.[64]

Protecting speech that helps to facilitate and check self-government indeed is a central purpose of the Free Speech and Free Press Clauses from the perspectives of constitutional structure and principle more broadly. The Speech and Press Clauses naturally should be read in conjunction with the larger document of which they form a part.[65] As we have seen, a major feature of that document's separated powers system is its scheme for containing executive energy. Recall the importance placed by the founders on the ability of the people and the other branches to discover presidential misconduct, exemplified by one commentator's assurance that "[t]he *United States* are the *scrutinizing spectators* of [the president's] conduct, and he will, always, be the distinguished object of *political jealousy.*"[66] The Free Speech and Free Press Clauses fit like puzzle pieces into this constitutional design. Without broad freedoms to gather and disseminate information from within the executive branch, the larger structure would crumble.

That the First Amendment serves in part to contain executive power is in no way undermined by its framing as a directive to Congress. As we have seen, the Constitution grants the lawmaking power to Congress alone. It does not accord the president prerogatives to restrain speech unilaterally. It thus would have been nonsensical for the First Amendment to admonish the president to "make no law." Indeed, Anti-Federalists made clear their fears that Congress would pass speech-restrictive laws absent textual guarantees of free speech and a free press.[67] Such fears would not have applied to the president, who had no lawmaking power.

The history underlying the Free Speech and Free Press Clauses highlights their role in supporting the larger constitutional structure. For example, the American colonists were deeply influenced by a series of British essays published in the 1720s under the pseudonym "Cato." In Essay Number 15, Cato wrote:

> Whoever would overthrow the Liberty of a Nation must begin by subduing the Freeness of Speech; a thing terrible to publick Traytors.
>
> . . .
>
> That Men ought to speak well of their Governours, is true, while their Governours deserve to be well spoken of, but to do publick Mischief without Hearing of it is only the Prerogative and Felicity of Tyranny.
>
> . . .
>
> Freedom of Speech is the great Bulwark of Liberty; they prosper and Die together. . . .[68]

Cato's "bulwark of liberty" language was repeated often by Americans both before and after the Revolution in explaining the necessity of a free press[69] and free speech.[70] Eighteenth-century Americans also consumed, penned, and circulated similar sentiments.[71] For instance, shortly before the Revolution,

> hoping to make allies of the settlers in Quebec, [the Continental Congress] approved a declaration explaining to the northern neighbors the goals of the American endeavor: "The last right we shall mention, regards the freedom of the press. The importance of this consists, besides the advancement of truth, science, morality, and arts in general, in its diffusion of liberal sentiments on the administration of Government, in its ready communication of thoughts between subjects, and its consequential promotion of union among them, whereby oppressive officers are shamed or intimidated, into more honourable and just modes of conducting affairs."[72]

In the constitutional ratification process, the role of speech and press freedoms as pillars of democracy and the rule of law were acknowledged by Federalists—who insisted that the original Constitution implicitly protected speech and press—and Anti-Federalists—who demanded the explicit textual protection that became the First Amendment—alike.[73] Those who went on to "draft[] the First Amendment," like "their mentors ... placed great emphasis on the role free expression can play in guarding against breaches of trust by public officials."[74] In short, there was no dispute among members of the founding generation that government oversight was among the most important ends of free speech and a free press.

The First Amendment's promise would be empty indeed if its protections did not extend to information that the president wishes to keep secret. This includes information from government insiders, who alone are structurally situated to reveal it. Indeed, both Federalists and Anti-Federalists, in the framing and ratification debates, deemed it crucial that the presidential office be designed to prevent insiders from hiding executive misconduct. Federalists boasted that by declining to annex a council to the president through Article II, they had deprived the president of a group that would eagerly do his bidding and hide his secrets. Anti-Federalists, on the other hand, insisted that the department heads would form a de facto council to play the same sycophantic, secret-keeping role on the president's behalf.[75] These debates highlight the nature of the government—one whose integrity is protected by mechanisms internal and external to the executive branch—that the Free Speech and Free Press Clauses are designed to support.

Returning to classified information leaks and publications, then, the question is whether there is something about classification status that justifies a much weaker level of First Amendment protection than should otherwise apply to those prosecuted for leaking or disseminating information about government. The answer is no for reasons both logical and empirical. Logically, free speech principles demand that executive inclinations to punish speech about itself be checked by forces independent of the executive. Nor does it suffice to leave the extent of such checks to Congress's discretion. After all, the First Amendment explicitly limits Congress's lawmaking power in the realms of speech and press. Beyond the obvious textual point, statutes that deem speech punishable in part or in whole for its classified status, where classification decisions are matters of executive discretion, effectively place the First Amendment status of government information in the hands of the executive.

Experience confirms that the political branches are woefully inadequate at self-policing against overreach in the classification system. For one thing, the president largely determines classification policy unilaterally, through executive orders that can change between administrations.[76] Furthermore, the application of these broad policies is delegated to an enormous number of government employees and contractors. At present, well over a million persons have such authority. Of that number, 2,326 had "original classification" authority as of the end of fiscal year (FY) 2012.[77] The average number of original classifiers between FY 1980 and FY 2008 was 5,400.[78] Original classifiers are "authorized to determine what information, if disclosed without authorization, could reasonably be expected to cause damage to national security."[79] Additionally, original classifiers create classification guides. Such guides are instructions for "derivative classifiers." A guide "is a set of instructions ... which identify elements of information regarding a specific subject that must be classified and establish the level and duration of classification for each such element."[80] The remaining million-plus persons with classification authority are derivative classifiers.[81] In theory, derivative classifiers lack policy discretion because their decisions are derived from original classification decisions.[82] In actuality, determining what is derivative of already classified information—short of exact replicas of the latter—itself entails discretion. This is particularly so where the basis for derivative classification is the following of classification guides.

Given this background, it is not surprising that experts across the political spectrum long have acknowledged rampant overclassification. J. William Leonard, the former director of the Information Security Oversight Office—a position sometimes called the "classification czar"—in the George W. Bush administration, acknowledges a problem of "excessive classification." Leonard says that he has "seen information classified that [he's] also seen published in third-grade textbooks."[83] At a 2004 congressional hearing, both Leonard and Carol Haave, then the Defense Department's undersecretary for intelligence, estimated that "probably about *half* of all classified information is overclassified."[84] In 1991, Rodney McDaniel, who had been executive secretary of the National Security Council in the Reagan administration, estimated that "only 10% of classification was for 'legitimate protection of secrets.'"[85] Former New Jersey governor and 9/11 Commission chair Thomas Keane has said that "three-quarters of the classified material he reviewed for the [9/11] Commission should not have been classified in the first place."[86] The Moynihan Commission, a committee led by Senator Patrick Moynihan in the 1990s to study government secrecy, observed in its 1997 report that "[t]he classification system ... is used too often to deny the public an understanding of the policymaking process, rather than for the necessary protection of intelligence activities and other highly sensitive matters."[87] Erwin N. Griswold, former solicitor general under Richard Nixon, deemed it "apparent to any person who has considerable experience with classified material that there is massive overclassification and that the principal concern of the classifiers is not with national security, but rather with governmental embarrassment of one sort or another."[88] And the Public Interest Declassification Board, whose members are appointed by the president and by majority and minority leaders in the House and Senate, declared in their 2012 report to the president that "[t]he system is compromised by overclassification."[89]

Statistics give an additional sense of the classification system's reach. As noted above, there presently are well over a million persons with some form of classification authority. The number of new classification decisions—including combined original and derivative decisions to classify—averaged 16.1 million per year from FY 1996 through FY 2009.[90]

Coupled with overclassification is the widespread practice of selective "authorized" leaking from the top.[91] The White House itself orchestrates leaks so frequently as to have spawned the well-worn joke that "the ship of state is the only vessel that leaks from the top."[92] By selectively leaking only self-serving information, an administration can steer public sentiment in its favor. Administrations also leak information as "trial balloons to test public reaction to policy options without formally committing to them."[93] Theodore Roosevelt is credited as the original master of strategic leaking from the White House.[94] Yet Roosevelt was hardly the last to employ this technique. The four most recent books of journalist Bob Woodward alone are "'filled with classified information that [Woodward] could only have received from the top of the government'" in the Obama and George W. Bush administrations.[95] Given the ubiquity of leaks from the top and the enormous number of secrets kept by the government, "leaks of classified information, including classified national security information, have become one of the primary ways the government communicates information to the public."[96]

Given the twin realities of massive overclassification and widespread selective leaks from the top, a broad executive discretion to prosecute classified information leaks is a powerful means for the executive—both through actual prosecutions and through fear of the same—to manipulate information flow. Such discretion can generate a deeply slanted chilling effect. Those who leak information that paints an administration in a bad light have much to fear in an environment where prosecutions occur or are threatened regularly.

These realities complement the theoretical problems of any scheme that enables the executive to qualify First Amendment protections for speech about itself. Such a scheme is profoundly in tension with a constitutional structure designed to ensure executive accountability and to do so partly through free speech and a free press.[97]

THE DOCTRINAL STANDARDS THAT COURTS SHOULD APPLY. When we turn to the question of doctrinal standards—that is, to the standards that courts should apply to implement the principles just articulated—an important distinction emerges. The distinction is that between government insiders who leak classified information and newspapers or other third parties who publish the same. While both merit robust protections, third-party publishers merit weightier ones than do insider leakers.

Third-party publishers are not government employees or other insiders in relationships of trust with the government. They have made no explicit or implicit promises of confidentiality to the government in exchange for receiving classified information. Constitutionally, their only role is that of potential check on the government through their participation in the flow of information. As such, the same very broad First Amendment standards that apply to unclassified speech should apply to third-party publications of classified information. Concretely, this means that something akin to the standard for assessing punishments of speech that threaten to incite violence—whereby punishment is constitutionally permissible only if the speech is intended to, and is likely to, incite imminent illegal activity— must apply.[98]

The constitutional position of executive branch insiders, whether government employees or contractors authorized to access classified information, is more complicated than that of outsiders. On the one hand, insiders are a part of the executive branch's machinery. As such, they properly are subject to executive control beyond that to which ordinary citizens are subject. At the same time, insiders' constitutional significance is not exhausted by their role as servants of the branch. They occupy other, equally important positions in the constitutional structure—those of potential checks on abuses or mistakes to which they alone may be privy.

The constitutional balance between executive control and checks on the executive thus calls for a nuanced calibration of protections and permissible punishments for insider leakers. The calibration should reflect two factors. First, it must be grounded partly in the relationship between the employee's institutional role and the punishment sought by the government. Second, it must reflect a considered balance between the constitutional value in deterring leaks and that in avoiding overdeterrence of leaks.

Several outcomes of this calibration warrant note. First, classified leaks should be treated like other government employee speech when employment sanctions such as dismissal or demotion are at issue. As we shall see in chapter 6, this means that a balancing test applies when employees are disciplined for leaks. Second, the government must meet a considerably higher threshold to impose criminal or civil, rather than employment-based administrative penalties. As a matter of institutional position, the government as employer is very differently situated from the government as law enforcer. In a free society, government necessarily has far less control over persons qua persons than it has over persons qua government employees. This translates to a much narrower discretion on the government's part to punish employees criminally or civilly than to punish them through the terms and conditions of their employment. The need to strike a balance between underdeterring and overdeterring leaks also militates in favor of a high law enforcement burden. Certainly, a job loss, demotion, or security clearance loss can be devastating. This is why the government must not have unfettered power to impose such sanctions, given the free speech value in insider leaks. Yet employment sanctions may pale next to the prospect of a lengthy prison sentence or bankrupting fines. At the same time, even with a high burden, the possibility of prosecution or civil punishment surely retains a chilling effect, as does the likelihood of employment-based repercussions.

Additionally, courts should consider varying the precise nature of the government's burden with the severity of the criminal or civil penalty sought. I propose that efforts to impose severe sanctions—for example, prosecutions seeking several years in prison or civil actions seeking potentially bankrupting monetary penalties—require a showing that the leaker lacked an objectively reasonable basis to believe that the public interest in disclosure outweighed identifiable national security harms. Efforts to impose less severe sanctions—for instance, prosecutions that raise the possibility of little if any incarceration time—may warrant a lesser standard. I would propose that the government in the latter cases be required to demonstrate that the leaker lacked an objectively substantial basis to believe that the public interest in disclosure outweighed identifiable national security harms.[99]

Leakers also should categorically be protected from any punishment for leaks that disclose illegal government conduct. To be clear, such protection would not suffice were it leakers' only constitutional shield. Controversy inevitably will surround questions of what is "illegal," particularly insofar as administrations can be expected to argue that some statutory violations are legal from an exclusivist perspective.[100] More fundamentally, such protection, standing on its own, would misallocate the appropriate burdens. Both constitutional reasoning and the reality of classification militate against embedding into constitutional law the presumption that classified information leaks are punishable unless they reveal particular categories of information, such as illegal conduct. Rather, the centrality of speech about government to our system, the risk of a chilling effect on speech, and well-justified fears that government will abuse secrecy and censorial powers warrant broader-based leaker protections. Nonetheless, the categorical permissibility of illegal activity leaks, while inadequate standing alone, is a useful supplement to the other protective elements suggested above.

CHAPTER FOUR

Supremacy Explained and Critiqued

The case for substantive accountability is comprised partly of the affirmative arguments detailed throughout chapter 3. The remainder of the case amounts to a rejoinder to supremacy. This chapter details and counters supremacy and its major rationales.

Supremacy: An Overview

Substantive Categories of Supremacist Argument

Supremacists read the president's constitutional powers to preclude Congress or the courts from limiting, overseeing, or otherwise checking presidential actions in many cases. Rather than a single theory, supremacy is better described as an interpretive tendency with multiple manifestations. Its manifestations include executive privilege; state secrets privilege; an exclusivist prerogative to violate statutes in secret as the president deems necessary to protect national security or the autonomy of his office; and a presidential prerogative to effectively criminalize speech—without triggering the usual strict judicial review required by the First Amendment—by deeming information classified.[1]

The first two claims sometimes are asserted as subsets of exclusivity, or of a right to violate statutes. In other words, supremacists sometimes argue that a particular statute can constitutionally be circumvented or should not be passed in the first place because it violates the president's constitutional discretion to protect executive privilege or state secrets. But the claims can also take forms distinct from exclusivity, such as where the president objects to disclosing information on executive privilege or state secrets grounds when the disclosure is sought not as a matter of stat-

utory right but of inherent judicial power or a congressional committee's
internal rules.

The fourth type of claim is somewhat different in nature from the first
three. While the executive branch at points has argued that Congress cannot constitutionally interfere with its classification powers, the claim on
which this book focuses is triggered where Congress has delegated power
to the executive branch. Specifically, it is triggered in cases where Congress has criminalized certain speech based at least partly on its classified nature. Supremacy comes into play when the executive responds to
speakers' First Amendment defenses. A typical response is that the executive's decision to classify information effectively removes it from the purview of the First Amendment. The supremacist argument, in short, is that
the executive's decision to classify speech essentially replaces—and thus
precludes—the rigorous inquiry in which the judiciary would otherwise
engage where speech is punished for its content. As a matter of terminology, this book uses the term "classified speech" to refer to both the leaking of classified information by government insiders to the press or other
third parties outside of the context of espionage or spying, and the conveying of such information by third-party publishers.

Supremacy as One End of a Spectrum

Supremacist claims exist on a larger spectrum of arguments—ranging
from more to less radical—that champion presidential power in relation
to checks by the other branches. In the classified speech context, for example, the executive might appeal for serious judicial consideration of its
views on the dangerousness of certain speech, without seeking to preclude
the judiciary's making the ultimate substantive determination under the
First Amendment. Such an appeal is not particularly radical and does not
warrant the supremacist label. This is a very different thing from an argument to the effect that the executive's decision to classify a piece of information effectively removes any First Amendment protections—and thus
any substantive judicial role—regarding dissemination of the same.

Chapter 5 goes into greater detail on the relative radicalism of different claims. For now, three points suffice. First, while this book at times
refers loosely to executive privilege, state secrets, and classified speech
claims as "supremacist," some incarnations of these claims are so low in
radicalism as to be nonsupremacist. Like classified speech claims, executive privilege and state secrets arguments can range from nonsupremacist

to supremacist in nature. Supremacist versions might assert, for example, that presidential determinations of the need to keep certain information secret must be conclusive, and that it would undermine Article II for the judiciary to review such information in camera. On the other hand, the executive might argue only that the judiciary should give weight to its position and perform a balancing test. The latter claim is not supremacist in nature.

Second, exclusivist claims—that is, claims of a right to circumvent statutes beyond the narrow confines of extraordinary prerogative— categorically are supremacist. Such claims include, but are not limited to exclusivist executive privilege and state secrets arguments. Exclusivity intrinsically undermines the central protections of macro-transparency and the legislative process. As chapter 5 details, some exclusivist claims are more radical than others. Nonetheless, all are sufficiently radical as to be supremacist.

Third, outside of the exclusivity context—and thus in the realm of classified speech or nonexclusivist executive privilege and state secrets claims—there is no exact science by which one can cleanly divide supremacist claims from nonsupremacist claims. Roughly speaking, however, the higher the level of radicalism—that is, the more deference demanded by the executive to its judgment—the more likely that the claim is supremacist in nature.

Supremacist Reasoning

Because supremacy is an interpretive tendency with multiple manifestations, it has no single, universally agreed-upon set of justifications. Each of the four subsets of supremacy just cited has unique interpretive features on which chapter 5 elaborates. Furthermore, different authors with different roles—ranging from scholarly to executive to legislative—writing at different times on different aspects of supremacy offer varied textual, structural, and historical justifications. These writers also vary in the clarity with which they address certain points.

Still, by mining major supremacist works, one can piece together a composite set of constitutional arguments in which supremacists ground their shared interpretive tendency. Starting at the most basic level, one core justification for supremacy is that the president has a duty to protect national security that cannot constitutionally be compromised by legislative or judicial restrictions. The second core justification for supremacy—

manifesting itself in the executive privilege context—is that the president has a constitutional discretion to protect the confidentiality of high-level executive branch communications and that this discretion may not be hindered unduly by legislative or judicial information-sharing demands.

SUPREMACY AND THE ORIGINAL MEANING OF EXECUTIVE POWER.   Supremacy's core justifications are not always linked explicitly to particular constitutional clauses. When supremacists do draw such links, however, they tend to focus on one or both of two clauses. The first is Article II's Vesting Clause. It reads, "The executive Power shall be vested in a President of the United States of America."[2] In drawing on this clause, supremacists often start with the notion—sometimes called the "Vesting Clause thesis"[3]— that the clause does not merely introduce the more specific powers and duties subsequently detailed in Article II, such as the power to appoint judges and executive branch officers "by and with the Advice and Consent of the Senate."[4] Rather, the clause is itself a grant of substantive power.[5] The Vesting Clause thesis is confirmed by constitutional text and structure, say its proponents. For example, they contrast the language of Article II's Vesting Clause with that of Article I's Vesting Clause. Article I vests Congress only with "all legislative Powers *herein granted.*"[6] The difference in language, they say, indicates that Article II's Vesting Clause does more than simply reference powers enumerated elsewhere in Article II. Rather, it grants all powers that the founders understood to be executive in nature, with the exception only of those explicitly delegated elsewhere.[7]

To frame the Vesting Clause thesis in modern originalist terms, the Vesting Clause locks in the original public meaning of the executive power, which encompasses substantive powers. Of course, even if one supports the Vesting Clause thesis, one still must determine the content of those powers and the aspects thereof that were left to the president and not delegated elsewhere in the Constitution. Depending on one's answers to these questions, supremacy need not follow from the thesis.[8] For example, some modern proponents of the Vesting Clause thesis have advanced it only to support a fairly modest set of powers—such as powers to articulate foreign policy or "protective" powers—that are subject to statutory limits.[9] Furthermore, some scholars who rely on the Vesting Clause thesis to support unitary executive theory have explicitly distanced themselves from aspects of supremacy.[10]

What sets supremacists apart in their use of the Vesting Clause is this: Through their readings of "the executive power" and of constitutional clauses that distribute parts of that power away from the presidency, they find a wide berth of presidential discretion that is supreme over contrary congressional or judicial actions. Some supremacists argue that, at the time of the founding, the term "executive power" was understood to encompass the prerogatives of the British Crown, including exclusive control over foreign affairs and national security. Through the Vesting Clause, the founders bequeathed these prerogatives to the president, excepting only those parts explicitly delegated to the Senate or the Congress as a whole in other parts of Article I or II.[11] Supremacists also meld originalist reasoning with functional reasoning about the president's characteristic energy. They conclude that the founders deliberately embraced so broad a meaning of executive power because they believed that only the president, with his energetic capacities, was functionally equipped to have the final word on matters of national security and foreign affairs.[12]

Gary Lawson employs such reasoning, albeit somewhat tentatively and indirectly, to conclude that the Vesting Clause empowers the president to conduct wartime intelligence gathering operations that Congress likely cannot restrict. In explaining that the Vesting Clause encompasses such exclusive powers, Lawson cites among other things to a defense of the Terrorist Surveillance Program (TSP)[13] by John C. Eastman. Eastman deemed the TSP within the president's powers and not subject to congressional restriction partly because "[o]ur nation's Founders created ... [an executive] strong enough to 'protect the community against foreign attacks,' with 'secrecy' and 'dispatch' if necessary."[14]

Arguments similarly melding history and functional reasoning were ventured in the late 1980s. They reflected conservative fears of a fettered presidency stretching back to the post-Watergate era and more immediately triggered by perceptions that Congress had overreached in response to the Iran-Contra affair. For example, Robert F. Turner invoked the Vesting Clause thesis as partial explanation for his view that some of the statutory restrictions at issue in Iran-Contra were unconstitutional usurpations of executive power that could legally be circumvented. Turner observed that foreign affairs powers traditionally belonged solely to the executive because "legislative bodies were [deemed] 'incompetent' to manage foreign affairs because they lacked the essential qualities of unity of design, secrecy, and speed of dispatch."[15]

SUPREMACY, ORIGINALISM, AND THE COMMANDER-IN-CHIEF CLAUSE. The second major textual hook that supremacists invoke is the Commander-in-Chief Clause of Article II, which reads: "The President shall be Commander-in-Chief of the Army and Navy of the United States."[16] Supremacists sometimes cite this clause alone and sometimes in tandem with the Vesting Clause for the proposition that the president's judgment is supreme as to which national security activities and secrecy measures are necessary to further a wartime effort, to defend against future attacks, or otherwise to protect the national security.[17] Supremacists often deem it self-evident that the Commander-in-Chief Clause precludes Congress from directing battlefield tactics—for example, from telling the president "take that hill." They analogize from that example to other directives that they deem unconstitutional.[18] In defending the TSP, for example, the Department of Justice argued in a public memorandum released shortly after the *New York Times* revealed the program's existence, that the TSP involved "tactical military decisions" on a global "battlefield."[19]

Supremacists treat it largely a matter of common sense that the commander-in-chief title entails indefeasible discretion on the battlefield and in analogous settings.[20] They tie this reading to founding assurances of the president's energetic capacities. These capacities, supremacists explain, equip the president far better than the legislature to conduct a war. From this, supremacists draw a broad and exclusive prerogative for the president to exercise those capacities as he deems necessary to further military objectives or protect national security.[21] Thus, Congress may not constitutionally tell the president which hill to take. Nor, by extension, may it restrict intelligence gathering, detention, or other measures that the president deems necessary to a military campaign or to national security.[22]

Supremacists claim additional support from the framers' decision at the Philadelphia convention to replace draft language empowering Congress to "make war" with language empowering it to "declare war." The impetus for the change was the wish to "leave[] to the Executive the power to repel sudden attacks." Furthermore, to quell Oliver Ellsworth's objection to the change, Rufus King explained that "'*make*' war might be understood to 'conduct' it which was an Executive function."[23] From the framing concern over sudden attacks, some supremacists infer a broad and exclusive prerogative for the president to act as he deems necessary to stave off attacks, irrespective of temporal imminence.[24] As for the framing reference to "conducting" war, it is sometimes invoked to bolster the force of analogies from the president's control over military tactics to presidential control over a host of national security decisions.[25]

SUPREMACIST REASONING FROM CONSTITUTIONAL PRINCIPLES AND EVOLVING HISTORY.   As we have just seen, supremacists often combine arguments about original meaning with functional reasoning grounded in constitutional principles. Functional reasoning also can be deployed as an independent basis for supremacy; for example, through the argument that supremacy is necessary to support constitutional principles of energy and accountability. Superficially—that is, without distinguishing between formal and substantive accountability or uncontained and contained energy—the principles invoked by supremacists mirror those underlying the substantive accountability framework.

In addition to invoking constitutional principles alone or to bolster originalist analyses, supremacists sometimes meld principles with evolving history. In so doing, they treat instances of supremacy in American history as affirming and reflecting founding principles. As we saw in chapter 2, evolving history arguments generally rest on one or both of two premises. First, presidential supremacy over time reveals the true and intended nature of the constitutional presidency and its relationship to the other branches. Second, a history of presidential supremacy and congressional acquiescence reflects an implicit interpretive consensus in favor of supremacy by both branches.

The first justification was voiced prominently in the Iran-Contra Minority Report. The report cites the founding premises that the president will be capable of "'decision, activity, secrecy, and dispatch'" and that he will be readily accountable for his actions. From this, the Minority Report draws a constitutional presumption that activities that call for such capacities or that involve case-by-case decision making for which a single person can most readily be held to account belong to the president alone. Among the activities in this category are "the deployment and use of force (but not declarations of war), together with negotiations, intelligence gathering, and other diplomatic communications (but not treaty ratification)."[26]

The Minority Report argues that this founding design has been borne out by actions of the political branches throughout history. It cites instances in which the president took unilateral action without seeking congressional approval, including covert operations, intelligence gathering, uses of force, and actions taken pursuant to the president's interpretation of treaties. The report deems it unsurprising that presidents frequently have asserted rights to act without congressional sanction. It quotes Gary Schmitt's observation to the effect that such assertions follow naturally from the president's structural capacities:

To some extent, the enumerated powers found in Article II are deceiving in that they appear understated. By themselves, they do not explain the particular primacy the presidency has had in the governmental system since 1789.

What helps to explain this fact is the presidency's radically different institutional characteristics, especially its unity of office. Because of its unique features, it enjoys—as the framers largely intended—the capacity of acting with the greatest expedition, secrecy and effective knowledge. As a result, when certain stresses, particularly in the area of foreign affairs, are placed on the nation, it will "naturally" rise to the forefront.[27]

The second supremacist justification for evolving history—that a history of presidential supremacy and congressional acquiescence represents an implicit interpretive consensus by the political branches—fits nicely into the "fettered presidency" narrative that presidentialists developed in the 1970s and 1980s. For example, an essay in the 1989 book *The Fettered Presidency* argues that early congresses "[appear] to have understood [their] power to 'make all laws . . . necessary and proper for carrying into execution . . . all other powers' as mandating that [they] 'facilitate the exercise of executive power in the realm of foreign affairs.'" In contrast, the essay's authors use the example of congressional oversight of covert action to lament that more recent congresses have overstepped their traditional constitutional role.[28]

The Minority Report is rife with similar sentiments. Referring to the use of force without congressional authorization, for example, the report concludes that "[u]ntil recently, the Congress did not even question the President's authority." It also observes that "[f]or the Congresses that had accepted the overt presidential uses of military force summarized [elsewhere in the report], the use of Executive power for . . . covert activities raised no constitutional questions." The Minority Report explicitly links these examples to the case for presidential exclusivity, concluding that

> [c]ongressional actions to limit the President in [the area of foreign policy] should be reviewed with a considerable degree of skepticism. If they interfere with core presidential foreign policy functions, they should be struck down. Moreover, the lesson of our constitutional history is that doubtful cases should be decided in favor of the President.[29]

The Trouble with Supremacy

The Vesting Clause Does Not Lock in Supremacy

PRERATIFICATION MATERIALS.   Supremacists glean the original meaning of executive power partly from the works of Locke, Montesquieu, and

Blackstone, whom they explain deeply influenced members of the founding generation. These writers, supremacists argue, make clear that the executive power encompasses the prerogatives associated with the Crown.
These prerogatives include all foreign affairs powers, all powers of war
and peace, and the Lockean prerogative to suspend statutes in times of
emergency.[30] Supremacists also emphasize the functional reasons given
by these authors as to why these powers belong to the same government
entity charged with executing statutes. Turner explains that "[a]ll three
of these writers viewed the control of foreign affairs to be the exclusive
province of the Executive. They argued, in essence, that legislative bodies were 'incompetent' to manage foreign affairs because they lacked the
essential qualities of unity of design, secrecy, and speed of dispatch." For
instance, while Locke distinguished between the "'executive' powers to
'execute' the laws enacted by the legislature" and the "'federative' power
over [foreign affairs,]" Locke deemed the powers "almost always united"
in the same hands because they call for similar functional advantages.[31]
Given their view of the original meaning of executive power, and of the
functional reasons for its breadth, supremacists deem the Vesting Clause
to grant wide zones of indefeasible discretion to the president. For the
same reasons, they argue that any textual exceptions to the clause must be
very narrowly construed.[32]

These arguments reflect the presidentialist tendency to claim robust
founding-era directives by overreading the evidence for original meaning or intent. When original public meaning is invoked, the problem of
overreading derives partly from the use of hypothetical founders through
whom meaning is channeled. As we saw in chapter 2, the technique enables interpreters to identify the primary documents that they deem essential, interpret those documents themselves, equate their interpretation with that of designated hypothetical founders whose characteristics
they define, and deem their interpretation locked in as a matter of original
meaning. Through this approach, is it all too easy to unearth intricate
constitutional directives even where the evidence suggests that actual
founding-era understandings were uncertain, mixed, or directly contrary
to these interpretations.

As also observed in chapter 2, some supremacists couch their analyses
in the language of framers' intent or ratifiers' understanding.[33] Yet their
reasoning remains materially the same as that of works framed in terms
of public meaning. As such, both sets of works share the same difficulties. Rather than overreading selected primary documents and deeming
the resulting interpretations those of hypothetical founders, original in-

tent or understanding based works derive the same conclusions but attribute them to actual founders. In both cases, overreach is facilitated partly through a selective focus on a handful of statements or founders. Both sets of works also deemphasize evidence of the broader framing, ratifying, and intellectual histories that call into question the nature and certainty of the constitutional meanings that supremacists deem locked in by the constitutional text. Because originalist supremacist approaches do not differ materially, regardless of whether they reference original public meaning, original intent, or original understanding, this book groups them together as "original meaning" or simply as "originalist" arguments except where otherwise noted.

Originalist overreach infects supremacist reliance on Locke, Montesquieu, and Blackstone in two key respects. First, supremacist interpretations of these materials in their own rights are strained. Second, the interpretations are at odds with substantial evidence of actual founding-era understandings. That evidence suggests that founding views of executive power fluctuated, leaned toward modesty, and approached consensus only on the point that the executive power is the power to implement the laws created by the legislature.

Supremacist interpretations of Locke, Montesquieu, and Blackstone evince far greater certainty about the intrinsic content of executive power than do the three writers themselves. For example, Locke argued that the federative power over foreign affairs and national security should, for functional reasons, be held by the same person who executes the laws. As a matter of definition, however, he clearly distinguished between the federative and executive powers.[34] Montesquieu, for his part, shifted between definitions of executive power at different points in *The Spirit of the Laws.* He also veered between suggesting that certain powers categorically are executive in nature, and indicating instead that those powers should be held by the person who executes the law for functional reasons.[35] And Blackstone's description of executive powers is colored both by the functional nature of some of his arguments and the fact that he wrote from the perspective of the British mixed government system. In this system, government branches were not distinguished primarily by function, but by the different parts of society that each represented. As Curtis Bradley and Martin Flaherty observe, "although Blackstone contends that the prerogatives of the Crown include particular foreign relations powers, he justifies these assignments of power by a combination of functional arguments and arguments relating to the nature of the British monarchy."[36]

Indeed, historian M. J. C. Vile quotes Jeremy Bentham's expressed doubt in the late eighteenth century that "Blackstone, or anyone else, had given enough thought to the terms *legislative power* and *executive power,* which they used so freely, and so vaguely."[37]

As for American understandings of executive power in the founding period, historians identify much flux and inconsistency. They attribute this partly to the uneasy intellectual transition from mixed government to the separation of powers. As Jack Rakove writes:

> The conceptual confusion which arose as Americans sought to define executive power in nonmonarchical terms generated further uncertainty. They embraced the theory of separated powers without wholly abandoning the language of mixed government; they struggled to distinguish the administrative parts of governance from other powers that the British crown had exercised as its prerogative; and they were further puzzled to decide whether foreign relations was more nearly executive or legislative or a hybrid of both.[38]

In addition to the confusion intrinsic in the transition from mixed government, postindependence developments disrupted any preconceptions that royal prerogatives attach to the government actor who executes the laws. Gordon Wood notes that "[m]ost Americans in 1776 ... agreed with William Hooper of North Carolina that 'for the sake of Execution we must have a Magistrate [as state governor],'" but it must be a magistrate 'solely executive,' a governor."[39] Wood adds, "[t]he ruler in American thought would never again be what it had been in English constitutionalism. In most states the governors remained, but they remained, as one Virginian said, 'wholly executive of the political Laws of the State.'"[40] These passages demonstrate two things. One, as Wood summarized, "Americans in their early constitutions had so enervated the traditional conception of the magistracy as an independent constituent of the society that it became in time increasingly impossible for them to think of their governors as anything but the repository of the executive functions of government."[41] Two, it was common for Americans, at least by the postindependence period, to conceive of pure executive power as nothing more than the power to execute the laws.[42]

This is not to say that state or national constitution makers could not opt to attach other prerogatives to the executive. Indeed, in the so-called critical period just prior to framing and ratification, states and the Continental Congress began to rethink the wisdom of weak, "purely executive" executives. But because historical experience had detached the executive from royal prerogatives, there would have been even less reason than there might have been previously to deem those prerogatives intrinsically "executive."[43]

This mix of approaches to executive power—ranging from ambiguity and inconsistency in defining it, to clearly narrow visions of it—were echoed in the framing and ratification debates. Several statements from the opening day of debate on executive power at the Philadelphia Convention nicely capture this mix. "Charles Pinckney opened debate … by declaring that 'he was for a vigorous Executive but was afraid the executive powers' it would inherit from [the Continental] Congress 'might extend to peace & war &c which would render the Executive a Monarchy.'"[44] "John Rutledge similarly stated that 'he was for vesting the executive power in a single person, tho' he was not for giving him the power of war and peace.'"[45] Yet James Wilson explained "that the royal prerogative did not provide 'a proper guide in defining the Executive powers.' Some of those prerogatives were actually legislative, including matters of 'war & peace &c. The only powers he conceived strictly executive were those of executing the laws, and appointing officers' not otherwise 'appointed by the Legislature.'"[46] Echoing Wilson's understanding, Roger Sherman "stated that 'he considered the Executive magistracy as nothing more than an institution for carrying the will of the Legislature into effect.'"[47]

Statements like Wilson's and Sherman's were echoed by federalists throughout the ratification debates to quell fears that the president would be a monarch in all but name. Federalist commentators repeatedly cited the careful delineation and limits of the president's powers. As a commentator from Connecticut put it, "[t]here is nothing of any great importance in his power *solely,* I think no man of considerable discernment can have fears from this quarter unless he has also very weak nerves."[48] Elaborating on this theme at the Virginia ratification convention, Edmund Randolph posed a rhetorical question:

> What are his powers? To see the laws executed. Every Executive in America has that power. He is also to command the army—This power also is enjoyed by the Executives of the different States. He can handle no part of the public money except what is given him by law. At the end of four years he may be turned out of office. If he misbehaves he may be impeached. … I cannot conceive how his powers can be called formidable.[49]

Similarly, Alexander Hamilton took to the *Federalist Papers* not only to mock arguments likening the king to a monarch,[50] but to deny that the president's powers would extend even to dismissing executive officers without Senate approval.[51]

Federalist commentators also emphasized the absence of presidential privileges or prerogatives and hence the president's susceptibility to examination and punishment. These comments very much echoed, and often were made in tandem with, arguments that the president's capacities for secrecy, vigor and dispatch would be contained through legislative directives and through public and interbranch vigilance.[52]

Finally, the problems of presidentialist originalism reflected here intersect with presidentialism's other core flaw—its conflating of formal and substantive accountability, and its corollary conflation of presidential capacities and presidential prerogatives. Where early writers deem the executive well equipped to use kingly prerogatives, supremacists understand them to have said that the executive power categorically *includes* those prerogatives. Similarly, supremacists view founding boasts of the president's energetic capacities as confirmation that the founders wished for him to exercise those capacities free from much interbranch checking and that they accorded him this privilege through the Vesting Clause.

POSTRATIFICATION MATERIALS.   Supremacists also emphasize Alexander Hamilton's postratification statements in support of the Vesting Clause thesis. Under the pseudonym Pacificus, Hamilton wrote that the Vesting Clause granted substantive executive powers. Those powers, he argued, encompassed a right on President Washington's part unilaterally to declare neutrality in the war between France and Britain. Hamilton acknowledged that Congress could declare war and effectively eliminate the state of neutrality. Nonetheless, until that point, and so long as Washington interpreted existing treaty obligations to permit a neutrality declaration, the executive power encompassed his right to make such a declaration.[53]

Furthermore, supremacists seek to minimize the significance of the negative posture that Madison and Jefferson adopted in response to Pacificus. At Jefferson's comically enthusiastic urging,[54] Madison wrote a series of essays under the pseudonym Helvetius, mocking Pacificus's expansive views of executive power. Pacificus's views, said Madison/Helvidius, reflect not the U.S. Constitution, but rather *"royal prerogatives in the British government."*[55] Supremacists suggest that the Helvetius writings do not reflect Jefferson's and Madison's true views. The writings, they argue, were politically opportunistic, inspired by the opposition of both men to neutrality.[56] As a matter of principle, supremacists say, Madison likely supported the Vesting Clause thesis that he had earlier articulated to support the removal power, as he had had no obvious political stake in the removal case.[57] As for Jefferson, supremacists point out that, as Washington's secretary of state, he had advised Washington that "[t]he transaction of business with foreign nations is executive altogether; it belongs, then, to the head of that department, except as to such portions of it as are specially submitted to the Senate. Exceptions are to be construed strictly."[58] They also observe that, as president and after his presidency, Jefferson embraced a governmental prerogative to transcend constitutional limits. Supremacists do criticize Jefferson, however, for deeming the prerogative extra-constitutional, rather than embedded in the constitutional grant of executive power.[59]

Supremacists also cite Hamilton's Pacificus writings to downplay the import of the statements that he made as Publius before ratification. They argue that the latter statements, in which Hamilton minimized the reach of presidential power, were less reflective of Hamilton's true vision than were the former. Hamilton's statements as Publius, they explain, were meant to quell Anti-Federalist fears of a monarchical presidency.[60]

In these postratification analyses, supremacists seem to rely partly on a framers' intent based reasoning to demonstrate not only what Hamilton, Madison, and Jefferson publicly said but what they truly meant. Presumably this evidence also is meant to confirm, from a public meaning perspective, that reasonable founders would have supported supremacist versions of the Vesting Clause thesis. Even if we take for granted the methodological validity of this reasoning, none of the examples cited are clearly supremacist in nature. Madison invoked the Vesting Clause in 1789 to support a presidential removal power.[61] At best, this supports the case for a unitary executive with full control over the executive branch, an issue that will be revisited in chapter 7. It does not, however, speak to presidential supremacy. And as Pacificus, Hamilton argued only for an executive power to declare neutrality insofar as it did not conflict with treaty obligations or other commitments—such as war declarations—within Congress's sphere of action.[62] Even Jefferson, who as president and postpresidency defended a right to transcend constitutional limits in the national interest, suggested that this prerogative belonged to the president and Congress as a whole, not to the president alone. Indeed he made clear his view that it was ultimately for Congress to accept or reject any extra-constitutional presidential actions or commitments, and for the people to determine whether the president and Congress had acted properly.[63]

Supremacists' postratification arguments seek to advance the same false sense of definitional clarity as do their preratification claims. Yet aspects of the arguments—such as the assertion that Hamilton exaggerated his belief, preratification, in the presidency's limitations, and that Madison and Jefferson opportunistically shifted their positions on executive power—only demonstrate the malleability of executive power's meaning, beyond the power to carry out the law, during the founding period. In this respect too, supremacists simply overread the available evidence. They seek, again, to lock in supremacy as a matter of original meaning where neither text nor history warrants it.

The Commander-in-Chief Clause Does Not Lock in Supremacy

In contrast to their positions on the Vesting Clause, supremacists generally do not cite to detailed evidence of original meaning when they invoke the Commander-in-Chief Clause. Instead, they rely primarily on common-sense assumptions about the term and inferences from presidential energy. For example, Michael Paulsen argues that

> Congress's power to declare war is an on-off switch, not a thermostat. Congress has the power to initiate war and the President does not. But once the switch is flicked on, the President has the power to conduct war and Congress does not.... [I]f it were otherwise, the Commander-in-Chief Clause would be a title only, not an independent, substantive presidential power.[64]

From the commander-in-chief power to control battlefield operations, Paulsen draws the classic supremacist analogy to presidential control over a wide range of national security activities.[65] Like other supremacists, he deems his conclusions bolstered by "evidence of the framers' design in creating the office of the presidency," particularly the office's energetic capacities.[66]

Whatever their intuitive appeal, such arguments are simply wrong. They are wrong as a matter of original meaning, and they are wrong as inferences from constitutional principles involving presidential capacities. As we have seen, the argument from principle is deeply flawed insofar as it equates the president's energetic capacities with a prerogative to exercise the same free from containment mechanisms. As for original meaning, the supremacist case is eviscerated by evidence compiled in two separate studies, one by legal scholars David Barron and Martin Lederman and another by legal scholar Saikrishna Prakash. Both studies acknowledge that the commander-in-chief sits atop the military hierarchy as a matter of original meaning.[67] Yet both conclude that the military actions and objectives that the commander-in-chief oversees, even minute tactical decisions, can be dictated by Congress consistent with original meaning.

As Prakash explains, the title of commander-in-chief apparently "originated in mid-seventeenth-century England.... In the seventeenth and eighteenth centuries, there were hundreds of commanders in chief, none of whom had any exclusive powers."[68] He elaborates:

> [T]he President does not succeed to the Crown's military powers because the Crown was not known as the "Commander in Chief." Rather, the President enjoys authority akin to the English Commander in Chief of the British Army, an officer who was subservient to the Crown and Parliament.... [Additionally,] during the Revolutionary War, America had numerous commanders in chief wholly subordinate to other entities, thus making it clear that Americans of that era did not regard commanders in chief as enjoying any exclusive power. The most famous commander in chief, George Washington, was subject to congressional direction throughout the War..... Regarding state constitutions, Professors Barron and Lederman point out that many expressly made the state commanders in chief subject to legislative control. Apparently no state commander in chief was ever thought to have any exclusive, absolute military powers. Taken together, these materials from the Continental Congress and the states fairly prove that prior to the Constitution, there was no general sense that the various commanders in chief enjoyed any exclusive military powers. Instead, every American commander in chief prior to the Constitution's creation was subject to direction by other entities, be they superior commanders in chief, state legislatures, or the Continental Congress.[69]

As Prakash suggests, these findings comport with those of Barron and Lederman.[70] Furthermore, as Prakash observes and Barron and Lederman detail at length, early postfounding practices reflected the assumption that the commander-in-chief was subject to legislative direction on even minute, tactical matters.[71]

The historical evidence thus belies the oft-repeated intuition that the Commander-in-Chief Clause demands national security supremacy as a matter of original meaning. Indeed, the evidence presents a challenge not only to supremacists who rely on the Commander-in-Chief Clause, but to those who rely on the Vesting Clause. While acknowledging his support for the Vesting Clause thesis, Prakash observes that "there is no reason for supposing that [the Vesting Clause] cedes the President any additional military powers or that it somehow ensures the exclusivity of the Commander in Chief's military powers." To make such a construction, he explains, "is to imagine that the Constitution conveys a familiar and limited power in one clause [, the Commander-in-Chief Clause] and simultaneously expands it beyond all recognition in another [, the Vesting Clause]."[72]

Here too we see the impact of supremacy's two major flaws. First, supremacists seek to lock in a robust definition of the commander-in-chief power that, at best, is far from clear as a matter of original meaning and at worst runs counter to the same. Second, they justify their position partly by pointing to structural and historical support for presidential energy. In so doing, they mistake the president's energetic capacities for a prerogative to exercise the same free from containment mechanisms that protect substantive accountability.

How Supremacists Misread Constitutional Principles and Misuse Evolving History

Supremacists thus err in their analyses of original meaning, and these errors intersect with their mistaken reading of constitutional principles. With respect to the latter, supremacists repeatedly confuse the president's historically celebrated structural capacities with legal prerogatives to exercise the same without containment. They also assume that accountability follows from supremacy by construing accountability in formal rather than substantive terms.

Similar problems are reflected in supremacist uses of evolving history. Recall the first type of supremacist argument from evolving history: that acts of supremacy and legislative acquiescence arise naturally from the president's and Congress's respective capacities and thus reflect the proper constitutional order. Such an argument rests on the premise that the president's energetic capacities constitute legal prerogatives. For example, to defend the TSP, the Bush administration argued that many past presidents had engaged in wiretapping on their own initiative.[73] At least one administration supporter argued that FDR had done so in the face of a prohibiting statute.[74] Yet this history supports the TSP only if one assumes that a capacity to initiate and undertake a warrantless wiretapping program is the same as a legal prerogative to do so in the face of a contrary statute. If the two are not the same, then the fact that prior administrations have harnessed their capacities to take such initiative, possibly in the face of contrary legislation, hardly proves that such actions are legal prerogatives of the president. Indeed, if one starts from a substantive accountability based perspective, such past instances are better read as cautionary prods to the people and the Congress—reminders of James Madison's warning that the Constitution's "parchment barriers" are meaningless if not actively guarded.[75]

The second rationale—that evolving history reflects an interpretive consensus within the political branches—is flawed where the facts show anything less than a long-standing pattern of explicit and ongoing congressional consent. It would be reckless to infer Congress's interpretive agreement under any other set of facts, given the respective capacities of Congress and the president. The president may, for example, manage to act for years in the face of contrary legislation due not to active congressional agreement but to his sheer capacity for unilateral action or for secrecy.[76]

In this respect too, the warrantless wiretapping example is instructive. In the wake of revelations about the TSP, the Bush administration cited decades of foreign intelligence surveillance activities, deeming them to reflect a "consistent understanding" that programs like the TSP are constitutional.[77] Yet upon closer inspection, there is no evidence of anything approaching a long-standing consensus that the president may wiretap without a warrant in contravention of statutory authority. For example, while members of the FDR through Kennedy administrations acknowledged publicly that they wiretapped and at times lobbied Congress for legislation "clarifying" their authority to do so, there is a near absence in the extensive legislative hearings on wiretapping and in administration statements of anything resembling an exclusivist argument. To the contrary, the relevant discussions and statements of that time-frame overwhelmingly assume that Congress, even in the midst of a World War, has the legal power to prohibit or restrict national security wiretapping.[78]

How Supremacy Undermines Substantive Accountability

This chapter elaborates on supremacy and its practical implications. It provides examples of supremacist positions taken in the legislative, executive, and judicial branches as well as in scholarship. It breaks these examples into the four major categories of supremacist argument introduced earlier. These categories include executive privilege, state secrets privilege, justifications for "secret law," and arguments for according persons or entities who leak or publish classified speech little if any First Amendment protection from prosecution. The chapter catalogues these examples toward three ends. First, their concreteness helps to illuminate supremacy's practical impact. Second, by demonstrating the extent to which supremacy can be, and often has been, directed against aspects of substantive accountability, the examples betray the incompatibility of supremacy and substantive accountability. If one is persuaded that the Constitution embodies a substantive accountability framework, then the framework's incompatibility with supremacy undermines supremacy's constitutional legitimacy. Third, the examples demonstrate the upward historical trajectory of supremacy. For example, as we shall see, the earliest executive privilege claims were so low in radicalism as arguably not to be supremacist at all. By the mid-twentieth century, however, such claims were increasingly radical. Recognizing differing radicalism levels, as well as radicalism's historical trajectory, is important because supremacists often invoke low-radicalism examples from history to support later, high-radicalism actions. Relatedly, one must understand the importance of fact-specific differences between claims—for example, between claims defending temporary, transparent statutory suspensions versus those justifying long-term, secretive suspensions—in order meaningfully to assess each claim.

Although this chapter's examples are drawn partly from the judiciary, the chapter does not purport to summarize comprehensively the major case law for each category. The chapter's goal is not to map out the doctrinal "big picture," but to illustrate supremacy's applications and impact on substantive accountability, as well as supremacy's historical trajectory across political and legal realms alike. The chapter thus draws examples from a variety of contexts, including executive statements, academic commentary, and judicial reasoning in majority and nonmajority opinions. The chapter that follows this one does provide an overview of the relevant case law. It does so in order to assess how the substantive accountability framework squares with existing doctrine, and how best to frame substantive accountability based arguments from a doctrinal perspective. The instant chapter, in contrast, draws from judicial among other sources to demonstrate supremacy's concrete implications for information control and substantive accountability, and to illuminate the evolution of supremacist claims over time.

Levels of Radicalism, Elaborated

Exclusivist Claims

The most radical exclusivity claims are those that most threaten macro-transparency. Claims of a right not only to circumvent statutes, but to do so in secret for indefinite periods of time, are at the apex of radical exclusivity. Through the TSP, for example, the Bush administration secretly circumvented existing statutory protections over the course of several years. During this time, the OLC issued a classified, very closely held memorandum deeming the TSP legal based on exclusivist reasoning.[1] These actions were extremely radical with respect to macro-transparency. They replaced publicly determined and publicly known statutes with secret, and secretly justified, executive branch law.

Somewhat less radical in nature are ex ante claims against passing particular statutes in the first place on the basis of exclusivity. Such claims are openly made and thus do not directly generate secret, executive-made law. Nonetheless, they seek to avoid statutory limits on executive discretion and thus to give the executive greater room to operate, quite possibly in secret, without macro-transparent constraints. Such claims also may implicitly or explicitly condone secret law by indicating that the executive branch could circumvent particular proposed laws were they to pass. For example, in the years after the TSP's existence was revealed by the *New York Times*, Congress considered new legislation to govern electronic surveillance. Ultimately, a Democratic Congress passed the FISA Amendments Act of 2008 (FAA). The FAA granted the Bush administration much of the wiretapping discretion that it had sought.[2] In a fascinating exchange in one of the congressional hearings held to consider legislation before the FAA's passage, an administration official urged the Senate Judiciary Committee to grant the administration wide discretion to avoid unconstitutionally constraining it. The official suggested that present or future administrations might circumvent a more restrictive statute. He said, "I believe that you'll ... see that if we have a scheme which is much more—which we can use much more easily to protect the nation, there's going to be even less need for this president or future presidents to go outside of FISA."[3]

A still less intrinsically radical claim is one that raises a case-specific objection to a particular disclosure request, where the disclosure right was created by statute. In this case, macro-transparency is not deeply threatened, as the statute is neither circumvented in secret nor blocked from existing in the first place. What is undermined, however, is the ability of the macro-transparent legislative process to generate effective accountability tools. The radicalism of such a claim also depends on the scope of executive discretion that it demands. For example, where a court reviews an information-sharing dispute, a claim that the court must defer entirely to the executive's view and should not even review the disputed information in camera, is quite radical. Less radical is an argument that the court should apply a presumption in the executive's favor but must ultimately make the call by independently reviewing the disputed information and weighing the costs and benefits of disclosure.

Not all exclusivist claims thus are equally radical. Nonetheless, all threaten macro-transparency by challenging the efficacy or very creation of macro-transparent, statutory restrictions and accountability tools. As such, all are sufficiently radical to be deemed supremacist in nature.

Other Claim Types

There is more radicalism variation among claims that raise case-specific objections to particular disclosure requests, where the disclosure rights were not created by statute but stem from internal congressional chamber rules or inherent judicial power. In such cases, the various costs and benefits of disclosure were not already assessed through the macro-transparent legislative process. There thus is room for debate, whether with members of Congress or with a court and opposing counsel, over the merits of a particular disclosure. While macro-transparency is not directly impacted in such a case, accountability tools—such as independent judicial review and congressional oversight—can be very much at stake. In such cases the degree of radicalism hinges on the scope of executive discretion claimed.

Similarly, claims involving "classified speech" and the First Amendment can range from high to fairly low in radicalism, depending on the nature of the claim. Such claims do not directly challenge macro-transparency as they arise in cases involving statutes that criminalize certain speech. Yet they do threaten a crucial accountability tool that supports macro-transparency. Classified information leaks by government employees—ranging from civil service personnel to the White House inner circle—are the lifeblood of journalism. And leaks by government employees to journalists about secret statutory violations at times have been the only means through which the public and members of Congress eventually learned of such activities. The radicalism of a particular claim thus varies by the extent to which it seeks to diminish the judicial scrutiny that would ordinarily apply to criminal punishments of speech if the speech were not deemed classified. At one end of the spectrum is the very radical claim that anyone who disseminates classified information—whether a government employee or the *New York Times*—can be criminally punished consistent with the First Amendment. Less radical are claims that do not deem First Amendment concerns fully vitiated by classification status, but that call for some lesser level of judicial scrutiny than would apply in the context of nonclassified speech. Less radical claims may also allow for other fact-specific elements to be taken into account, such as whether the speech at issue was leaked by a government employee or disseminated by the press.

Executive Privilege

The earliest executive privilege claims in postfounding America were relatively narrow objections to information requests by Congress and, less frequently, by courts. The case-by-case nature of early claims is evidenced partly by the absence of a standard label for them until 1958, when the Eisenhower administration coined the term "executive privilege."[4] For clarity's sake, I use that label to refer to all such claims, including those made before 1958.

The first executive privilege episode in American history occurred when a congressional committee sought papers from the Washington administration regarding a failed military expedition led by General St. Clair. According to the memoirs of Thomas Jefferson—then Washington's secretary of state—Washington and his cabinet were of the view that the president should withhold papers that might damage the public interest. Yet as the memoirs and subsequent events reflect, the cabinet decided that the release of the St. Clair papers would not be damaging. Washington thus complied with the congressional committee's request.[5] Washington took a similarly fact-tailored approach in the second information-sharing episode of his administration. In that case, the Senate sought correspondence involving Gouverneur Morris, U.S. ambassador. Washington transmitted portions of the requested documents, explaining to the Senate that "I directed copies and translations to be made; except in those particulars, in my judgment, for public considerations, ought not to be communicated. These copies and translations are now transmitted to the Senate; but the nature of them manifest the propriety of their being received as confidential."[6]

In the third and final episode of President Washington's administration, the House of Representatives sought the instructions that the president had given to Chief Justice John Jay to negotiate a treaty with Britain. Washington refused the request on the ground that the House had no constitutional role in the treaty process—treaties are negotiated by the president and subject to supermajority approval by the Senate. Washington explained that disclosing negotiations, even after their completion, would fly in the face of the secrecy concerns that led the founders to delegate treaty consideration to the president and the Senate alone. Washington stressed that he had provided the Senate with all papers relevant to approving the treaty.[7] The House, which had sought the papers to help decide whether to appropriate funding to implement the treaty, passed two nonbinding resolutions in response to Washington's refusal. The first affirmed the House's constitutional role in passing legislation necessary to implement treaties. The second "insisted that the House need never declare the purposes or application of the information, so long as the information related to 'Constitutional functions of the House.'"[8]

It is disputable whether these early claims can be considered supremacist. In the first two cases, Washington did not assert a preclusive legal right—as opposed to policy judgments subject to negotiation or even statutory directive—to withhold information from a body with a constitutional interest in receiving it.[9] In the third case, Washington did suggest that the House generally had no entitlement to information regarding treaty negotiations, as the House conducted no business involving the same. However mistaken this claim, it nonetheless is distinct from that of a right to withhold information from a body with a legitimate need for it.

If supremacist, these early claims nonetheless are fairly low in radicalism. For one thing, each claim was made and explained openly. Each of the first two claims was defended in a fact-specific manner. To the extent that President Washington viewed these responses as legal claims, they were legal claims contingent on facts and hence conducive to debate and negotiation. This is distinct from legal claims that seek effectively to preclude debate by cloaking their justifications in secrecy or asserting a legal discretion so sweeping as to elide fact-specific objections. As for the third claim, again, however incorrect its underlying premise—that the House has no legitimate interest in treaty negotiations—it is distinct from a claim of right to withhold information from a body with a legitimate interest in the same. Furthermore, even the third claim was subject to challenge on a fact-specific basis. Indeed, House members contested it on the ground that they required the requested information to cast informed votes on funding the treaty negotiated by John Jay.

In any event, these early claims hardly reflected a consensus across branches or administrations. The congressional committee investigating the St. Clair expedition had nothing to contest, as Washington turned over all requested papers. In the dispute involving Gouverneur Morris, the Senate did not object to Washington's redactions, but this silence could have meant many things. As Prakash points out, "the Senate's unwillingness to challenge Washington's deletions may have reflected nothing more than a changed political calculus. . . . [Alternatively,] it is entirely possible that the Senate found the furnished materials sufficient for the Senate's needs."[10] In the third case, House members adopted "strong resolutions of protest" in response to Washington's refusal to turn over the instructions that he had given John Jay.[11] Washington's approach in the Jay Treaty case also was implicitly repudiated by his successor President Adams, who transmitted to the House and Senate instructions that he had provided to three special envoys to France.[12]

The seeds of more radical executive privilege claims began to be planted around the mid-nineteenth century, becoming relatively standard by about the mid-twentieth century.[13] Claims are now typically framed as matters of constitutional right, with the right extrapolated partly from the president's capacity to keep secrets. Such extrapolation often takes the form of historical argument. For example, executive privilege proponents infer a constitutional right to keep secrets from postfounding examples of presidential secret keeping, including the Washington administration examples discussed above.[14] They also infer such a right from founding-era statements celebrating secrecy as one of the president's energetic traits.[15]

Modern claims are also much broader than those of the Washington administration. For example, the Eisenhower administration expressed the view that "the President and the heads of departments have an uncontrolled discretion to withhold . . . information and papers in the public interest."[16] President Eisenhower also "was the first to claim explicitly an executive privilege based simply on an undifferentiated interest in preserving the confidentiality of deliberations and advice throughout the Executive Branch."[17] The latter claim is generally framed as the "candor" rationale—that is, the notion that the president may shield high level executive branch communications when he determines that disclosing the same could inhibit candor in future communications.[18] An early reference to the rationale by the Obama administration demonstrates its long reach.[19] In the wake of a controversy over security procedures for the White House state dinner, the administration explained that the White House social secretary is immune from testifying before Congress "[b]aced on the separation of powers" and the need for "the White House staff to provide advice to the [P]resident confidentially."[20]

Modern, relatively radical claims have substantial shadow effects in light of their far-reaching rationales. Consider the impact, for example, of the Supreme Court's 1974 decision in *United States v. Nixon.*[21] *Nixon* arose from Richard Nixon's refusal to turn over tapes of oval office conversations subpoenaed in the Watergate prosecutions.[22] While rejecting President Nixon's claim of privilege under the extraordinary circumstances of the case, the Court for the first time recognized executive privilege as a valid constitutional doctrine. Citing the candor rationale, the Court deemed the privilege a presumptive one in favor of the president.[23] The Court also suggested that where the claim rests on a different rationale— that of national security—the presumption is even stronger, requiring extreme if not absolute judicial deference.[24] Since the *Nixon* case, the candor and national security rationales have been invoked many times by Democratic and Republican administrations alike to oppose information access demands.[25] Administrations also routinely cite to a federal appeals court decision that preceded *United States v. Nixon* by two months and validated the Nixon administration's refusal to refuse to turn over White House tapes requested by the Senate Select Committee on Presidential Campaign Activities. The court in that case, *Senate Select Committee v. Nixon,* held that a congressional body can overcome the presumption favoring executive privilege only by showing that the information sought "is demonstrably critical to the responsible fulfillment of the Committee's functions."[26] Administrations regularly invoke that standard in refusing to disclose information in a wide range of settings.[27] Such demurrals fuel a cycle whereby administrations invoke previous administrations' positions to support their own. This cycle, and the ever-present possibility of future intransigence, can discourage congressional inquiries in light of their possible futility and provide a welcome escape hatch for congresspersons who prefer not to probe the executive branch for partisan or other political reasons.[28]

The most radical executive privilege claims are exclusivist in nature—that is, they embrace a right to circumvent statutes that impose disclosure requirements. Before considering examples of such claims, it is helpful to understand the different ways in which exclusivist objections to statutes can manifest themselves. The most obvious form of such an objection is an explicit claim to the effect that a statute is unconstitutional on its face or as applied. Yet exclusivity can also manifest itself through aggressive statutory interpretation. That is, through strained statutory readings that lead to the conclusion that particular presidential actions are permitted by statute. Two marks of an exclusivity-infused statutory reading are (1) the tenuousness of the statutory interpretation and (2) the linking of the interpretation to a broad view of the president's power under Article II. The link can take one of two forms. It can take the form of an argument that a statute authorizing presidential power is most naturally read broadly given the breadth of the president's constitutional discretion to execute laws. Or it can amount to the position that the statute must be read very broadly if reasonably possible because a more constraining statute would violate the president's constitutional powers or would raise a serious question to that effect.

An important example of an exclusivity-infused statutory interpretation involving executive privilege arose in the midst of the Iran-Contra controversy. In 1986, the OLC was asked to offer an opinion on the legality of the decision previously made and implemented by President Reagan to withhold notice to the congressional intelligence committees of the decision to sell arms to Iran until roughly ten months after the deal was complete.[29] The statutory requirement at issue was Section 501 of the National Security Act. For any covert actions about which the intelligence committees were not given prior notice, the act required the president to inform them "in a timely fashion" and to provide a "statement of the reasons for not giving prior notice."[30] The OLC concluded that the word "timely" had to be interpreted to give the president "virtually unfettered" discretion to withhold notice for however long he deemed necessary. Otherwise, the act would raise serious constitutional questions.[31] Among other things, the OLC cited *United States v. Nixon,* explaining that while the *Nixon* Court rejected President Nixon's claim, "the Court repeatedly and emphatically stressed that military or diplomatic secrets are in a different category: Such secrets are intimately linked to the president's Article II duties, where the "courts have traditionally shown the utmost deference to Presidential responsibilities."[32]

Another indirect use of executive privilege to avoid a statutory disclosure requirement can occur when an administration warns that executive privilege concerns might be raised if statutory disclosure rights are pursued. This technique proved successful in the 2004 case of *Cheney v. United States District Court.*[33] The *Cheney* Court admonished lower courts that the vice president need not invoke executive privilege in order to seek court protection from disclosing information under an openness law. Instead, the Court explained, it was enough for the vice president to object to an entire discovery request on separation of powers grounds, including the ground that it would unduly burden him to have to claim executive privilege with respect to particular pieces of information.[34] Hence, the very possibility that executive privilege problems might be raised by aspects of a discovery order was enough to get the order struck (and ultimately, on remand, to have the case dismissed) although executive privilege was never claimed.[35]

Administrations also invoke the concept of executive privilege to object to proposed legislation and thus to keep macro-transparent disclosure obligations from arising in the first place. For example, the Obama administration objected to proposed legislation to require notice to the congressional intelligence committees in cases where administrations currently may notify a smaller group known as the "Gang of Eight."[36] The administration deemed the proposal to "raise significant executive privilege concerns by purporting to require the disclosure of internal Executive branch legal advice and deliberations." It also cited "the President's responsibility to protect sensitive national security information."[37] The administration also threatened to veto an amended proposal, written in response to its initial objection, to allow Gang of Eight notice while requiring some general information—including the fact that more detailed notice was given to the Gang of Eight—to be provided to the full intelligence committees.[38]

In another striking example, administrations of both parties have objected to proposed statutes that would require executive branch employees to report directly to Congress on certain matters without enabling the president or a department head first to review and revise such reports. As discussed in chapter 8, these objections rest partly on unitary executive theory. Yet administrations also routinely cite executive privilege as an independent basis to render such provisions unconstitutional.[39]

State Secrets Privilege

There is some debate over the precise parameters of the state secrets privilege, including the extent to which it overlaps with executive privilege.[40] This book proceeds on the conventional assumption that there is some overlap between the two privileges and some applications unique to each privilege. This assumption entails three main points. First, national-security-based executive privilege claims made in response to congressional requests for information do not overlap with state secrets claims, as the latter are limited to evidentiary privileges in litigation. Second, state secrets claims that do not involve high-level executive branch communications—such as discussions with the president—do not overlap with executive privilege claims. Third, there is some potential for overlap between state secrets and executive privilege where a national security–based secrecy claim is made in response to a litigation-driven request for information involving presidential or other high-level executive branch communications.

The state secrets privilege enables the government to argue to a court that it would endanger national security to reveal certain evidence in open court or even in a closed setting to the court alone.[41] The doctrine's basis and origins are somewhat disputed. Some argue that it developed solely as a common law privilege with no constitutional content, while others treat it as a presidentialist privilege with roots in both the common law and constitutional law.[42] The debate has significant practical implications. If the privilege is grounded solely in the common law, it can be overridden by statute. If it is grounded in the president's constitutional powers to protect national security, then it is subject to the supremacist positions that Congress may not curtail it and courts must defer deeply when the executive asserts it. Given this dispute, it is not surprising that the Supreme Court's seminal state secrets case bears elements of both low-level and high-level radicalism. The case, 1953's *United States v. Reynolds*,[43] marked the Court's first explicit recognition of the doctrine.[44]

Reynolds stemmed from lawsuits brought under the Federal Tort Claims Act (FTCA) by the widows of three civilian observers on a B-29 aircraft that crashed during a test flight. The widows claimed that the crash was caused by air force negligence.[45] They sought the production of the air force's official accident report.[46] The air force sought to quash the request, claiming a constitutional privilege to protect state secrets.[47] The air force explained that the plane had carried "'confidential equipment on board and any disclosure of its mission or information concerning its operation or performance would be prejudicial to [the air force] and would not be in the public interest.'"[48]

The widows argued that Congress had overridden any privilege by passing the FTCA and that it was within Congress's constitutional power to do so.[49] The Supreme Court concluded that it need not weigh in on either side of the constitutional issue. Instead, it read the FTCA to incorporate the state secrets privilege.[50] The Court thus explored the privilege's content but did not address whether it was constitutionally based and whether Congress could override it.

As for the privilege's content, the Court outlined the following principles:

> The privilege belongs to the Government and must be asserted by it; it can neither be claimed nor waived by a private party. It is not to be lightly invoked. There must be formal claim of privilege, lodged by the head of the department which has control over the matter, after actual personal consideration by that officer. The court itself must determine whether the circumstances are appropriate for the claim of privilege, and yet do so without forcing a disclosure of the very thing the privilege is designed to protect.[51]

The Court added that "[t]he latter requirement is the only one which presents real difficulty."[52] With respect to that requirement, the Court cautioned the judiciary not to abdicate their judgment over evidentiary matters "to the caprice of executive officers."[53] This point was coupled with the Court's earlier warning to the executive branch not to invoke the privilege lightly. Yet the Court declined to

> go so far as to say that the court may automatically require a complete disclosure to the judge before the claim of privilege will be accepted in any case. It may be possible to satisfy the court, from all the circumstances of the case, that there is a reasonable danger that compulsion of the evidence will expose military matters which, in the interest of national security, should not be divulged. When this is the case, the occasion for the privilege is appropriate, and the court should not jeopardize the security which the privilege is meant to protect by insisting upon an examination of the evidence, even by the judge, alone, in chambers.[54]

The Court also suggested that judicial assessments as to whether disclosure would create a "reasonable danger" should be weighed against the strength of the interests in disclosure. However, "even the most compelling necessity [for disclosure] cannot overcome the claim of privilege if the court is ultimately satisfied that military secrets are at stake."[55]

The *Reynolds* Court deemed the widows' need for the accident report "dubious" because the widows could have, but did not, interview the surviving crew members.[56] The Court thus concluded that "a formal claim of privilege, made under the circumstances of this case, will have to prevail" based on the government's affidavits. The Court did not look beyond the affidavits to review the accident report itself or deem it necessary for the lower court to do so on remand. The Court remanded the case to the trial court for further proceedings consistent with its decision.[57]

Certain aspects of the *Reynolds* opinion lay the foundation for a privilege low in radicalism. The Court left open the possibility that the privilege could be overridden by statute. Of equal importance, it stated that the judiciary must independently determine whether and how the privilege applies in any given case, as "'[i]t is the judge who is in control of the trial, not the executive.'"[58] Still, in applying the privilege, the Court planted the seeds of a far more radical doctrine by refusing to require in camera judicial review of the evidence at issue. As one commentator explained in reflecting on *Reynolds*, "if the court does not examine the information, it must decide in the dark. Thus, the executive will almost always determine the legal question of privilege."[59]

The risk of executive abuse when judges do not independently examine evidence is sharply illuminated by the factual developments that followed *Reynolds*. As noted, the *Reynolds* Court remanded the case back to the lower courts. At that point, the widows' attorney noticed depositions of the surviving crew members. The attorney subsequently wrote to one of the widows that "'we went ahead and took the depositions'" and that the crew members stated that the secret equipment that the government claimed would be revealed in the accident report "'had absolutely nothing to do with the accident and had not even been put into operation.'"[60] According to the widows' recollections, the attorney at that point "seemed inclined to take the issue back to district court, using the depositions as evidence that access to the accident report was needed."[61] However, the widows decided against a further round of litigation. The advice of one widow's family lawyer might have played a role. He wrote to her of his "doubts now, as we are deprived of most essential proof to make out a case." The accident report "was of official character and carries in it the determinable cause of the failure in the plane which precipitated the tragedy." Statements by surviving crew members "might and might not spell out negligence sufficient to base a judgment in your favor thereon; but inasmuch as these are all that is left to us to proceed on, [the plaintiffs' attorney] will have to make the best of them on the trial."[62] The widows agreed to settle with the government rather than continue to trial.[63]

Nearly fifty years later, the daughter of one of the deceased civilian observers obtained the accident report, which by then was declassified, after learning on the internet that it was available.[64] She discovered that the report contained no military secrets about experimental equipment or otherwise. "But there was incriminating evidence showing government negligence. According to the report, the crash was most likely caused by an engine fire. Contrary to air force directives, a protective shield designed to prevent engine overheating had not been installed."[65]

Reynolds's impact has been substantial, with the decision's high-radicalism potential increasingly realized. For one thing, many lower courts have upheld privilege claims based solely on government affidavits or declarations, without themselves reviewing the disputed materials.[66] Indeed, courts at times have upheld claims based solely on government declarations even when the disputed information had once been in the public domain and was retroactively classified after the plaintiff's lawsuit was filed.[67] Courts have also upheld claims based on government declarations that invoke the theoretically limitless "mosaic theory."[68] The mosaic theory encompasses "the notion that the government may withhold otherwise trivial or innocuous information because it might prove dangerous if combined with other information by a knowledgeable actor (especially a hostile intelligence agency)."[69]

More so, state secrets doctrine has been used as a basis not only to exclude pieces of evidence, but to dismiss entire cases because the very subject matter of the litigation is deemed a state secret or because the plaintiff is deemed unable to make their case or the defendant to offer a defense without disclosing state secrets. Research by Robert Chesney reveals that the government, as reflected in published cases, requested dismissal on state secrets grounds five times between 1971 and 1980 (with three of the five requests granted), nine times between 1981 and 1990 (with eight of the nine requests granted), thirteen times between 1991 and 2000 (with twelve of the thirteen requests granted), and sixteen times between 2001 and 2006 (with ten of the sixteen requests granted).[70]

As noted, assertions of the privilege and judicial applications of the same are often underscored by supremacist reasoning. For example, both the Bush and Obama administrations sought the dismissal of entire cases under the privilege. Each took the position that the privilege, while developed at common law, "has a firm foundation in the constitutional authority of the President under Article II to protect national security information."[71]

Supremacist invocations of the state secrets privilege tend to conflate presidential energy with a prerogative to use that energy with little containment. For example, courts applying the state secrets privilege first and most ubiquitously reason that the executive branch, by virtue of the fact that it has access to so many secrets and that it often plays a predominant role in national security matters, has an expertise that courts cannot safely second-guess. As Amanda Frost and Justin Florence explain, "[j]udges repeatedly assert that they must defer to the executive because they lack the ability to make independent judgments about the executive's claimed need for the privilege, and frankly concede that they are reluctant [to] second-guess the executive's assertions that disclosure will put the nation at risk."[72] Second, the expertise rationale is sometimes explicitly intertwined with the more straightforward notion that national security secrecy decisions belong to the executive branch as a matter of constitutional right.

The opinion of the U.S. Court of Appeals for the Fourth Circuit in *El Masri v. United States* exemplifies both lines of reasoning.[73] In *El Masri,* the court dismissed a case brought by a German citizen of Lebanese descent who claimed that the CIA mistakenly identified him as a terrorist, captured him, tortured him and sent him to Afghanistan where he was jailed for four months before being released on the side of an abandoned road in Albania months after the CIA discovered his innocence.[74] The court relied on declarations by the CIA director to dismiss the case on state secrets grounds.[75] Describing the constitutional backdrop against which it made its decision, the Fourth Circuit, echoing similar reasoning by the district court whose opinion it affirmed, explained that "the Executive's constitutional authority is at its broadest in the realm of military and foreign affairs. The [Supreme] Court accordingly has indicated that the judiciary's role as a check on presidential action in foreign affairs is limited."[76] The Fourth Circuit cited, among other things, to Supreme Court precedent that prescribes a "limited judicial role in foreign policy matters, especially those involving 'information properly held secret'"[77] and that deems the "'authority to protect [national security] information'" to belong to "the President as head of the Executive Branch and as commander-in-chief."[78] The *El Masri* Court joined its constitutional reasoning to analysis based on executive expertise. It invoked the mosaic theory and the president's unique vantage point to determine when disclosures will cause international embarrassment or otherwise harm foreign relations.[79]

The state secrets privilege casts a very long shadow. As Laura Donohue notes, the impact of the privilege goes far deeper than its appearance in published judicial opinions can tell us. Donohue searched court dockets to examine the use of the privilege in litigation to assess how it influences cases including those that do not result in published opinions or those that result in opinions that do not mention the privilege. She found that

> from January 2001 to January 2009, the privilege played a significant role in the executive branch's national security litigation strategy. In one case, the Administration asserted the state secrets privilege some 245 times. More to the point, the government has invoked the states secrets privilege in more than one hundred cases. . . . And it is not just the executive branch that benefited from the privilege: in scores of additional cases, private industry claimed that the state secrets doctrine applied, with the expectation that the federal government would later intervene to prevent certain documents from being subject to discovery or to stop the suit from moving forward. Beyond these, there are hundreds of cases on which the shadow of the privilege fell.[80]

Donohue's research reveals a substantial shadow effect. For instance, she notes that in cases against private government contractors, "[e]ven where the government never becomes involved in the suit, the threat of the state secrets privilege gives the companies a tactical advantage. It shapes litigation in important and prejudicial ways, often dropping out of the picture by the time the court issues its opinion resolving the case."[81] More broadly, she concludes that the case files "suggest that the shadow of state secrets is much longer than previously realized—indeed, that the state secrets doctrine has expanded well beyond the framing of *Reynolds* to become a powerful litigation tool for both private and public actors."[82]

Finally, exclusivist state secrets claims have been made to argue that Congress may not constitutionally limit the doctrine. In an April 2009 brief urging dismissal of a case against the National Security Agency on state secrets grounds, for instance, the Obama administration "incorporate[d] by reference [the government's] prior detailed discussion" to the effect that the statute under which the plaintiffs brought suit should not be read to preempt the state secrets privilege.[83] The referenced prior argument was made in two Bush administration briefs in a related case.[84] There, the government had argued, among other things, that a preemptive reading of the statute should be avoided because "any effort by Congress to regulate an exercise of the Executive's authority to protect national security through the state secrets privilege would plainly raise serious constitutional concerns."[85]

The Bush administration also objected, on exclusivist and other grounds, to 2008 legislation that would have limited the doctrine.[86] While the Obama administration declined to comment on similar legislation introduced in 2009, its exclusivist response to the claim that another statute preempts the state secrets privilege obviously could be applied to that legislation. Furthermore, while the Obama administration announced a policy in 2009 whereby it would seek to invoke the privilege only when necessary and as narrowly as possible in each case, that policy is entirely self-imposed and self-enforced.[87]

Secret Law

Recall the distinction between extraordinary prerogative claims and ordinary prerogative claims. The former are assertions of an extraordinary right to circumvent existing laws where time constraints foreclose congressional action. The circumvention must be transparent so that the people and the other branches are able to respond. Ordinary prerogative—which this book uses interchangeably with the term exclusivity—encompasses a far broader presidential discretion to circumvent laws, one not limited by temporal or transparency requirements. Ordinary prerogative claims tend to be tautological because they hinge on the president's own judgment as to what national security, and in some cases the autonomy of his office, demand.[88] This is the essence of Richard Nixon's infamous statement: "[W]hen the President does it, that means it is not illegal."[89] Ordinary prerogative thus can justify long-term statutory circumvention, so long as the president deems it essential. Most important for our purposes, ordinary prerogative does not demand transparency because public judgment, outside of that reflected at the ballot box once every four years, is not essential to it. To the contrary, ordinary prerogative intrinsically leaves room for presidential judgments to the effect that statutory circumventions must remain secret.

At the apex of the supremacy/secrecy mix, then, is secret law. Secret law occurs when the executive deems it necessary to the national interest not only to circumvent a statute, but to do so in secret.[90] To be sure, the concept of secret law is complicated by the fact that the executive may contest the notion that it has violated a statute in any given case. As explained above, exclusivity can manifest itself not only in admitted statutory violations, but in aggressive statutory interpretations grounded partly in supremacy. Furthermore, at times there is a genuinely fine line between executing legislation and going beyond or even violating it. Additionally, where legislation is extremely broad—like the 2001 AUMF, for example—it may leave room for an array of potential programs so vast and varied that they can constitute secret law if undisclosed.

For simplicity's sake, this book treats as secret law only those executive branch actions or programs that secretly violate existing statutes. Yet to detect or prevent secret law, Congress and the courts logically must be able to learn of executive programs beyond those that the executive freely admits violate the law. As such, this book counts as claims that facilitate secret law assertions of a presidential right to resist disclosing the existence of executive branch programs or the internal legal opinions that justify them. This is so even where the executive branch maintains that the programs at issue are consistent with existing statutes or where the executive refuses to confirm or deny the programs' existence and hence their legality.

One very important means to facilitate secret law is the issuance of secret legal opinions by the OLC.[91] Recall that the OLC, which has been called "the attorney general's lawyer,"[92] advises the president on the legality of government actions.[93] Its role gives it tremendous influence, particularly over matters relating to national security. As Jack Goldsmith, who headed the OLC from 2003 to 2004 explains, "most legal issues of executive branch conduct related to war and intelligence never reach a court, or do so only years after the executive has acted. In these situations, the executive branch [i.e., the OLC] determines for itself what the law requires, and whether its actions are legal."[94] Furthermore, an opinion from the OLC deeming an action legal is understood, in practice, to immunize the president and others from prosecution if they later take that action.[95] As Goldsmith puts it, the OLC possesses "one of the most momentous and dangerous powers in the government: the power to dispense get-out-of-jail-free cards."[96]

In the wake of 9/11, drafting of and access to controversial OLC opinions reportedly were restricted to a small group that called itself "the War Council." It consisted of vice presidential counsel David Addington, OLC Deputy Assistant Attorney General John Yoo, White House counsel (later attorney general) Alberto Gonzales, Timothy Flanigan of the White House Counsel's Office, and Pentagon general counsel Jim Haynes.[97] The War Council's most important players were Addington and Yoo.[98] Addington's influence stemmed from his ability to speak for the vice president (who, in turn, was largely responsible for intelligence matters in the administration), his intimidating personality, his tendency toward political retribution, and his relative expertise in constitutional and national security law.[99] Yoo, meanwhile, was "crucial" to the war council's plans as its only member who "was an OLC deputy with authority to issue legal opinions that were binding throughout the executive branch."[100] According to Goldsmith, Yoo, "[i]n close coordination with the War Council . . . pumped out [OLC] opinions on all manner of terrorism-related topics."[101] Meanwhile, the War Council shielded their work from prying eyes by classifying opinions and bypassing ordinary review and access channels within the executive branch.[102]

The War Council thus was able to craft what amounted to secret amendments to existing statutes—in other words, secret law. It did so by issuing very closely held opinions that authorized the executive branch to secretly contravene statutory restrictions, including limits on torture and warrantless wiretapping. For example, a 2003 OLC opinion asserted that certain federal criminal laws should not be construed to apply to military interrogations and that they are unconstitutional if they do so apply. The justification was exclusivist: "In wartime, it is for the President alone to decide what methods to use to best prevail against the enemy."[103] This memorandum not only was classified, it was so closely held that it was kept from even "the top lawyers for each branch of the military."[104] It was declassified on April 1, 2008, in response to a Freedom of Information Act lawsuit by the American Civil Liberties Union (ACLU).[105]

In written testimony for a hearing of the Senate Judiciary Committee, Subcommittee on the Constitution held on April 30, 2008 (in which I participated as a witness), former classification czar J. William Leonard expressed dismay that the interrogation memorandum had been classified in the first place. He wrote:

> [T]his memorandum represents one of the worst abuses of the classification process that I had seen during my career, including the past five years when I had the authority to access more classified information than almost any other person in the Executive branch. This memorandum is purely a legal analysis—it is not operational in nature. Its author was quoted as describing it as "near boilerplate." To learn that such a document was classified had the same effect on me as waking up one morning and learning that after all these years, there is a "secret" Article to the Constitution that the American people do not even know about.[106]

Leonard stressed the dangers of secret presidential assertions of power to circumvent law. He also cautioned that multiple such assertions can compound one another's effects. He wrote:

> The combination of these two powers of the President—that is, when the President lays claim to [powers to circumvent statutes], but does so in secret—can equate to the very open-ended, non-circumscribed, executive authority that the Constitution's Framers sought to avoid in constructing a system of checks and balances. Added to this is the reality that the President is not irrevocably bound by his own Executive Orders, and this administration claims the President can depart from the terms of an Executive Order without public notice. Thus, at least in theory, the President could authorize the classification of the OLC memo, even though to do so would violate the standards of his own governing Executive Order [on classification policy]. Equally possible, the President could change his Executive Order governing secrecy, and do so in secret, all un-

beknownst to the Congress and the courts. It is as if Lewis Carroll, George Orwell, and Franz Kafka jointly conspired to come up with the ultimate recipe for unchecked executive power.[107]

Partly as a result of testimony by Bradford Berenson and Dawn Johnson at the same hearing at which Leonard appeared, Senators Feingold and Feinstein introduced legislation—the details of which had first been suggested in an article by Trevor Morrison[108]—addressing the use of OLC opinions as conduits for secret law.[109] The bill would have required the attorney general to disclose to Congress any "authoritative interpretation" of a statute by the Justice Department that deems a law unconstitutional on Article II grounds or purports to interpret a statute in such a way as to avoid a constitutional difficulty under Article II.[110] The bill sought, in other words, to prevent the Department of Justice from secretly and authoritatively advising the executive branch that it need not obey a statute or that it may follow a strained interpretation of a statute on exclusivist grounds.

Yet from an exclusivist perspective, such a bill is unconstitutional because it could conflict with the president's judgment that the opinions must be kept secret for purposes of national security or to preserve candor in executive branch discussions. This was the view taken by Attorney General Mukasey. He explained that "to the extent [OLC opinions] are generated or used to assist in presidential decision-making," they are subject to executive privilege.[111] He argued, for example, that the bill "could chill the Department's ability or willingness to provide full and candid legal assessments of statutes or government actions."[112] He concluded that the bill "violates constitutional limits and undermines the public interest protecting the confidentiality of legal advice vital to the integrity and legality of government decision-making."[113]

The Obama administration too has asserted a right to withhold opinions that would reveal the legal parameters of certain programs. As of this writing in fall 2013, the administration for some time has been engaged in litigation with the *New York Times* and the ACLU in response to the groups' respective FOIA requests for such information. The *Times* sought all OLC opinions since 2001 that "address the legal status of targeted killings" of persons, including U.S. citizens, suspected by the U.S. of terrorism.[114] The ACLU similarly sought materials "pertaining to the legal basis in domestic, foreign and international law upon which U.S. citizens can be subjected to targeted killings."[115] The ACLU also sought OLC opinions "pertaining to the legal basis in domestic, foreign and international law upon which the targeted killing of Anwar al-Awlaki was authorized."[116]

The administration has declined, thus far, to release any responsive OLC opinions. Initially it refused even to confirm or deny the existence of materials responsive to the FOIA requests insofar as they pertained to the CIA.[117] Eventually, given its own official disclosures—including disclosures by President Obama and the attorney general designed to assure the American public of drone strikes' efficacy and legality[118]—the administration conceded the existence of some previously unacknowledged responsive materials, though it declined to describe their contents. Moreover, the administration continues to maintain that "whether or not OLC provided legal advice to the CIA is itself exempt from disclosure."[119]

While the administration has framed its FOIA defenses predominantly as matters of statutory interpretation—hinging, among other things, on the scope of FOIA's exemption for properly classified information[120]—those defenses are underscored by supremacy and its shadow. The administration's legal briefs rely heavily on judicial decisions that disparage courts' institutional capacity for and constitutional role in closely scrutinizing executive branch secrecy.[121] Indeed, there is a long history of nearly conclusive judicial deference to executive branch invocations of FOIA's classification exemption, despite a clear congressional directive to courts to assess such claims independently to ensure that classification is proper.[122]

The District Court for the Southern District of New York, in a recent opinion concerning the *New York Times* and ACLU lawsuits,[123] cites this tradition of judicial deference in declining to evaluate whether an acknowledged OLC legal memorandum advising the Defense Department on the legality of targeted killing was properly classified as a substantive matter. The court explained that "[a]ll a court can do with a document that has been classified using proper procedures is determine whether classification protection has been waived."[124] On the waiver question, the court again cites judicial precedent counseling deference, explaining that the government can waive classification status through disclosure only where the disclosure was made through official channels and where the classified information "[i]s as specific as," and "matches" the disclosed information.[125] Accordingly, the district court deemed it inappropriate to order the disclosure of the OLC memorandum or even to examine it in camera. It based this conclusion on the fact that the administration's publicly stated legal justifications, particularly those made in a speech by Attorney

General Holder at Northwestern University Law School, did not "reveal[] *the exact* legal reasoning behind the government's conclusions that its actions comply with domestic and international law."[126] Nor did the administration's many other official public statements "reveal[] the necessarily detailed legal analysis that supports the Administration's conclusion that targeted killing, whether or [sic] citizens or otherwise, is lawful."[127]

Discretion to Prosecute Classified Speech

The final example involves executive defenses against First Amendment claims by persons prosecuted for engaging in classified speech. Classified speech defenses rest on the notion that executive classification decisions are decisive as to the harmful nature of the information classified. By this logic, the decisions preclude much if any independent judicial role in assessing the same. Under ordinary First Amendment doctrine, a speaker cannot be punished for speech that could harm national security unless the courts determine that the speaker intended to, and was likely to, incite imminent illegal action through the speech. And while the government has more leeway to punish its employees' speech under First Amendment doctrine, employees retain some protection even against employment-based discipline.[128] From a supremacist perspective, however, such protections do not apply where the speech at issue is classified. Rather, classification effectively transforms speech into something akin to government property. Alternatively, if still speech, it is transformed into speech that *ipse dixi* can be deemed to cause sufficient national security harm to be unprotected.

In seeking to prosecute insider leaks or possession or—in the case of the George W. Bush administration—third-party transmittal of classified information, the Obama, Bush, and Reagan administrations all have argued that such prosecutions do not implicate the First Amendment in any way. For example, the Obama administration argued in prosecuting alleged leaker Thomas Drake that "[a] restriction upon the retention of classified documents is an inhibition of action, not protected free speech."[129] In the alternative, the administration argued that even if the possession of such documents is speech, it is speech "integral to criminal conduct" and thus unprotected.[130]

Anticipating the Obama administration's first two arguments, the Bush administration argued in *United States v. Rosen & Weissman* that even third-party oral dissemination of classified information is not speech and warrants no First Amendment protection. The administration deemed classified information property, and its unauthorized dissemination pure theft.[131] Alternatively, the administration urged that even if such transmission constitutes speech, it is categorically unprotected speech because it is classified and "relates to the national defense."[132] The Reagan administration also appears—extrapolating from the court opinions in *United States v. Morison*—to have made arguments very similar to those later employed in the Bush and Obama administrations. That is, in prosecuting Samuel Morison for leaking classified information to the press, the administration apparently argued that Morison had engaged in no speech, but instead had committed theft.[133]

In keeping with supremacy's general trajectory, prosecutions and threatened prosecutions for classified speech are on an upswing. Prior to the George W. Bush administration, only one person in American history had been successfully prosecuted for leaking classified information, and only two prosecutions had been brought.[134] No third-party publisher of classified information, such as the press or a lobbyist, had been prosecuted for disseminating classified information. In indicting two lobbyists in *United States v. Rosen & Weisman,* the Bush administration brought the first case in history against private citizens for exchanging classified information outside of the context of espionage or spying. The Bush administration also placed greater heat on insiders who leak classified information to the press or other third-party publishers. It successfully prosecuted one leaker and opened investigations against others.[135] In the Obama administration, the heat has been turned up to levels that are stifling. As of this writing in fall 2013, the administration has charged eight persons—six government employees and two contractors—with violating the Espionage Act by leaking information to the press, more than twice the number of persons so charged by all past administrations combined.[136]

Former *Washington Post* editor Leonard Downie Jr., who recently authored a report on the Obama administration and the press for the Committee to Protect Journalists [CPJ], deems "[t]he [Obama] administration's war on leaks and other efforts to control information . . . the most aggressive I've seen since the Nixon administration. . . . The 30 experienced journalists at a variety of news organizations whom [Downie] interviewed for [the CPJ] report could not remember any precedent."[137] Veteran news anchor Bob Schieffer attributes the Obama administration's unprecedented aggression to the ratchet effect of presidential power and

secrecy. He explains: "Every administration learns from the previous administration. They become more secretive and put tighter clamps on information. This administration exercises more control than George W.
Bush's did, and his before that."[138]

As we will see in chapter 6, the case law relating to classified speech
prosecutions is not all bad news for classified speakers. Still, supremacy is
manifest in aspects of the relevant precedent. For example, the majority
opinion in *United States v. Morison,* which was decided by the U.S. Court
of Appeals for the Fourth Circuit in 1988, expressed the view that classification turns information into government property and removes it from
the purview of the First Amendment when it is transmitted by government employees to unauthorized persons. Importantly, two of the three
judges on the panel in *Morison* wrote concurring opinions expressing
somewhat more moderate views. Nonetheless, the majority opinion represents one extreme to which supremacy can take the executive's power
to prosecute classified speakers.[139]

Supremacy's impact—specifically, that of the notion that the First
Amendment does not stand in the way of broad executive prerogatives to
prosecute classified speech—can be deep even where prosecutions do not
culminate in judicial merits decisions. Indeed, supremacy's shadow effect
makes it politically and legally viable for the executive to obtain favorable
plea bargains or indirectly to impose heavy financial, professional and
personal costs on prosecutorial targets without going to trial. Consider,
for example, the case of former FBI translator Shamai Leibowitz, who
served a year in prison after pleading guilty to leaking classified information to a blogger. At Leibowitz's sentencing hearing, the judge handling
the case acknowledged that he did not know what information Leibowitz had disclosed or whether the disclosures were damaging. As Josh Gerstein reports:

> [Judge] Williams [said] that while he assumed that the disclosures had a seri-
> ous impact on national security, he really didn't know because he wasn't privy
> to what information was disclosed and what impact it had. "The court is in the
> dark," the judge said. "I'm not a part and parcel of the intricacies of that. . . . I
> don't know what was divulged, other than some documents."[140]

Another leak prosecution and subsequent plea bargain are particularly
striking examples of the risks of supremacist overreach. The prosecution
was of linguist and computer expert Thomas Drake. Drake worked for

the National Security Agency (NSA), first as an outside contractor and then as a full-time employee, for well over a decade.[141] During his time at NSA, Drake and several colleagues became alarmed over the NSA's decision to reject surveillance technology called ThinThread that had been developed within NSA for $3 million. NSA instead turned to private contractors to develop a new program (called Trailblazer) for more than $1 billion. Drake and his colleagues believed that 9/11 might have been avoided had ThinThread been adopted. In their view, the technology would have flagged key Al Qaeda communications that were swept up by NSA's technology but unnoticed by analysts prior to 9/11.[142]

After 9/11, Drake brought his concerns to the congressional intelligence committees and to the Defense Department's inspector general, in the latter case by helping the inspector general (IG) investigate a complaint ("the IG Complaint") about the ThinThread/Trailblazer matter. Concerned that these efforts were having little effect and alarmed at revelations that the NSA was secretly wiretapping and data mining the communications of Americans, Drake leaked information to a reporter from the *Baltimore Sun*. Drake maintains, however, that he never knowingly conveyed classified information.[143] The *Baltimore Sun* stories triggered an FBI investigation to locate their sources. The FBI's interest reportedly was piqued because they thought that the *Sun* stories might share a source with the 2005 *New York Times* story revealing that the NSA was secretly engaged in warrantless wiretapping. FBI agents raided the houses of all four persons who had signed the IG Complaint with which Drake had assisted. "Under the law, such complaints are confidential, and employees who file them are supposed to be protected from retaliation. It's unclear if the Trailblazer complaint tipped off authorities, but all four people who signed it became targets."[144] Drake, who had not signed the IG Complaint despite assisting in its investigation, was the next to have his house raided. After the 2007 raid, Drake remained in limbo for over two years. Despite his initial hopes that the Obama administration would drop the case, Drake was indicted on April 14, 2010. The indictment alleged ten counts, including five counts of retaining classified information.[145]

Just a few days before the case was scheduled to go to trial in June 2011, Drake and the government reached a plea agreement. On June 9, 2011, Drake pled to a single misdemeanor count of misusing a government computer. About a week later, he was sentenced to one year of probation with no incarceration time and no fine. Many commentators, including the judge overseeing the case, expressed dismay that Drake's long ordeal—during which time he was investigated without charge for over two years, indicted for crimes that could have landed him in jail for several decades, saw his career end, and lost his eligibility for a government pension after years of government service—was precipitated by a case that ultimately collapsed.[146] The government attributed the last-minute plea deal to its conclusion that it could not present certain information to the jury without posing a threat to national security. Some commentators deemed that explanation a disingenuous attempt to save face and to avoid taking a weak case to trial.[147] Indeed, J. William Leonard, who had served as classification czar during the administration of George W. Bush, had been scheduled to appear at Drake's trial, without pay, as a witness for Drake's defense. Leonard was prepared to testify that the classified information at issue posed no national security threat and should never have been classified in the first place.[148]

With respect to the NSA activities that first gave rise to Drake's case, the Trailblazer program ended up costing the government $1.2 billion before being abandoned in 2006.[149] As for the IG Complaint, it culminated in a classified 2004 report that was finally declassified—albeit in heavily redacted form—on June 22, 2011, less than two weeks after Drake's sentencing. Among the report's unredacted passages were the following from the "results" section of the executive summary: "the National Security Agency is inefficiently using resources to develop a digital network exploitation system that is not capable of fully exploiting the digital network intelligence available to analysts from the Global Information Network"; and "the NSA transformation effort may be developing a less capable long-term digital network exploitation solution that will take longer and cost significantly more to develop."[150]

Supremacy's impact extends well beyond those who are actually prosecuted. Increased prosecutions or threats thereof can have a chilling effect, particularly on those who leak information that may anger or embarrass an administration. This is the core concern expressed by many journalists over the Obama administration's unprecedented aggression toward leakers. As *New York Times* reporter Scott Shane observes, "[m]ost people are deterred by those leaks prosecutions. They're scared to death. There's a gray zone between classified and unclassified information, and most sources were in that gray zone. Sources are now afraid to enter that gray zone."[151]

The chilling effect is compounded by developments of the past several years whereby the current administration has shown that it is willing to, and possesses tools enabling it to pursue information from and about journalists more vigorously than ever before. For example, administrations for roughly forty years have abided by self-imposed Justice Department regulations substantially restricting the occasions and procedures whereby journalists or their communications records will be subpoenaed.[152] The regulations require, among other things, that such subpoenas be used only as "last resort[s]" in federal investigations, that they be "'as narrowly drawn as possible,' and that the targeted news organization[s] 'shall be given reasonable and timely notice' to negotiate the subpoena[s] with Justice or to fight [them] in court" except where "such negotiations would [] pose a substantial threat to the integrity of the investigation."[153] Yet despite these guidelines and past practices respecting them, the Obama administration acknowledged in May 2013 that it had, in investigating a 2012 AP story a few months earlier, "secretly subpoenaed and seized all records for 20 AP telephone lines and switchboards for April and May of 2012."[154] Although the targeted story involved only five AP news reporters and an editor, the seized records covered "'thousands and thousands of newsgathering calls' by more than 100 AP journalists using newsroom, home, and mobile phones."[155] This example illustrates the current administration's willingness to seize journalists' records en masse without notice or opportunities for negotiation. Their willingness is complemented by their increasing technological capacity to bypass journalists by turning to "electronic evidence," including telephone and e-mail records of journalists' communications.[156]

Disclosures by one of the leakers targeted most recently for prosecution—Edward Snowden—further illuminate the tremendous technological resources by which the government can access Americans' communications, including those of journalists and their sources. News stories driven by Snowden's leaks detail "secret NSA operations that acquire, store, and search huge amounts of telephone call, text, and e-mail data from American telephone and internet companies, under secret FISA court authorization, to find and track communications that might be tied to terrorist activity."[157] These revelations, along with the government's leak prosecutions and other anti-leaking measures, contribute to the chilled "atmosphere surrounding contacts between American journalists and government sources."[158]

The justifications underlying aggressive anti-leaking measures, as well as the measures' intimidating effects, also create a political atmosphere conducive to government pressure on private actors to retaliate against classified speakers. For example, Senator Joe Lieberman success-fully launched a call for Internet service providers "hosting WikiLeaks to immediately terminate [their] relationship with them" following a series of high-profile disclosures in 2010. Other entities also followed suit, with credit card companies and additional service providers boycotting WikiLeaks.[159]

At their core, these linked phenomena—increased leak prosecutions, enhanced means to target leakers and journalists, private cooperation to supplement government measures, and a heightened chilling effect among journalists and their sources—rest in no small part on suprem-acy. As we have seen, the legal positions taken by the executive branch in classified speech prosecutions encompass the notion that executive classification decisions remove virtually all First Amendment protections that would otherwise apply to the speech at issue. The perceived legiti-macy of these legal positions, in turn, provides justification for aggressive measures to facilitate prosecutions. Such measures, along with actual and threatened prosecutions, cast a long and chilling shadow over journalistic communications.

CHAPTER SIX

Presidential Supremacy in the Courts

This chapter, like the preceding one, proceeds through each of supremacy's four manifestations. Its focus, however, is exclusively on judicial precedent. For each of the four supremacy types, the chapter summarizes the major case law and explains where it overlaps with and departs from the substantive accountability approach. It also suggests, for each area, arguments that a substantive accountability advocate might make in light of the relevant precedent. Such arguments contemplate both how substantive accountability can be fostered within the parameters of the existing case law, and respects in which the U.S. Supreme Court (or lower courts in areas where the Supreme Court has not ruled) ought to reconsider existing precedent.

Thinking strategically about the case law is important for at least two reasons. First, while separation of powers issues are only rarely resolved by courts, those cases that are decided on the merits have important shadow effects. The mere possibility that an executive privilege or state secrets claim might at some point be raised in a dispute, that the executive might someday invoke supremacy to defend circumventing a statute, or that the executive might prosecute a government employee for leaking information or a newspaper for publishing it, naturally factors into the actions of those engaged in relevant disputes or decision making. How it factors in will, of course, vary with the content of the relevant precedent. Second, when assertions of supremacy do reach the courts, judicial precedent naturally is of central importance.

Executive Privilege

The seminal case on executive privilege is *United States v. Nixon*. The *Nixon* Court deemed the privilege a presumptive one, citing the candor rationale. The Court suggested that the presumption is considerably greater in the national security context. Although the *Nixon* Court cautioned that its analysis did not necessarily apply outside of the criminal discovery context, the Court and lower courts have assumed that the *Nixon* approach, or something much like it, governs executive privilege disputes that arise in other contexts, including those in which a congressional body requests information or individuals invoke public access statutes to obtain documents.

Courts not only apply the *Nixon* framework to congressional requests and statutory public access inquiries, they suggest that *Nixon*'s pro-privilege presumption may be stronger in those settings than in the criminal discovery context. For its part, the executive branch routinely relies on the U.S. Court of Appeals' opinion in *Senate Select Committee v. Nixon* for the proposition that a congressional subpoena can overcome executive privilege only where the information sought "is demonstrably critical to the responsible fulfillment of the Committee's functions."[1] And in *Cheney v. United States District Court,* the Supreme Court took the view that the plaintiffs' discovery requests, by which they sought to determine whether an open government statute applied to a series of energy policy meetings chaired by the vice president, raised interests less weighty than those at issue in *Nixon.* The *Cheney* Court expressed skepticism about the plaintiffs' interpretation of the open government statute, and thus about whether discovery could prove it applicable to the energy policy meetings. It observed that "[t]he District Court ordered discovery . . . not to remedy known statutory violations, but to ascertain whether [the statute's] disclosure requirements even apply to the [energy committee] in the first place." It added, however, that even if the statute's "objectives would be to some extent frustrated" by the denied discovery request, "it does not follow that a court's Article III authority," as in *Nixon,* "or Congress's central Article I powers would be impaired."[2]

Yet the case law is not all bleak for substantive accountability proponents. *Nixon* and its progeny leave the door open for vigorous, case-by-case arguments that the need for disclosure outweighs executive secrecy needs. Indeed, the *Nixon* Court itself ordered the White House tapes turned over to the district court for examination. And lower courts have emphasized that *Nixon*'s balancing test demands only a pro-privilege presumption, not abdication to executive judgments. In its 1976 opinion in *United States v. AT&T,* the U.S. Court of Appeals for the D.C. Circuit admonished the district court for deferring too strongly to the executive's national security-based executive privilege claim. The claim had been raised in response to a subpoena by a House Subcommittee investigating warrantless surveillance practices. The district court had echoed the *Nixon* Court's statements counseling deference to the executive in the realm of foreign policy and purported to balance the interests of the subcommittee and the executive.[3] The appeals court determined, however, that the lower court had not exercised independent judgment, but had "basically accepted the Executive's assertion of ultimate authority."[4] The appeals court also took the view that the matter would best be resolved through negotiations between the political branches and directed the district court to facilitate such negotiations. Those negotiations, stressed the appeals court, should be grounded in assumptions of shared congressional and executive responsibility for foreign affairs, not executive supremacy.[5]

The U.S. District Court for the District of Columbia struck a similarly moderate note in the recent case of *Committee on the Judiciary v. Miers.* The *Miers* court made clear that the candor rationale does not justify absolute immunity for high-level White House advisors from having to testify before Congress. Rather, such advisors must appear if subpoenaed, and at that point may raise objections to specific questions. Such objections, when raised, can be resolved through interbranch negotiation or through judicial balancing. Absolute immunity, in contrast, would "totally insulate[]" White House advisors from congressional scrutiny, a result "[t]hat would eviscerate Congress's historical oversight function."[6] Importantly, the *Miers* court distinguished its facts from those in *Cheney v. United States District Court. Cheney,* said the *Miers* court, did not establish a blanket privilege for high-level advisors or officials. Rather, the vice president was allowed to forgo making specific objections only because the "civil subpoenas [at issue] were unacceptably overbroad."[7] Given reasonable discovery requests, the vice president and other advisors presumably are required to make case-by-case objections.[8]

Supreme Court and lower court precedent also catalogue the important public interests served by open government laws and congressional investigations. In *Nixon v. Administrator of General Services* [AGS], decided in 1977, the Supreme Court rejected an executive privilege challenge to Title I of the Presidential Recordings and Materials Preservation Act. The act prohibited the destruction of the Nixon presidential papers and recordings, including the infamous White House tapes, and required their transfer to the custody and control of AGS. In rejecting Richard Nixon's challenge to the act, the Court focused predominantly on the act's modest burden on executive secrecy interests. The Court pointed out that Nixon was no longer president at the time of the challenge and that his challenge was actively opposed by both Gerald Ford (president when the litigation was initiated) and Jimmy Carter (president at the litigation's conclusion). It also emphasized that the act preserved rights to raise privilege claims against AGS regulations promulgated under it, and that AGS itself was a part of the executive branch.[9] Yet the Court considered the other side of the balance too, making clear that the public interests furthered by the statute were quite heavy:

> An incumbent President should not be dependent on happenstance or the whim of a prior President when he seeks access to records of past decisions that define or channel . . . current governmental obligations. Nor should the American people's ability to reconstruct and come to terms with their history be truncated by an analysis of Presidential privilege that focuses only on the needs of the present. . . . . Other substantial public interests that led Congress to seek to preserve appellant's materials were the desire to restore public confidence in our political processes by preserving the materials as a source for facilitating a full airing of the events leading to appellant's resignation, and Congress's need to understand how those political processes had in fact operated in order to gauge the necessity for remedial legislation. Thus by preserving these materials, the Act may be thought to aid the legislative process and thus to be within the scope of Congress's broad investigative power.[10]

The *AGS* Court also cited the interdependent nature of information gathering. It observed that Congress, in passing the act, "repeatedly referred to the importance of the materials to the Judiciary in the event that they shed light upon issues in civil or criminal litigation, a social interest that cannot be doubted."[11]

More recently, the district court in *Miers* highlighted the public interests and constitutional values served by congressional investigations, observing that

> Congress's power of inquiry is as broad as its power to legislate and lies at the very heart of Congress's constitutional role. Indeed, the former is necessary to the proper exercise of the latter: according to the Supreme Court, the ability to compel testimony is *"necessary to the effective functioning of courts and legislatures."* [citation omitted] Thus, Congress's use of (and need for vindication of) its subpoena power in this case is no less legitimate or important than was the grand jury's in United States v. Nixon. Both involve core functions of a coequal branch of the federal government.[12]

The same district court echoed this reasoning in denying the Obama administration's motion urging the court to decline jurisdiction over an executive privilege dispute that stemmed from a House committee investigation of the botched "Fast and Furious" program. The court concluded that "[t]o give the Attorney General the final word would elevate and fortify the executive branch at the expense of the other institutions that are supposed to be its equal, and do . . . damage to the balance envisioned by the Framers."[13]

The existing case law, then, is rife with tools for friends of substantive accountability. Certainly, advocates might urge the Supreme Court (or lower courts on matters where the Supreme Court has not yet ruled) to revisit those aspects of precedent that are in tension with substantive accountability. Yet advocates also can make their cases with vigor under the existing doctrine, explaining why the facts in particular matters tip the balance toward disclosure. More fundamentally, advocates should urge courts to exercise independent judgment in weighing the benefits of disclosure against the need for secrecy under *Nixon*. At minimum, a court evaluating an executive privilege claim should require the executive to disclose the disputed information in camera and explain with specificity why it cannot be disclosed more broadly. In disputes outside of the judicial realm, such as those between the political branches that have not reached a court, advocates can help to shape the doctrinal shadow against which the disputes occur. They can do so by reminding participants of the extent to which the existing case law acknowledges the value in, and protects Congress's investigative function and the people's ability to monitor their government.

State Secrets Doctrine

United States v. Reynolds (1953) remains, to this day, the Supreme Court's major pronouncement on the state secrets doctrine. As we saw in chapter 5, the *Reynolds* Court did not reach a conclusion on the privilege's constitutional status. That is, it did not determine whether the privilege is grounded solely in the common law and thus fully subject to congressional curtailment, or whether it has constitutional dimensions that limit Congress's power to restrict it. The *Reynolds* Court also sent mixed signals on the extent to which courts should defer to privilege claims. The Court admonished lower courts not to abdicate "judicial control . . . to the caprice of executive officers."[14] Yet the Court famously refused to require disclosure of the contested documents. Lower courts on a number of occasions have followed the Supreme Court's example in refusing to order disclosure or examine disputed materials. And as Donohue's research reveals, the doctrine casts a very long shadow. Its impact extends to cases before they are filed, those in which the doctrine is not officially invoked, and those in which the government is not directly involved.

State Secrets Doctrine as a Basis to Dismiss Cases

Increasingly, the privilege has been invoked not merely to prevent the use of certain evidence, but to dismiss cases against the government. As a doctrinal matter, this can happen through one of two precedential vehicles. First, courts sometimes conclude, using the *Reynolds* framework, that evidence must be barred and that its omission will prevent the plaintiff from making out an affirmative case or the defendant from offering a defense or that "litigating the case to a judgment on the merits would present an unacceptable risk of disclosing state secrets."[15] For example, an en banc panel of the U.S. Court of Appeals for the Ninth Circuit recently ordered the dismissal of a complaint against Jeppesen Dataplan, Inc. The complaint alleged that Jeppesen provided flight planning services to the CIA for its program of extraordinary rendition, whereby the CIA sent the plaintiffs and other persons to overseas locations to be detained and tortured.[16] The en banc panel concluded that litigating the plaintiffs' claims posed an unacceptable risk of disclosing state secrets. It explained that

> all seven of plaintiffs' claims . . . describe Jeppesen as providing logistical support in a broad, complex process, certain aspects of which, the government has persuaded us, are absolutely protected by the state secrets privilege. Notwithstanding that some information about that process has become public, Jeppesen's alleged role and its attendant liability cannot be isolated from aspects that are secret and protected.[17]

The second precedential vehicle for dismissing cases is the so-called *Totten* bar. The term derives from the 1875 case of *Totten v. United States.* In *Totten,*

> the administrator of a self-styled Civil War spy's estate brought a breach-of-contract suit against the United States. He alleged that his testator had entered

into a contract with President Lincoln to spy on the Confederacy in exchange for $200 a month. After the war ended, the United States reimbursed expenses but did not pay the monthly salary. [The Court] recognized that the estate had a potentially valid breach-of-contract claim but dismissed the suit. The contract was for "a secret service," and litigating the details of that service would risk exposing secret operations and other clandestine operatives "to the serious detriment of the public."[18]

At minimum, the *Totten* bar "precludes judicial review in cases ... where success depends on the existence of [the claimant's] secret espionage relationship with the Government"[19] or—as in the 1981 case of *Weinberger v. Catholic Action of Hawaii*—where plaintiffs invoke regulatory requirements that can be triggered only if the government confirms the location of proposed nuclear weapons storage facilities.[20] Furthermore, courts sometimes describe the *Totten* bar as having "evolved into the [broader] principle that where the very subject matter of a lawsuit is a matter of state secret, the action must be dismissed without reaching the question of evidence."[21]

As evidenced by *Jeppesen* and other recent cases, the state secrets doctrine can be a powerful weapon for dismissing claims. Yet the case law is not without its own tools to limit its reach. At the most basic level, advocates can cite judicial warnings to the effect that state-secrets based dismissal, whether framed under *Totten* or *Reynolds*, is an "option of last resort, available in a very narrow set of circumstances."[22] Such advocates can link this point to fact-specific reasons why the extraordinary remedy is not warranted in given cases.

A somewhat bolder argument can be ventured to the effect that state-secrets based dismissals are categorically inappropriate in certain cases. At minimum, such cases include those in which a claim of illegal government conduct is stated, the government deems the existence or nonexistence of that conduct itself is a secret, and the claimant did not contract to participate in the alleged secret activity. The handful of Supreme Court cases countenancing state-secrets based dismissals are readily distinguishable from the category of cases just described. Indeed, the logic of the former cases affirmatively militates against its extension to the latter cases. From this perspective, a number of recent lower court decisions including *Jeppesen* and the Fourth Circuit's opinion in *El Masri* misread the relevant Supreme Court precedent.

Three of the four Supreme Court cases ordering state secrets based dismissals involve alleged breaches of contracts to which those resisting the privilege were parties. In two cases, self-described spies sued for breaches of their espionage contracts.[23] In the third and most recent case—2011's *General Dynamics Corp. v. United States*—the government sued the petitioner contractors for defaulting on an agreement to develop carrier-based stealth aircraft. The contractors invoked the defense of superior knowledge, arguing that their default was excusable because the government failed to share its superior knowledge of stealth technology with them. The defense, explained the Court, is inextricably tied to "some of the Government's most closely guarded military secrets." Indeed, state secrets inadvertently had been revealed in discovery proceedings. The Court deemed the situation similar to those presented in *Totten* and *Tenet,* and concluded that the same result—contractual nonenforcement—should follow.[24]

The *General Dynamics* Court identified a strong link between the *Totten* bar cases and contract law. Indeed, the cases' shared contractual aspects led the Court to group *General Dynamics* with *Totten* and *Tenet* rather than with *Reynolds*. The Court explained that "*Reynolds* decided a purely evidentiary dispute by applying evidentiary rules: The privileged information is excluded and the trial goes on without it."[25] In contrast, the Court characterized *General Dynamics,* like *Totten* and *Tenet,* as calling upon its "common-law authority to fashion contractual remedies in Government-contracting disputes."[26] The *General Dynamics* Court noted that "[a]s in *Totten,* our refusal to enforce this contract captures what the *ex ante* expectations of the parties were or reasonably ought to have been. Both parties 'must have understood,' that state secrets would prevent courts from resolving many possible disputes under the . . . agreement." The use of the extraordinary *Totten* bar was warranted in these cases as a contractual fix, one that placed the parties in a position that they could reasonably have anticipated when they agreed to the contractual terms.[27]

In the remaining Supreme Court case involving state secrets based dismissal—*Weinberger v. Catholic Action of Hawaii*—Defense Department regulations arguably required the navy to prepare an environmental impact statement for its own reference for locations in which nuclear weapons storage was proposed. Citing *Totten,* the Court deemed the case one in which "'public policy'" counsels against judicial inquiry into proposed nuclear weapons storage locations. The Court thus was unable to examine "whether or not the Navy has complied with [its regulations implementing the relevant statutory scheme]."[28] *Weinberger* is readily confinable to its facts. For one thing, the *Weinberger* Court minimized the strength and certainty of the applicable legal directive. Having concluded that the relevant statute did not require public access to the environmental impact statement sought by the respondents, the Court found that the Defense Department's implementing regulations nonetheless "can fairly be read to require that an EIS be prepared solely for internal purposes, even though such a document cannot be disclosed to the public."[29] Indeed, Justice Blackmun, joined by Justice Brennan, cautioned in concurrence that the case was resolvable solely by reference to the fact that the relevant statute did not require disclosure of the materials sought by respondents. The concurrence deemed it "unnecessary to address the applicability or vitality of [*Totten*], which suggested as a matter of 'public policy' that certain suits involving confidential data could not be maintained."[30]

More broadly, the judicial reasoning in all four cases emphasizes fairness and the rule of law. In each case, the court appears satisfied, for highly fact-specific reasons, that these values are unharmed. In the three contract-based cases, the Court makes clear its view that the parties resisting the privilege claim helped to create the circumstances out of which the claim arose. Furthermore, they should have anticipated that the contracts upon which they relied could prove unenforceable. In *Weinberger,* the Court suggests uncertainty as to whether the law required the report sought by the plaintiffs in the first place. And if it did require as much, it did so through a Defense Department regulation rather than a directive from another branch or from the Constitution. Furthermore, the *Weinberger* respondents did not allege that the purportedly secret activity itself was unlawful.

A profoundly different situation presents itself where a plaintiff states a claim alleging illegal government conduct to which they were not a contracting party and where the government asserts that the alleged activity—including the truth or falsity of its very existence—itself is a state secret. Plaintiffs in such cases have done nothing to give rise to the secrecy claim. Furthermore, in light of standing rules, they necessarily allege that they in some way are victimized or endangered by the challenged conduct. As in *Jeppeson,* for example, claimants may allege that they were transported abroad, detained without a hearing, and tortured. Finally and most fundamentally, both the rule of law and the separation of powers are deeply incompatible with a procedural device by which the government can immunize alleged illegal conduct from judicial scrutiny by deeming that conduct a secret. This incompatibility is sharpest where dismissal occurs at the pleadings stage. Given procedural rules, dismissal at this stage amounts to a judicial decision to the effect that a plaintiff's allegations, even if they truthfully and accurately describe unconstitutional or otherwise illegal behavior, can receive no judicial forum because the illegal behavior's existence or details is a state secret. Such consequences illuminate the value in the Supreme Court's admonition that state secrets based dismissal is a tool of "last resort," and the danger of straying beyond the fact-driven rationales of the existing Supreme Court precedent.

State Secrets Doctrine as Evidentiary Bar

Even when used as an evidentiary bar rather than a direct basis for dismissal, state secrets doctrine can prove supremacist in application. As in *Reynolds* itself, courts may bar disputed evidence without reviewing it and thus leave executive representations—such as the government's claim in *Reynolds* that the accident report contained national security secrets—judicially unchecked. Yet despite *Reynolds* and numerous lower court decisions upholding state secrets claims without judicial review of the disputed evidence,[31] advocates have a strong doctrinal basis on which to urge courts, case-by-case, to review disputed evidence themselves, and to demand that the government defend its privilege claims with some precision. For one thing, the holding in *Reynolds* and in all judicial opinions as to whether particular evidence must be barred under the state secrets doctrine, is highly fact-specific. Litigants thus can distinguish privilege claims to which they object from past claims that were upheld, and particularly from those that were upheld without judicial review of the disputed materials.

More fundamentally, advocates should emphasize that while the *Reynolds* Court expressed and effectuated the view that "[i]t may be possible to satisfy the court" that information cannot safely be divulged without the court examining the information itself, the Court also cautioned that "[j]udicial control over the evidence in a case cannot be abdicated to the caprice of executive officers."[32] In refusing to order the accident report disclosed, the *Reynolds* Court made a fact-specific judgment that the report was unnecessary to the plaintiffs because they could get the same information by interviewing the surviving crew members. The Court deemed this determination consistent with both national security and the judicial checking function. Even if history had not proven this calculation misguided, one could urge courts to apply the *Reynolds* framework differently to different facts—for example, to demand to review incident reports or other evidence to supplement witness testimony in light of the risk of inaccurate testimony. *Reynolds'* subsequent history can and should bolster such arguments. It is not the case, of course, that the subsequent history alters the legal framework outlined in *Reynolds*. The history does, however, call into question the belief that the framework—particularly its call to protect national security while guarding against executive caprice—can be satisfied without judicial review of disputed evidence.

The Doctrine's Constitutional Status

Precedent also leaves open the possibility that state secrets privilege— whether because it is a product of the common law or because, if constitutionally grounded, it does not belong exclusively to the president—can be limited by statute. The *Reynolds* Court explicitly left this question open. And while the question is not addressed directly in *Totten, Tenet, General Dynamics,* or *Weinberger,* the Court in the first three cases refers to the privilege as a matter of "public policy."[33] The *General Dynamics* Court further situates the privilege within the Court's "common-law authority to fashion contractual remedies in Government-contracting disputes."[34]

Individual Justices and lower courts on occasion have stated or assumed that Congress is free to limit the state secrets privilege. Concurring in *Tenet,* Justice Stevens, who also joined the majority opinion, explained that "Congress can modify the federal common-law rule announced in *Totten.*"[35] In *Jeppesen,* the U.S. Court of Appeals for the Ninth Circuit, en banc, "reluctantly"[36] dismissed the case on state secrets grounds, but added that "[o]ur holding today is not intended to foreclose—or to prejudge—possible *nonjudicial* relief, should it be warranted for any of the plaintiffs."[37] It observed that "Congress has the authority to enact remedial legislation authorizing appropriate causes of action and procedures to address claims like those presented here."[38]

Finally, a federal district court in 2008 wrote a particularly detailed and instructive opinion to the effect that Congress is free to curtail the state secrets privilege. In the opinion, Judge Walker of the U.S. District Court for the Northern District of California held that, in litigation brought under FISA, FISA's provisions for handling national security information override the state secrets privilege.[39] Judge Walker explained that "*Reynolds* itself, holding that the state secrets privilege is part of the federal common law, leaves little room for [the] argument that the state secrets privilege is actually rooted in the Constitution."[40] Furthermore, he rejected the notion that there is a sharp dichotomy between the common law and constitutional principles, or that a privilege rooted partly in presidential power is indefeasible by Congress. He explains:

> [I]t would be unremarkable for the privilege to have a constitutional "core" or constitutional "overtones." Article II might be nothing more than the source of federal policy that courts look to when applying the common law state secrets privilege. But constitutionally-inspired deference to the executive branch is not the same as constitutional law.[41]

Judge Walker put a somewhat finer point on the matter in discussing a 1988 Supreme Court case upon which the defendants had relied. He observed that the case, *Department of the Navy v. Egan*,

> recognized the president's constitutional power to "control access to information bearing on national security," stating that this power "falls on the President as head of the Executive Branch and as Commander in Chief" and "exists quite apart from any explicit congressional grant." But *Egan* also discussed the other side of the coin, stating that *"unless Congress specifically has provided otherwise,* courts traditionally have been reluctant to intrude upon the authority of the Executive in military and national security affairs." *Egan* recognizes that the authority to protect national security information is neither exclusive nor absolute in the executive branch. When Congress acts to contravene the president's authority, federal courts must give effect to what Congress has required.[42]

Secret Law

Secret law results when an administration circumvents a statute or statutes in secret. In such cases, the public record reflects that a particular law or set of laws controls in a given area, while in reality different rules apply. The TSP, for example, was a warrantless surveillance program that operated in violation of FISA, that was authorized at the top levels of the executive branch, and that the Justice Department justified through legal memoranda. Yet because its existence was unknown to the public, to most members of Congress, and to all but a small handful of persons in the executive branch, it amounted to secret law.[43]

The achievement and maintenance of secret law depends on a variety of supremacist tools, including executive privilege, state secrets doctrine, and the punishment or threatened punishment of classified speech. Furthermore, secret executive override of statutes requiring disclosure, itself a form of secret law, can protect other secret legal regimes. In these respects, too, the example of the TSP is highly instructive. The TSP's secrecy was facilitated partly by executive circumvention of statutory requirements to keep the congressional intelligence committees informed of such programs. It also was partly facilitated, of course, by classification. Additionally, it is fair to infer that the risk of classified speech prosecutions played some role in deterring potential whistleblowers and in the *New York Times'* decision to postpone revealing the program for more than a year after they learned of it. Indeed, both the Bush and Obama administrations initiated leak prosecutions and threatened others in the wake of the Times' revelation of the program. To this day, much about the program and possible sister programs remains secret due partly to post-revelation state secrets and executive privilege claims.[44]

Plainly, it takes a village of supremacist tools to support secret law. As such, all of the judicial precedents discussed throughout this chapter have some bearing on the topic. Yet the case law most directly related to secret law is the small body that concerns exclusivity, or the executive's ability to override statutes. On the one hand, this body of law reveals a judicial openness toward the notion that, under limited circumstances, certain statutory restrictions on the president's power to protect national security may be unconstitutional. Yet the same cases also indicate that any such circumstances would have to be extraordinary. More to the point, there is a solid basis to argue that the *secret* circumvention of statutes falls well outside of any limited exclusivity supportable under the case law.

The judicial opinion most closely identified with exclusivity is Justice Jackson's celebrated concurrence in *Youngstown Sheet & Tube Co. v. Sawyer.* In *Youngstown,* a majority of the Court rejected the Truman administration's efforts to seize steel mills in the United States to prevent a labor dispute from stopping steel production in the midst of the war in Korea. The majority held that existing statutes prohibited the administration's action.[45] The administration, for its part, did not argue that it has a constitutional prerogative to override the statutes. Rather, it argued that the statutes did not prevent its actions and that those actions were authorized implicitly by legislation to fund U.S. efforts in Korea.[46] The dissent echoed the government's position.[47]

Though agreeing with the majority's conclusion and rationale, Justice Jackson concurred separately to offer guidance for future cases involving presidential power and statutory authority. While acknowledging that his analysis necessarily was "somewhat over-simplified," he grouped acts of presidential power into three zones, creating a framework that a majority of the Court has embraced in subsequent cases.[48] In zone one of this framework, presidential power "is at its maximum." There, the president "acts pursuant to an express or implied authorization of Congress." Zone one actions can be invalidated only where "the Federal Government as a whole lacks power." In zone two, the president "acts in absence of either a congressional grant or denial of authority." There,

> he can only rely upon his own independent powers, but there is a zone of twilight in which he and Congress may have concurrent authority, or in which its distribution is uncertain. Therefore, congressional inertia, indifference, or quiescence may sometimes, at least as a practical matter, enable, if not invite, measures on independent presidential responsibility. In this area, any actual test of power is likely to depend on the imperatives of events and contemporary imponderables rather than on abstract theories of law.

In zone three, the president's power is "at its lowest ebb." There, he acts against Congress's "express or implied will." Zone three actions can be sustained only where Congress is constitutionally prohibited from limiting the presidential powers at issue. "Presidential claim to a power at once so conclusive and preclusive must be scrutinized with caution, for what is at stake is the equilibrium established by our constitutional system."[49]

The very concept of the "lowest ebb" suggests that executive actions in that realm—that is, acts that contravene legislative authority—bear a strong presumption of illegality. This impression is bolstered by Justice Jackson's ready dismissal of the notion that Article II provides preclusive authority for the steel mill seizure.[50] It is also bolstered by Chief Justice Marshall's opinion for a unanimous Court in the 1804 case of *Little v. Barreme*.[51] The *Little* Court held that a statute authorizing the president to detain U.S. ships traveling to France implicitly prevented him from detaining U.S. ships traveling away from France. The statute was directed toward ending commerce between the United States and France in furtherance of the United States' "quasi-war" with France. The executive deemed seizures *to and from* French ports necessary to achieve this statutory end. Nonetheless, the *Little* Court deemed the seizure of ships sailing from France implicitly prohibited, and thus illegal, in light of the statutory authorization to capture ships sailing to France.[52] "[T]here is no suggestion in [Chief Justice Marshall's] opinion, or that of any Justice of the Court—and no evidence that any of the parties, including the Executive, argued—that Congress could not limit the President's tactical flexibility in this respect."[53] More than two centuries after *Little,* the Supreme Court in *Hamdan v. Rumsfeld* invalidated military commissions whose procedures it deemed to violate statutory specifications. Citing Justice Jackson's "lowest ebb" discussion in *Youngstown,* the *Hamdan* Court declared: "Whether or not the President has independent power, absent congressional authorization, to convene military commissions, he may not disregard limitations that Congress has, in proper exercise of its own war powers, placed on his powers."[54]

In contrast to the relevant opinions in *Youngstown, Little,* and *Hamdan,* the authorities typically cited to support presidential exclusivity do not, in fact, uphold exclusivist actions. Rather, these cases involve presidential actions taken either in the absence of governing statutory authority (and hence in Justice Jackson's "zone of twilight") or with statutory authority (and thus in Jacksonian zone one).[55] This phenomenon is epitomized by the 1936 case of *United States v. Curtiss-Wright Export Corp.*[56] Justice Sutherland's majority opinion includes a sweeping passage describing

the very delicate, plenary and exclusive power of the President as the sole organ of the federal government in the field of international relations-a power which does not require as a basis for its exercise an act of Congress, but which, of course, like every other governmental power, must be exercised in subordination to the applicable provisions of the Constitution. It is quite apparent that if, in the maintenance of our international relations, embarrassment—perhaps serious embarrassment—is to be avoided and success for our aims achieved, congressional legislation which is to be made effective through negotiation and inquiry within the international field must often accord to the President a degree of discretion and freedom from statutory restriction which would not be admissible were domestic affairs alone involved. Moreover, he, not Congress, has the better opportunity of knowing the conditions which prevail in foreign countries, and especially is this true in time of war. He has his confidential sources of information. He has his agents in the form of diplomatic, consular and other officials. Secrecy in respect of information gathered by them may be highly necessary, and the premature disclosure of it productive of harmful results.[57]

As Harold Koh recounts, "[a]mong government attorneys, Justice Sutherland's lavish description of the president's powers is so often quoted that it has come to be known as the '"Curtiss-Wright, so I'm right" cite.'"[58]

Justice Sutherland's analysis has been heavily criticized over the years, not least for invoking the concept of the president as "sole organ" in a manner that belies the term's original, nonsupremacist usage.[59] Yet even taking the opinion at face value, its utility for exclusivists is limited. The most basic reason for this limitation is that the executive action upheld by the Court was undertaken pursuant to a joint resolution. For our purposes, joint resolutions are equivalent to statutes because the Constitution requires that they be passed through the same arduous procedures. The joint resolution at issue in *Curtiss-Wright* established a means to criminalize arms sales to Paraguay and Bolivia. Specifically, such sales would become criminal if the president proclaimed—after making certain findings and consulting with particular nations—that halting the sales would further peace between Paraguay and Bolivia. After President Roosevelt made such a proclamation, the Curtiss-Wright Company was prosecuted for selling arms to Bolivia. Curtiss-Wright argued that the joint resolution was unconstitutional because it delegated too much discretion to the president. In Jacksonian terms, then, the executive action upheld in *Curtiss-Wright* took place in zone one, not zone two or three. To the extent that Justice Jackson's sweeping rhetoric suggests the legitimacy of zone two or zone three actions, it is pure dicta.[60]

More so, the reasoning of the *Curtiss-Wright* dicta is not clearly supremacist when read in light of its factual and historical context. True, the opinion refers to "the very delicate, plenary and exclusive power of the President as the sole organ of the federal government in the field of international relations." Yet this statement's reach depends on the meaning of the term "sole organ." The phrase, as used in the 1800 speech by then-congressman John Marshall from which Justice Sutherland quotes, has widely been interpreted to reference the president's role as the nation's instrument for communicating with foreign nations, and possibly his role in executing—as opposed to formulating—treaties and other foreign policy instruments.[61] If this is the meaning of *Curtiss-Wright*'s "sole organ" power, then even its "plenary and exclusive" nature cannot transform it into a right to circumvent statutes, resolutions, or treaties. Furthermore, a narrow reading of the *Curtiss-Wright* dicta is consistent with the majority opinion as a whole. The opinion is overwhelmingly directed toward explaining that Congress is constitutionally permitted, and well advised, to pass legislation that grants the president substantial discretion in the realm of foreign affairs.[62] A modest interpretation also is called for in light of the historical context in which *Curtiss-Wright* was decided. In 1936, the proposition that the president constitutionally could override statutes in the name of national security or foreign affairs was deeply radical and rarely raised as a possibility in any forum.[63] The position was nowhere suggested in the lower court opinions or by any of the parties in *Curtiss-Wright*.[64] Furthermore, even in very recent times, it is not uncommon for otherwise sophisticated commentators to conflate inherent, zone two presidential power with exclusive, zone three presidential power.[65] Given that such confusion reigns even today, it would be a tremendous stretch to interpret *Curtiss-Wright*'s dicta as clear support for exclusivity by a 1936 Supreme Court majority. On balance, then, the imprecision of the *Curtiss-Wright* dicta, the rarity of exclusivity at the time, and the fact that exclusivity was not raised in the lower court or by the parties, make the opinion a very thin reed on which to hang the case for exclusivity.

That said, precedent does leave room for the possibility that the Constitution permits some small zone of exclusivity. Yet it is equally plain that any such zone must remain exceptional and be carefully guarded against expansion and abuse. These limits require checks external to the executive branch. Secret statutory circumvention, which makes such checks impossible, thus should be recognized as categorically illegitimate. The necessity of checks on statutory circumvention, and hence the intrinsic illegitimacy of secret circumvention, can be inferred from at least three aspects of the relevant case law. First, as already noted, it can be inferred from the suggestion in existing precedent that any legitimate zone of exclusivity necessarily is small and exceptional. Second, it can be inferred from the very fact that the Court has reviewed national security cases on a number of occasions, including and beyond *Little, Youngstown,* and *Hamdan,* to assess the executive's statutory compliance.[66] Even if the Court had held an instance of statutory circumvention acceptable in any of these cases—which it has not, in fact, done—it would have done so only after assessing whether the circumstances warranted so extraordinary a holding. By definition, such review requires the fact of statutory circumvention to be known in the first place. Third, where courts discuss the limits of judicial review in national security or foreign affairs cases, they frequently add the caveat that the executive remains accountable politically.[67] Yet for political safeguards to exist, the people and nonexecutive political actors must have the ability meaningfully to judge and respond to executive actions. Long-term, secretive statutory circumvention is the very antithesis of such a system.

Classified Speech

Arguments supporting a broad executive discretion to prosecute classified speech fall into two rough categories. The first encompasses the view that classified speech on the whole—whether leaked by insiders or transmitted by third-party publishers—warrants little or no protection. The government has taken this position in litigating the small handful of classified speech prosecutions. A second set of arguments reflects the view that third-party publishers merit strong First Amendment protections while leakers warrant little if any such protection. The major rationale offered for this distinction is the concept of waiver. That is, insider leakers are said to have waived any First Amendment rights to disclose information where their access to the same was granted contingent on their explicit or implicit agreement not to disclose it to unauthorized persons.[68] While the former argument—that all classified speech is unprotected—is more radical than the latter—that only classified speech by insider leakers is unprotected—both are grounded in supremacy. In both cases, the bare fact of classification by executive fiat is said to remove or dramatically reduce the First Amendment protections that would otherwise apply.

The remainder of this section is divided into four subsections. The first details those aspects of judicial precedent that support pro-prosecution arguments. Specifically, it details doctrinal support for the arguments that classified speech is unprotected regardless of the speaker, and that insider leakers in particular warrant little if any protection from prosecution. The second subsection explores the limits of precedential support for each of the two pro-prosecution arguments. The third subsection considers the extent to which judicial doctrine lays the groundwork for an affirmative case to strongly protect both leakers and third-party publishers under the First Amendment. The fourth subsection explains that this doctrinal groundwork is compatible with the standards proposed in chapter 3 for evaluating classified speech prosecutions.

Doctrinal Support for Prosecuting Classified Speakers

SUPPORT FOR THE ARGUMENT THAT CLASSIFIED SPEECH WARRANTS LITTLE IF ANY CONSTITUTIONAL PROTECTION, REGARDLESS OF THE SPEAKER. The Supreme Court has decided no cases that directly involve prosecutions for leaking or publishing classified information. Nonetheless, some statements by the Court and individual Justices in related cases reflect the view that classification may effectively remove, or substantially diminish, any First Amendment protections that would otherwise attach to those who disseminate information. For example, while the Court famously refused, in *New York Times v. United States*, to authorize an injunction to stop the *New York Times* from publishing the Pentagon Papers, three members of the Court suggested in concurrences that postpublication criminal punishment of the *New York Times* might be permissible, and three members dissented on the ground that they would have granted a prior restraint.[69] In a dissenting opinion joined by Chief Justice Burger and Justice Blackmun, Justice Harlan deemed the judiciary's role in reviewing the executive's judgment on foreign affairs, including whether to suppress information, "very narrowly restricted."[70]

In the 1980 case of *Snepp v. United States*, the Supreme Court upheld a contract whereby former CIA agent Frank Snepp had agreed to submit any writings about the CIA to the agency for prepublication review. The Court also approved a constructive trust against proceeds garnered by Snepp for writings not submitted for review.[71] While the *Snepp* Court emphasized the existence of a contractual agreement, it also placed much weight on the review's purported purpose to protect classified information. The Court explained that "[w]hen a former agent relies on his own judgment about what information is detrimental, he may reveal information that the CIA—with its broader understanding of what may expose classified information and confidential sources—could have identified as harmful."[72] The Court suggested that the government's interest would be much less significant were the information unclassified. Indeed, some lower courts have cited *Snepp* for the proposition that "'[t]he government has no legitimate interest in censoring unclassified materials,'" and, thus, "'may not censor such material, contractually or otherwise.'"[73] For the *Snepp* Court and lower courts, then, the fact that information is classified greatly enhances the government's constitutional power to control its dissemination through contractual conditions of employment.

This theme is echoed in some other lower court opinions. Indeed, in the only federal appellate court opinion to rule directly on the constitutionality of prosecuting leakers, the U.S. Court of Appeals for the Fourth Circuit characterized an employee's leak of satellite photos to the press as pure theft. It deemed no "First Amendment rights . . . implicated" by his prosecution.[74] Judge Russell's 1988 opinion for the court in that case—*United States v. Morison*—relied heavily on Morison's position as a government employee who had signed nondisclosure forms. Yet the opinion also rested implicitly on the special status of classified information and the executive's control of the same. Among the cases invoked at length by Judge Russell were *Snepp* and an earlier Fourth Circuit case, *United States v. Marchetti*.[75] Like *Snepp, Marchetti* had involved a former CIA employee's prepublication clearance agreement. As the *Snepp* Court would later do, the *Marchetti* Court emphasized that the executive branch's control over employee speech is substantially heightened in the context of classified information, given the president's constitutional authority to keep secrets and protect national security.[76] Indeed, the *Marchetti* court stated that the First Amendment would preclude equivalent restraints on government employees "with respect to information which is unclassified or officially disclosed."[77]

Finally, a few recent district court opinions provide partial support for those who deem classified information unprotected or substantially less protected than other speech. In rejecting Thomas Drake's motion to dismiss the government's indictment against him for allegedly retaining classified information, the U.S. District Court for the District of Maryland, which sits within the Fourth Circuit, cited its circuit's controlling precedent in *United States v. Morison*. The *Drake* Court cited *Morison* for the position that the statute under which Drake was prosecuted was not overbroad in violation of the First Amendment, as Drake remained free under it to discuss unclassified information.[78]

Two opinions of the U.S. District Court for the Eastern District of Virginia—also within the Fourth Circuit—in *United States v. Rosen & Weisman*, are somewhat more mixed in assessing the First Amendment protections due third parties who disseminate leaked information. On the one hand, a 2006 opinion issued in response to the defendants' motion to dismiss the indictment on First Amendment grounds suggested that classification might effectively be decisive in making speech punishable.[79] Yet a subsequent opinion softened the potential extremity of the earlier one. Among other things, the second opinion, issued in February 2009, clarified that the jury must independently determine if the Espionage Act's criteria for illegal communications are met.[80] It explained:

> [E]vidence that information is classified is, at most, evidence that the government intended that the designated information be closely held. Yet, evidence that information is classified is not conclusive on this point. . . . Further, the government's classification decision is inadmissible hearsay on the second prong of the . . . [statutory definition of national defense information,] namely whether

unauthorized disclosure might potentially damage the United States or an enemy of the United States.[81]

Still, the February 2009 opinion marks a far cry from the First Amendment protections ordinarily applied when speech is prosecuted as a threat to national security. Ordinarily—that is, at least where speech does not include classified information—speech can be punished as a threat to national security only when it is intended to cause, and is likely to cause, imminent illegal activity.[82]

SUPPORT FOR THE ARGUMENT THAT LEAKERS DO NOT WARRANT SIGNIFICANT FIRST AMENDMENT PROTECTIONS, EVEN IF THIRD-PARTY PUBLISHERS MERIT THEM. The concept of waiver also figures prominently in *Morison* and in cases involving prepublication review. In *Morison,* Judge Russell's opinion for the Court emphasized that Morison had committed theft by stealing classified photographs to which he had special access as a security-cleared employee of the navy. The opinion also stressed that Morison had agreed, as a condition of his employment and security clearance, not to disclose classified information without authorization.[83] And in *Snepp,* the Supreme Court deemed Snepp's employment relationship with the CIA to have "involved an extremely high degree of trust."[84] The trust relationship was made explicit, said the Court, in the prepublication review agreement that Snepp signed.[85] Most important, the Court stressed that the remedy it approved—a constructive trust on Snepp's proceeds—was perfectly tailored to Snepp's "fiduciary and contractual" breaches.[86]

Waiver themes invoked by courts in other contexts also have been drawn upon by courts addressing classified information leaks. In 2009's *Wilson v. CIA,* the Second Circuit upheld Valerie Plame Wilson's prepublication agreement with the CIA as applied to stop the publication of information that, while public knowledge, remained classified.[87] In so holding, the Court cited the 1995 case of *United States v. Aguilar.* In *Aguilar,* the Supreme Court upheld the conviction of a federal judge for revealing the fact of a wiretap order to its subject.[88] The *Wilson* Court cited *Aguilar* for the proposition that

when a government employee "voluntarily assume[s] a duty of confidentiality, governmental restrictions on disclosure are not subject to the same stringent standards that would apply to efforts to impose restrictions on unwilling members of the public."[89]

And in 2011, the District Court for the District of Columbia, rejecting Stephen Kim's motion to dismiss his criminal leak prosecution, cited the D.C. Circuit's decision in *Boehner v. McDermott*. Specifically, it cited the *Boehner* Court's view that pursuant to *Aguilar,* "'those who accept positions of trust involving a duty not to disclose information they lawfully acquire while performing their responsibilities have no First Amendment right to disclose that information.'"[90]

Some commentators deem another line of judicial precedent—that involving the free speech protections due government employees against termination or other employment-based discipline—bad news for leakers seeking protection from prosecution. In these cases—sometimes referred to as the *Pickering* line of cases after the earliest in the series, *Pickering v. Board of Education*—the Court established that government employees sometimes are protected from being fired or disciplined for speech on matters of public concern. To determine whether an employee may be punished in a given case, courts must balance "'the interests of the [employee], as a citizen, in commenting upon matters of public concern and the interest of the State, as an employer, in promoting the efficiency of the public services it performs through its employees.'"[91] In the 2006 case of *Garcetti v. Ceballos*, the Court clarified that these protections do not apply to speech "made pursuant to the employee's official duties."[92] At least one academic commentator interprets *Garcetti* to mean that employees who leak classified information have no First Amendment protection from prosecution because they accessed the information as a result of their government employment.[93] Another commentator concludes that the *Pickering* balance applies to classified information leaks, but that the result is a broad government leeway to punish leaks through discharge or criminal prosecution.[94] The latter commentator does, however, consider leaks that reveal illegal government conduct protected under *Pickering* balancing.[95]

The Limits of the Doctrinal Case for Prosecuting Classified Speakers

THE LIMITS OF DOCTRINAL SUPPORT FOR PROSECUTING CLASSIFIED SPEAKERS GENERALLY.   While aspects of existing doctrine suggest that classified information deserves far less protection than unclassified speech warrants, the notion does not rest on rock solid ground. The shakiness of the foundation is due partly to the scarcity of the relevant case law. Many questions simply have not been decided by any federal court, or have been decided only by a single federal appellate court. Furthermore, of the few relevant judicial opinions, some are careful to note that greater protections might be warranted under different circumstances.

As we have seen, the only federal appellate court to rule directly on the constitutionality of prosecuting classified leaks or publications was the Fourth Circuit in *United States v. Morison*. There, the court considered Samuel Morison's prosecution for leaking classified satellite photos to the press. Judge Russell's opinion for the Court contained statements to the effect that the case involved pure theft and implicated no First Amendment rights. Nonetheless, two of the three panel judges concurred separately to make clear their view that the prosecution implicated the First Amendment. And while both concurring judges embraced a deferential role for the judiciary, the extent of deference prescribed by either— and thus agreed upon by a majority of the *Morison* court—is unclear. Concurring Judge Wilkinson suggested that very strong deference is in order, as the alternative "would be grave."[96] Yet he also expressed confidence that sources who reveal very important stories, such as "'corruption, scandal, and incompetence in the defense establishment,'" were unlikely to be prosecuted or convicted, and that if they were, the situation could be "cured through case-by-case [judicial] analysis of the fact situations."[97] Concurring Judge Phillips endorsed "Judge Wilkinson's ... view that the first amendment issues raised by Morison are real and substantial and require the serious attention which his concurring opinion then gives them."[98] He also accepted Judge Wilkinson's "general estimate" that leaks exposing important news will not be punished, deeming it "the critical judicial determination forced by the first amendment arguments advanced in this case."[99]

To be sure, the *Morison* court overall was exceedingly deferential to broad statutory prosecution authorizations as applied to classified information leaks. This is deeply problematic from the perspective of free speech theory, particularly given the realities of overclassification and selective leaking from the top. Nonetheless, the concurring statements in *Morison* of two of the three judges leave room, however narrow, for case-by-case arguments to the effect that some prosecuted speech is of such high value as to warrant tougher judicial scrutiny than that accorded Morison. Similarly, recall that the district court in *Rosen & Weissman*, a court within the Fourth Circuit, took a more protective view still of the case-by-case fact-finding demanded where third parties are prosecuted for publishing classified information.

While no Supreme Court precedent directly addresses classified speech prosecutions, some do, as we have seen, contain reasoning that could be deemed dismissive of any First Amendment concerns about the same. Yet there are forceful reasons against extending such cases beyond their facts. As for the Pentagon Papers case, it would be imprudent for courts to extrapolate very much from the dissenting or concurring opinions. For one thing, prosecutions—of either leakers or the press—simply were not at issue in the case. While this point alone counsels caution, it is further warranted in light of the tremendous time pressure under which the case was briefed, argued, and decided. As observed in Justice Harlan's dissenting opinion:

> Both the Court of Appeals for the Second Circuit and the Court of Appeals for the District of Columbia Circuit rendered judgment on June 23. The New York Times' petition for certiorari, its motion for accelerated consideration thereof, and its application for interim relief were filed in this Court on June 24 at about 11 A.M. The application of the United States for interim relief in the Post case was also filed here on June 24 at about 7:15 P.M. This Court's order setting a hearing before us on June 26 at 11 A.M., a course which I joined only to avoid the possibility of even more peremptory action by the Court, was issued less than 24 hours before. The record in the Post case was filed with the Clerk shortly before 1 P.M. on June 25; the record in the Times case did not arrive until 7 or 8 o'clock that same night. The briefs of the parties were received less than two hours before argument on June 26.[100]

The Court's decision, the concurrences, and the dissents all were issued just four days after oral argument, on June 30, 1971. Given the sense of urgency surrounding the case, one should hesitate to draw broad lessons from the dissenters' view that the prior restraint should have been continued long enough to permit thorough judicial consideration. The same caution applies to concurring statements to the effect that a prior restraint was out of order, but that the government might have other viable options including criminal prosecution.[101]

Snepp, too, can and should be limited to its facts. It is true that the *Snepp* Court emphasized the executive's prerogative to control classified information. Given that prerogative and given Snepp's employment with the CIA, the Court deemed a prepublication review agreement a reasonable and constitutional means for the CIA to protect classified information. Yet much of the opinion's force comes in its approval of the trial court's remedy for Snepp's breach of the agreement. Specifically, the Court approved a constructive trust on the proceeds of Snepp's book, which Snepp had failed to submit to the CIA for review. A constructive trust, the court explained, is "the natural and customary consequence of a breach of trust. It deals fairly with both parties by conforming relief to the dimensions of the wrong. . . . . [S]ince the remedy reaches only funds attributable to the breach, it cannot saddle the former agent with exemplary damages out of all proportion to his gain."[102] *Snepp* thus does not embrace an unfettered executive discretion to control classified information or an unfettered legislative discretion to authorize any means of control. To the contrary, it leaves room for fact-sensitive analyses to determine whether a given punishment for classified speech goes too far.[103]

Furthermore, Snepp was rife with procedural irregularities. In his petition for certiorari, Snepp had asked the Supreme Court to consider the constitutionality of the injunctive and damages remedies upheld by the appellate court. The government responded with a conditional cross-petition, asking the Court, if it granted Snepp's certiorari petition, also to review the appellate court's rejection of the constructive trust remedy that the trial court had approved.[104] The Supreme Court's per curiam opinion focused on the constructive trust issue. The Court's response to Snepp's First Amendment objections was shoe-horned into a single footnote. Because the Court barely addressed the issues raised by Snepp, the dissent argued that the Court had effectively denied Snepp's petition for certiorari and thus lacked jurisdiction over the case, given the conditional nature of the government's cross-petition.[105] More so, the Court decided the case without benefit of merits briefs or oral argument.[106] As Archibald Cox wrote at the time: "One would have supposed that the extent of the government's authority to silence its officials and employees and thereby deprive the public of access to information about government activity was not too obvious to deserve deliberate judicial consideration."[107]

THE LIMITS OF DOCTRINAL SUPPORT FOR PROSECUTING LEAKERS IN PARTICULAR.   The doctrinal strength of the waiver theory, too, has its stopping points. The limits of its reach in two important cases—*Morison* and *Snepp*—parallel the limits of the support that one can draw from those cases for prosecuting classified speech generally. As for *Morison,* the Court's opinion—despite its sweeping rhetoric to the effect that Morison engaged not in speech but in theft and a violation of his employment terms—again must be viewed in light of the separate opinions of two of the three judges on the panel. While those opinions too are broadly deferential to the executive, they acknowledge that serious First Amendment issues are at stake and suggest that *Morison* does not preclude future courts' taking into account the value of particular leaks in assessing prosecutions. As for *Snepp,* that opinion's reach again is limited by its remedy-specific reasoning. The *Snepp* Court did deem a former CIA employee to have waived his First Amendment rights when he agreed to submit future writings to the CIA for prepublication review so that the agency could check for classified information. Yet an important feature of the Court's reasoning was its attention to the tight fit between the remedy that it approved—a constructive trust against book proceeds—and the nature of the contractual breach at issue. Furthermore, *Snepp*'s procedural irregularities independently warrant caution in extending its holding beyond its facts.

Turning to other cases, it also is too great a stretch to read language in *Aguilar v. United States* to mean that government employees are fully unprotected in all contexts from revealing information that they have agreed not to reveal. Recall that the Supreme Court in *Aguilar* upheld a federal judge's conviction for revealing a wiretap order to its subject. Citing *Snepp,* the *Aguilar* Court explained that "[a]s to one who voluntarily assumed a duty of confidentiality, governmental restrictions on disclosure are not subject to the same stringent standards that would apply to efforts to impose restrictions on unwilling members of the public."[108] This statement tells us only that the voluntary commitment element is a factor that lowers the level of constitutional protection relative to what it otherwise would be. It does not mean that First Amendment protections fail to apply at all. Indeed, the *Aguilar* Court stressed that the relevant statute targeted only disclosures of wiretap orders or applications intended to impede the same. The court also cited the obvious state interests in preventing this narrow set of disclosures.[109] To the extent that lower courts cite *Aguilar* for the broader proposition that voluntary non-disclosure agreements erase a contracting party's First Amendment rights, they misread it. Furthermore, to the extent that the U.S. Courts of Appeals for the D.C. and Second Circuits in particular have cited *Aguilar* for this overly broad proposition, they have done so in a manner unnecessary to their holdings and in cases limitable to their facts.[110]

The *Pickering* cases also should not be construed to bear negatively on leakers' constitutional protections against prosecution. As with *Snepp,* the cases' reasoning is tied closely to particular remedies. Throughout the

Pickering cases, the Supreme Court considers government's discretion to act as an employer to discipline its employees—that is, to fire or demote them—for their speech. The Court engages in case-by-case balancing between "'the interests of the [employee], as a citizen, in commenting upon matters of public concern and the interest of the State, as an employer, in promoting the efficiency of the public services it performs through its employees.'"[111] Underlying the employer's side of the balance is the view that public employers, like private ones, need discretion to deal with employee speech that negatively impacts the workplace. To protect such discretion, the *Garcetti* Court went so far as to deem the *Pickering* test—and hence First Amendment protections—inapplicable to employees disciplined for "statements [made] pursuant to their official duties."[112] Such a limit was necessary, said the Court, to avoid "'constitutionali[ing] the employee grievance.'"[113]

The *Pickering* cases, in short, are concerned with the government's need for discretion *when it acts as an employer in disciplining or dismissing employees.*[114] The deference that the cases give government employers to fire or discipline employees for their speech—whether through the application of *Pickering* balancing or through *Garcetti*'s categorical exclusion of some speech from protection—does not translate to the realm of criminal punishment.

Finally, recall that at least one commentator reads *Garcetti*—which deemed *Pickering*'s protections inapplicable to speech "made pursuant to the employee's official duties"—to remove any First Amendment protections for classified information leaks because leakers access such information through their employment. Even if we assume that *Garcetti* applies to criminal prosecutions, its categorical exemption should not be construed so broadly. True, the *Garcetti* Court stated that "[r]estricting speech that owes its existence to a public employee's professional responsibilities does not infringe any liberties the employee might have enjoyed as a private citizen."[115] But the logic of *Garcetti* on the whole—and of the earlier cases on which it builds—cuts against interpreting the statement to preclude protection for information gleaned through government employment. Rather, the statement is best read to mean that speech that is itself part of one's job is not protected. The latter interpretation is tailored to the *Garcetti* Court's goal to avoid "'constitutionaliz[ing] the employee grievance.'"[116] The former interpretation, on the other hand, would dramatically undercut a premise—cited throughout the *Pickering* cases and reiterated in *Garcetti* itself—underlying the speech value side of the *Pick-*

ering balance. That is, government employees have special value to add to public debate by virtue of their inside knowledge, and the public has an important "interest in receiving [their] well-informed views."[117] Indeed, the D.C. Circuit in *Wilson v. CIA,* which involved Valerie Plame Wilson's efforts to include some classified information about her CIA service in a book, observed in a footnote that "[t]his case does not implicate the concerns discussed in *Garcetti.*"[118] Other federal courts similarly have found *Garcetti* inapplicable to speech conducted outside of one's employment responsibilities, even where the speech consists of information learned through, and about, that employment.[119]

The Seeds of an Affirmative Doctrinal Case for Robustly Protecting Classified Speakers from Prosecution

Precedent also contains the seeds of an affirmative case for strongly protecting classified speakers. Two foundational elements of the case are the notions that information about government is of central importance under the First Amendment and that suspicion is warranted when the government seeks to shield information about itself from public view. Both ideas find substantial support in precedent. On the first point, the Supreme Court has made clear that speech on matters of public importance is at the heart of the First Amendment.[120] Such speech not only benefits speakers, but is vital to the constitutional system. If elections and interbranch checks and balances are to be more than mere facades, the people must have opportunities to learn and convey information and debate ideas.[121] Expounding on these points, the Court has observed:

> The freedom of speech and of the press guaranteed by the Constitution embraces at the least the liberty to discuss publicly and truthfully all matters of public concern without previous restraint or fear of subsequent punishment. The exigencies of the colonial period and the efforts to secure freedom from oppressive administration developed a broadened conception of these liberties as adequate to supply the public need for information and education with respect to the significant issues of the times.[122]

Appreciation for the value of speech about government and public affairs is closely intertwined with fears that the government will abuse censorial powers to single out speech that it dislikes, including that which it perceives to threaten its comfort or credibility. As the material just quoted reflects, the Court recognizes the very real risk—and long history—of such abuse as important factors underlying its free speech jurisprudence. Fear of government abuse, combined with recognition of speech's affirmative value, are manifest in doctrines designed to limit government's discretion to punish speech for its content. Among these doctrines is the "content distinction" rule, which amounts to a strong presumption against laws or law enforcement based on the viewpoint, subject matter, or communicative impact of speech.[123]

Long experience also demonstrates the special risks posed where government seeks to punish speech that ostensibly threatens national security. From World War I through the early Cold War years, the Court regularly upheld prosecutions for antiwar, communist, and socialist speech. There is wide consensus in retrospect that the prosecutions were poorly justified and that the Court deferred unduly to the government in upholding them.[124] The Court appeared to have internalized these lessons by 1969, when it decided *Brandenburg v. Ohio*.[125] In *Brandenburg,* the Court announced that one cannot constitutionally be punished for speech linked to terrorism or to other dangerous activity unless the speech is intended to incite, and likely to incite, imminent, lawless action.[126] The *Brandenburg* Court also made clear that the judiciary has the final word in striking this balance.[127]

The Supreme Court's appreciation for the informing and deliberative functions of speech, and its wariness of government abuse, are manifest further in the Court's attentiveness to the chilling effect of speech restrictions. The Court has repeatedly observed that free speech is harmed not only by unwarranted punishments, but by the self-censorship of those who fear the same. Speakers may play it safe in the face of vague or far-reaching laws, saying nothing that risks angering powerful members of society. Such reasoning was central to the Supreme Court's opinion in *New York Times v. Sullivan* establishing strong First Amendment protections for speakers accused of defaming public officials. The Court deemed it better for protections to be so strong that some defamatory speech will go unpunished, than so weak that "would-be critics of official conduct may be deterred from voicing their criticism."[128]

These aspects of precedent lend support not only to protecting third-party publishers, but to protecting leakers as well. A government employee, lacking the high-level political support of an authorized leaker or the resources of many third-party publishers, is especially vulnerable to chilling with respect to classified speech that high-level officials are likely to deem unwelcome for its content.

The *Pickering* line of cases shines the most direct light on the unique constitutional value of leaks from government insiders. In *Garcetti,* the Supreme Court explained that "the First Amendment interests at stake extend beyond the individual speaker. The Court has acknowledged the importance of promoting the public's interest in receiving the well-informed views of government employees engaging in civic discussion."[129] Indeed, public employees can make uniquely important contributions to the speech marketplace precisely because of knowledge gained through their work. In *Pickering* itself, the Court observed that "[t]eachers are, as a class, the members of a community most likely to have informed and definite opinions as to how funds allotted to the operations of the schools should be spent. Accordingly, it is essential that they be able to speak out freely on such questions without fear of retaliatory dismissal."[130]

Such speech value does not disappear in the context of national security and classified information. To the contrary, the very secrecy of these contexts heightens the value of information flow, even as the state's interests on the other side of the balance may be heightened as well.

Proposed Doctrinal Standards against the Precedential Backdrop

The affirmative arguments just described add a doctrinal dimension to the case from constitutional text, structure, and principle—a case described in chapter 3—for strongly protecting classified speakers from prosecution. Chapter 3 also proposed standards by which courts should assess prosecutions of third-party publishers and leakers, respectively. Those standards follow as well from the precedent-based case for protecting classified speakers. Like the arguments from text, structure, and principle, the precedent-based case lays a foundation both for protecting third-party publishers and leakers, and for protecting the former more strongly than the latter. The distinction between the two groups can be justified partly by the case law's limited adoption of waiver theory. It also can be drawn partly from precedent's related embrace of the notion that the government has greater leeway when it acts in some institutional roles, such as that of employer, than in others, including that of prosecutor.[131] Additionally, defamation law provides some doctrinal grounding for chapter 3's suggestion that courts consider modulating the strength of leaker protections with the severity of the penalty sought. In the defamation setting, courts long have subjected plaintiffs to burdens that vary based partly on the level of damages that they seek.[132]

Substantive Accountability and Internal Checking

Internal Checks and Their Relationship to External Checks

This chapter brings us back to the case for and implications of the substantive accountability framework. Previous chapters explained the leeway that the framework provides Congress and the courts to create and protect external checks on executive power. This chapter and the next focuses on Congress's constitutional power—within the confines of the legislative process—to structure the executive branch to create and protect checks on presidential power from within the branch.

To be sure, the dichotomy between internal and external checks is not a clean one. Executive privilege and state secrets controversies arise when Congress, the courts, or the public attempt to retrieve information from within the executive branch. Mechanisms to curtail secret law include congressional oversight and other means to shed light on executive branch programs. And classified leaks of information come from within the executive branch, while leaker protections—apart from voluntary restraint by the executive branch—arise from legislation or judicial review. Nor are the "internal checks" discussed in this chapter purely internal. Rather, a more precise description of this chapter's topic is the extent to which the Constitution permits Congress, acting through the legislative process, to accord the president less than complete control over all discretionary executive decisions and those who make them.

Still, it is useful as a practical matter and conceptually meaningful to distinguish between external and internal checks. The distinction hinges primarily on the nature of the congressional or judicial mechanism that creates or protects the check. In the case of external checks, Congress or the judiciary limits the executive's ability to have the final word on whether information must be shielded to protect national security or to preserve candid discussions with the president. Such checks are enabled by a constitutional scheme that permits or requires certain substantive judgments to be shared with other branches. Internal checks, in contrast, are protected by legislation that imposes structural limits on unfettered presidential power within the executive branch. Such legislation might, for example, prevent the president from firing particular personnel without good cause. Or it might authorize only certain administrators to make specified decisions, and thus forbid the president from substituting his judgment for theirs. Put another way, an internal check "'does not concern the scope of executive powers, it concerns who controls whatever power the executive has.'"[1]

Considering internal checks in their own right also enables us to engage directly with the strain of presidentialism called unitary executive theory. To unity proponents, the Constitution requires full presidential control over all discretionary executive branch decisions and actors. From this perspective, a statute that limits the president to "good-cause" dismissals of certain executive branch actors is unconstitutional, as is a statute that directs a specific administrator to make certain decisions and forbids the president from overriding the same.[2] Unity-based objections also have been made to statutes that require executive personnel to testify before Congress without first clearing their testimony with the White House.[3]

The remainder of this chapter details the role and legitimacy of internal checks within the Constitution's substantive accountability framework. To summarize the case briefly, Congress—acting within the constraints of the legislative process—has substantial albeit not unlimited leeway to create zones of partial independence from presidential control within the executive branch. On the one hand, the president must maintain supervisory control throughout the branch. This is necessary partly to effectuate the textual demands of the Vesting and "Take Care" Clauses. It also is demanded by formal accountability, which is a necessary but not sufficient part of substantive accountability. Yet some limits on presidential control not only are consistent with substantive accountability, but can positively enhance it. Unfettered presidential control can be used, for example, to keep truthful information from emerging from the executive branch through White House vetting of congressional testimony, pressure to alter scientific findings for political reasons, or secretive influence over agency policy decisions. Congress has substantial constitutional leeway to pass statutes that create pockets of partial independence from presidential control to facilitate substantive accountability through information flow. This leeway is not unlimited. At some point, limits on presidential control become great enough to defeat the formal component of substantive accountability and the supervisory role mandated by the Vesting and Take Care Clauses. But the question is a functional one of degree within wide boundaries of congressional leeway. This scheme marks a far cry from the categorical directive of unfettered presidential control that unity proponents find in Article II.

This chapter's next two sections elaborate on the constitutional case for congressional leeway to create and protect internal checks. They also detail and counter the core justifications for unitary executive theory. The first section considers what relevant directives follow from the Constitution's text as a matter of original meaning. It discerns only a thin textual mandate, one that demands presidential supervision of the executive branch but does not preclude some limits on direct presidential control. In short, the first section finds that the original meaning of the Constitution's text demands functional limits on the degree of presidential estrangement from administrative decision making. The text does not establish a categorically unitary executive.

The first section adds to existing debates in two ways. First, it performs some brush-clearing that is necessary before we can return to the substantive accountability framework. That is, it counters unity-based arguments from text, structure, and history that would, if correct, preclude the internal checking features of the substantive accountability framework. Second, the section builds a bridge between anti-unity arguments from history and text and anti-unity arguments grounded in functional, substantive accountability-based concerns. It explains that unity proponents not only misread history, but that they do so in part because they mistake founding commitments to substantive accountability with commitments to purely formal accountability or with founding attachments to structure for structure's sake.

The second section turns directly to the substantive accountability framework and the place of internal checks in the same. It also elaborates on the flaws of functional, accountability-based arguments for unity.

Revisiting the Original Meaning of the Executive Power Clauses

Core Unity-Based Arguments from Original Meaning

In chapter 4, we saw that the original meaning of "executive power" is quite lean, entailing only the power to carry the laws of the legislature

into execution. It is largely on this point that nonsupremacists part ways
with supremacists, with the latter finding additional privileges and prerogatives in the executive power. Unity proponents and opponents part ways
on a somewhat finer point. Opponents read the Vesting and Take Care
Clauses to give the president a supervisory, rather than direct power over
all law execution. Unity proponents, on the other hand, read the clauses
to require presidential control over every discretionary executive decision
and decision maker in the U.S. government.

At the heart of unity's textual case is the Vesting Clause. The clause, as
we have seen, directs that "The executive power shall be vested in a President of the United States of America."[4] Unity proponents emphasize that
"[a]t bottom," as a matter of original meaning, "the executive power is the
power to execute the laws."[5] In this, they are in accord with this book's
views. Yet in their next analytical step, unity's proponents veer from the
path of opponents. Specifically, proponents reason that "if the [Vesting
Clause] grants the power to execute the laws, absent some powerful textual reason or historical understanding to the contrary, it must enable the
president to execute the laws himself."[6] They deem this point intuitive.
They also deem it bolstered by the fact that "[e]very other constitutional
provision that grants a power to an entity permits the recipient to exercise the power personally. For instance, no one doubts that federal judges
may exercise their federal judicial power over cases and controversies by
rendering judgments regarding such cases."[7] To unity's proponents, then,
the Vesting Clause plainly and obviously bequeaths full control of every
executive decision and decision maker to the president. From this starting
point, they find that other constitutional provisions—including the Take
Care and Opinions Clauses—do not contradict this bequeathal, and in
fact affirm it by implicitly assuming it.[8]

Unity proponents deem their textual understanding deeply supported
by history. They draw first from evidence of original meaning to deem the
executive power the power to execute the law. From there, they move to
the bolder point that executive power belongs exclusively and indefeasibly to the president. The latter, they say, is overwhelmingly evidenced by
the founding decision to create a single-headed presidency rather than a
plural executive or one with an annexed advisory council. In other words,
they equate the founding rejection of a plural presidency or an executive council with a decision to establish a fully unitary executive branch.
Unity proponents also conflate founding assurances of a singular presidency's accountability and energy with promises that a fully unitary exec-

utive would bear those same traits.[9] They also cite the "Decision of 1789" as further confirmation of their position.[10] In the latter case, the First Congress engaged in an epic debate over the removal power, culminating in legislation that assumed a presidential power to remove the secretary of foreign affairs.

Unity Proponents Overread Original Meaning

THE TEXT DOES NOT LOCK IN UNITY.   As we have seen, one must take great care in discerning constitutional rules ostensibly locked in by text. Caution is warranted particularly in light of the risk that one will miss the forest of underlying constitutional principles—and thus, ironically, undermine the constitutional scheme—in an effort to unearth thick directives from the past.

In conflating a unitary presidency with a unitary executive branch, unity supporters overread the original meaning of the executive power clauses. They begin on the right foot, defining the original meaning of executive power as the power to execute the laws. Yet they falter in leaping to the conclusion that the Vesting Clause must vest every discretionary aspect of every executive decision in the president. Even when one views the Vesting Clause in isolation from other constitutional text, the unitary interpretation is but one plausible construction. At least equally plausible is that the phrase, "[t]he executive power is vested in a President of the United States," demands that the president maintain the power to oversee or to supervise law execution—for example, that he retain the power to dismiss executive personnel "for good cause," if not to substitute his own decisions for theirs or to dismiss them for any reason. Even by itself, then, the Vesting Clause is logically consistent with the view that, as Peter Strauss puts it, the president is the "overseer and not [the] decider" of the executive branch.[11]

The Vesting Clause was written, read, and debated in full awareness of the fact that the executive would not and could not personally execute every aspect of every law. For one who read the clause knowing of this commonsense inevitability, the clause might still have implied that the president would personally control all law execution in that he could substitute his judgment for that of his subordinates or dismiss them for any reason at any time. But it would have been equally plausible for the clause to mean that the president would have supervisory powers, enabling his substantial if not unfettered control over the executive branch.

When one widens his or her view of constitutional text beyond the Vesting Clause, the case for the president as Straussian overseer becomes stronger still. Indeed, Strauss and other anti-unity scholars have looked predominantly beyond the Vesting Clause to make their respective textual cases.[12] For one thing, the text refers to other officers and departments apart from the president himself. The text thus makes explicit the otherwise inferable point that the president will not personally execute the laws. Indeed, the text permits the president to "require the Opinion, in writing, of the principal Officer in each of the executive Departments, upon any Subject relating to the Duties of their respective Offices." While the Opinions Clause is not flatly inconsistent with unity, it fits much more logically into a system whereby officers are not mere alter egos to the president but are subject to presidential oversight. The latter vision also is reflected in the Take Care Clause. The Take Care Clause does not order the president to execute all laws himself. Nor does it demand that he "assure" faithful execution of the laws, a command that would assume his full control over the same.[13] Rather, it admonishes him only to "take Care that the Laws be faithfully executed." Furthermore, the textually dictated system for appointments—whereby all officers are nominated by the president but must be approved by the Senate, and whereby Congress can vest inferior officers' appointments in persons other than the president—also reflects a scheme consistent with limits on presidential control over particular executive branch decisions and actors.[14]

Article II's anti-unity aspects are complemented by Article I's "Sweeping" or "Necessary and Proper" Clause. The latter explicitly grants Congress the power to pass legislation "necessary and proper for carrying into Execution" both Congress's own enumerated powers and "all other Powers vested by this Constitution in the Government of the United States, or in any Department or Officer thereof."[15]

HISTORY CONFIRMS THAT THE TEXT DOES NOT LOCK IN UNITY. A textual review thus casts serious doubt on the notion that the Constitution locks in unity as a matter of original meaning. When one looks to history, the notion is positively shattered. As we saw in chapter 4, the founding-era consensus on executive power's definition extended only to the power to carry into effect the laws of the legislature. Yet there was hardly clarity over the extent to which the Constitution bequeathed unfettered control over even this power to the president. History reflects at least two points of uncertainty. First, it was not self-evident what the power to carry out the law necessarily included. In particular, it was not clear whether it encompassed a right to appoint and remove subordinates. Second, whatever the power to carry out the laws entailed, there was no consensus that the Constitution granted every aspect of that power, undivided and indefeasibly, to the president.

Original Meaning and the Appointment and Removal Powers. It is far from clear that the executive power includes, as a matter of original meaning, unfettered appointment and removal powers. The appointment power was alternately referred to as an executive power or as a power that traditionally had been part of the royal prerogative but that was not intrinsically executive in nature.[16] And while the Constitution specified appointment procedures for executive officers, it nowhere specified removal procedures short of impeachment. Were the removal power clearly executive as a matter of original definition, this presumably would have been reflected in founding assumptions. To the contrary, however, two prominent Federalists assured Americans during the ratification period that the president would not possess such power. Writing as *An American Citizen* in "the first substantive essay published anywhere in favor of the Constitution,"[17] Tench Coxe explained that the president could not "take away offices during good behaviour."[18] In the *Federalist*, Alexander Hamilton expressed the view that senatorial consent would be needed to "displace as well as to appoint [officers]."[19]

The lack of a founding consensus on removal also was reflected in the First Congress's 1789 debate over presidential removal power, discussed in detail below. Suffice it for now to note that a number of participants expressed a belief similar to that expressed by Hamilton in the *Federalist*— the Senate had to consent to removals of executive officers. While others evinced the view that the president alone had constitutional discretion to effectuate such removals, others expressed confusion and uncertainty on the matter. The Debate of 1789 thus corroborates the lack of founding consensus on the scope of the president's removal power.

Original Meaning and Unfettered Presidential Control of Law Execution. Whatever the power to execute the law entails, unity proponents deem it clear that that power must belong, indefeasibly and without limit, to the president. As we have seen, however, the text alone is ambiguous on this point. The Vesting Clause could reasonably be interpreted to grant the president unfettered direct control over every executive decision. But it could just as reasonably mean that the president is the executive branch's Straussian "overseer" rather than the "decider" of each and every discretionary executive decision made within the federal government. And when the Vesting Clause is viewed in tandem with the other relevant provisions of the Constitution, the case for president as decider weakens considerably.

Preratification history, too, cuts against the notion that unity would have been evident, as a matter of constitutional directive, to members of the founding generation. The intellectual and experiential backdrop of the era conduced to flexible and functional, not rigid and formalistic readings of provisions like the Vesting Clause. This backdrop includes the uncertainty and malleability surrounding all but the thinnest meaning of the phrase "executive power" and the transition from mixed government to separated powers.[20] It also encompasses the period between the Revolution and the founding, when state constitutions regularly mixed formalistic references to separated powers with breaches of executive unity and independence.[21] "[S]tate constitutions not only permitted, but actually mandated legislative involvement in both personnel and superintendence. Nothing in the records of the Convention demonstrates that exclusivity suddenly became the norm in 1787."[22] To the contrary, participants in the framing and ratification debates likened the U.S. president's proposed executive powers to those of state governors.[23] Recall, for example, Edmund Randolph's rhetorical challenge at the Virginia ratifying convention to those who deemed the president too powerful: "What are his powers? To see the laws executed. Every Executive in America has that power."[24]

Postfounding practices also belie the notion that the Constitution conveyed a widely understood unity directive. In creating the federal government's first three administrative departments over the summer of 1789, the first Congress passed laws embodying functional flexibility rather than rigid formality. The laws varied the degree of presidential control over each department's secretary. The statutes creating the Departments of War and Foreign Affairs each directed the relevant secretary to "conduct the business of the said Department in such manner as the President of the United States, shall from time to time Order or instruct."[25] Yet in the statute creating the Treasury Department, such language was notably absent. Instead, the treasury secretary was directed to perform certain enumerated services "as may be by law required of him."[26] More important, the Treasury statute gave the secretary duties that effectively "made him in part an agent of Congress." As David P. Currie explains, "[t]he Secretary . . . was seen as an indispensable, direct arm of the House." And while "[t]he debate on [the Treasury] provisions was marked by deep concern over undue executive influence on the House . . . [n]o one seems to have made the converse argument that they gave Congress excessive power over the executive."[27]

The treasury secretary was hardly the only "mongrel" administrator created by the First Congress.[28] The 1789 Judiciary Act, which created the position of attorney general, did not direct him to take orders from the president, apart from a provision requiring him "to give his advice and opinion upon questions of law when required by the president of the United States, or when requested by the heads of any of the departments."[29] Indeed, in the office's early years, the attorney general was treated as a legal advisor to the president and to members of Congress alike.[30] Congress even directed the attorney general to bring specific legal actions.[31] The Judiciary Act also created a system of federal district attorneys, but nowhere indicated that they were to be under the direction of the attorney general or the president. When the attorney general sought such control in 1792, Congress did not grant his request.[32] Other examples abound of administrative offices and duties that were created in Congress's earliest years without being placed under direct presidential control.[33]

Susan Low Bloch aptly describes the view of administration reflected in Congress's earliest actions. "The question was one of degree—the degree of presidential control. The First Congress established varying levels of presidential control over various officials depending on the function of the officer involved. The early legislators established gradations of presidential control along functional, flexible lines."[34]

History, Functionalism, and Substantive Accountability

Unity proponents thus overread original meaning when they deem it conclusive of a unity directive. This point is fairly well tread. Less recognized, however, is the link between unity's textual and historical errors and its conflating of substantive and formal accountability. Unity proponents argue that unity not only is demanded by original meaning, but that it is functionally desirable because it fosters accountability. They point out that the president is the only nationally elected figure in American politics. If he controls all law execution in the United States, then the national electorate has a clear object of blame or reward for such activity. Unity supporters also argue that the founders shared their concerns about accountability. Evidence of such founding concerns, they say, further illuminates the founding decision to create a fully unitary executive.[35]

Accountability indeed was a central preoccupation of the founders. Yet their concerns extended beyond the ballot box mechanisms of formal accountability. Beyond those essential mechanisms, the founders assumed the need for myriad means to ensure the information flow necessary to add substance to formal accountability. This was no less true with respect to internal than external checks. Not surprisingly, then, while Federalists extolled the virtues of a single president, they coupled such analyses with assurances of the various checks that the president would encounter internally as well as externally. Accordingly, the divide between Federalists and Anti-Federalists over the presidency was not about unity versus nonunity as those terms are used today. Rather, the founding disagreements were fact-specific ones over the nuances of particular proposals for the very top of the executive branch—that is for the structure of the presidency itself—and over the proposals' predicted effects on substantive accountability.

This section develops this point by taking a closer look at three key founding-era moments: the rejection of a presidential advisory council, the debate and decision of 1789, and the adoption of the Opinions Clause. Each event reflects the absence of an uncompromising unity directive as a matter of original meaning. More important, each reflects a founding-era concern not with unity per se, but with the need to create an infrastructure to support substantive accountability, including through internal checks, in the executive branch.

SUBSTANTIVE ACCOUNTABILITY AND THE COUNCIL-LESS PRESIDENT.   In rejecting a presidential advisory council, the founders by no means embraced a unitary executive. The concerns expressed by the founders over the council—particularly those involving accountability—were very specific to the characteristics of the envisioned council. Indeed, the features of the council that they lamented were strikingly similar to unitary aspects of modern presidential relations with executive agencies. The founders' reasons for rejecting a council thus do not help the pro-unity case from history or principle. To the contrary, they parallel modern, substantive accountability-based objections to unity.

The work of Alexander Hamilton as Publius provides an excellent starting point. In extolling the virtues of a council-less president, Hamilton stressed several factors: The council would be small in number and thus susceptible to presidential persuasion to act against the public interest;[36] a nefarious council-president combination could act in relative secrecy;[37] and council members and the president would lack distinct roles, making it difficult or impossible for the public and the other branches to know who to blame for bad behavior.[38] Hamilton also isolated an additional problem relating to the council's role in appointments. Appointments made by the president and his council—unlike appointments made by the president and the Senate—would tend to reward sycophantic candidates who would place loyalty to the president above the public interest. As Hamilton artfully put it, presidents might be tempted to select candidates "possessing the necessary insignificance and pliancy to render them the obsequious instruments of his pleasure."[39]

All four of these concerns are encapsulated in a passage in *Federalist* No. 77 in which Hamilton disparagingly compares a proposed presidential council with the executive council system of appointment in New York:

> The council of appointment consists of from three to five persons, of whom the governor is always one. This small body, shut up in a private apartment, impenetrable to the public eye, proceed to the execution of the trust committed to them. It is known that the governor claims the right of nomination upon the strength of some ambiguous expressions in the Constitution, but it is not known to what extent, or in what manner he exercises it; nor upon what occasions he is contradicted or opposed. . . . Whether a governor of this State avails himself of the ascendant, he must necessarily have in this delicate and important part of his administration to prefer to offices men who are best qualified for them, or whether he prostitutes that advantage to the advancement of persons whose chief merit is their implicit devotion to his will and to the support of a despicable and dangerous system of personal influence are questions which, unfortunately for the community, can only be the subjects of speculation and conjecture.[40]

Other ratification debate statements from supporters and opponents of a presidential council alike demonstrate that the question addressed by those engaged in this debate was not whether the executive branch must in all respects be unified, but whether the council in particular would facilitate substantive accountability. Participants on both sides of the debate expressed a desire for an executive branch whose actions could be tracked, and rewarded or punished, by the people and the other branches.

They simply disagreed on whether the council in its envisioned particulars was the right way to achieve this goal. One council proponent argued, for example, that "the supreme executive powers ought to have been placed in the president, with a small independent council made personally responsible for every appointment to office or other act, by having their opinions recorded."[41] Similarly, George Mason lamented that

> [t]he President of the United States has no Constitutional Council (a thing unknown in any safe and regular government) he will therefore be unsupported by proper information and advice; and will generally be directed by minions and favourites ... or a Council of State will grow out of the principal officers of the great departments; the worst and most dangerous of all ingredients for such a Council, in a free country; for they may be induced to join in any dangerous or oppressive measures, to shelter themselves, and prevent an inquiry into their own misconduct in office.[42]

Opponents of the council countered that it would undermine substantive accountability, whereas a council-free president would be accountable. One council opponent explained that "the executive power is better to be trusted when it has no screen. Sir, we have a responsibility in the person of our President; he cannot act improperly, and hide either his negligence, or inattention; he cannot roll upon any other person the weight of his criminality."[43] Another similarly argued:

> It has also been objected, that a Council of State ought to have been assigned the President. The want of it, is, in my apprehension, a perfection rather than a blemish. What purpose would such a Council answer, but that of diminishing, or annihilating the responsibility annexed to the character of the President. From the superiority of his talents, or the superior dignity of his place, he would probably acquire an undue influence over, and might induce a majority of them to advise measures injurious to the welfare of the States, at the same time that he would have the means of sheltering himself from impeachment, under that majority.[44]

Finally, like Hamilton and Mason, others engaged in the ratification debate took it as a given that the executive branch ought not to be staffed by members whose primary loyalty is to the president. One constitutional proponent reasoned approvingly that, because the president could not appoint officers without Senate consent, there will be no problems of "patronage and influence, and of personal obligation and dependence."[45] Another constitutional proponent cited the same constitutional provision as "prevent[ing] the officers from looking up to the President alone as their master and benefactor."[46]

The founding decision to create a single president with no constitutional council thus cannot be equated with a decision to create a fully unitary executive branch. To the contrary, the founding decision reflects two conclusions. First, founders on both sides of the debate deemed it crucial that the people and other branches be able to track executive activity to ensure political and legal accountability. In short, there was widespread consensus on the importance of substantive accountability, particularly on mechanisms to ensure sufficient information flow to expose wrongdoing and to make formal accountability meaningful. Second, the prevailing side of the debate deemed the envisioned council—with its likely secrecy, small size, and lack of clearly delineated functions—antithetical to accountability. The founding decision thus reflects no formal unity directive. To the contrary, it supports the conclusion that Congress functionally must have discretion to create pockets of independence in the executive branch. Indeed, we shall see in chapter 8 that modern manifestations of administrative unity resemble the clannish and evasive council that the founders feared. Modern efforts to disrupt unity to prevent such conditions thus are very faithful to founding principles.

THE DEBATE OF 1789.   The Debate of 1789 further illuminates two core historical points. First, there was nothing approaching a founding consensus that the Constitution demanded a fully unitary executive branch. Second, founding discussions about the structure of the executive branch reflected a deep, shared commitment to substantive accountability.

No Consensus on Unity as a Constitutional Mandate.   The Debate of 1789, which took place in the House of Representatives during the first Congress, centered on whether the bill creating a Department of Foreign Affairs should explicitly grant the president the power to remove the secretary of foreign affairs. This question took the form of three proposed amendments to the bill. First, after four days of debate, the representatives voted 34 to 20 to retain a clause deeming the secretary "removable from office by the President of the United States." Second, after a short discussion on the day after the first vote, the representatives voted 30 to 18 to add language further implying a presidential removal power. The new clause stated that the department's chief clerk would have custody of all department books and records "whenever the [secretary] shall be removed from office by the President of the United States, or in any other case of vacancy." Third, the representatives voted later that same day, 31 to 19, to strike the words approved in their first vote by which they had explicitly granted a presidential removal power.[47]

There are two schools of thought as to whether the majority votes reflect a belief in a unitary executive. Supporters of the pro-unity interpretation—that the majority votes reflect the belief that the president has the constitutional prerogative to dismiss executive branch officers at his pleasure—acknowledge that the first vote, standing alone, could be interpreted either as a declaration of such a presidential prerogative or as reflecting Congress's belief in its own constitutional discretion to grant or withhold such power from the president. They argue that the subsequent two votes, however, reflect the majority's desire to clarify—by implying rather than explicitly granting a presidential removal power—that the power is constitutional in nature.[48] Opponents of the unity-based interpretation deem the votes inconclusive of any constitutional theory of presidential power on the part of a majority of the representatives. The votes and the legislative history, they argue, reflect disagreement and confusion among those who voted for the provisions as to whether they merely recognized a preexisting constitutional removal power on the part of the president or whether they exercised their own constitutional prerogative to grant such power by legislation.[49]

The anti-unity position is the stronger one for three reasons. First, let us assume for the sake of argument that a majority of the voting representatives clearly believed that the president has a constitutional right to dismiss officers at his pleasure. Even if this were the case, it tells us nothing more than that the issue was a highly contested one and that some in the founding era—including those representatives in the 1789 majority—supported unity whereas others—including those representatives in the 1789 minority—believed otherwise. The very fact of this division—again, assuming the best possible meaning of the votes for unity supporters—demonstrates that the concept of unity was not unambiguously embedded in the Vesting and Take Care Clauses as a matter of original definition. That unity was a position argued by some founders is a very different thing from its being so plainly reflected in the text's original meaning as to constitute a categorical mandate.

Second, the conditions surrounding the vote were not "best case" for unity. The representatives who spoke in favor of a removal power did not share a monolithic view. Rather, some deemed the removal power a constitutional prerogative of the president,[50] while others deemed it within

Congress's discretion to bestow pursuant to the Necessary and Proper Clause.[51] Still others took no clear position on the removal power's constitutional basis.[52]

Third, as with the constitutional council debate, the 1789 debate was too fact-specific to stand for a sweeping principle of unity throughout the executive branch. Most important in this regard was the alternative that the members of the majority rejected. The counterproposal to dismissal with pleasure was not dismissal for cause or some other relatively moderate restriction on the president. Rather, representatives in the minority predominantly argued that removal by the president should be permitted only with the consent of the Senate. They argued both that this was good policy and that it could be inferred as a constitutional command from the Senate's "advise and consent" role in appointing executive officers.[53] The latter position, of course, was the same one taken by Alexander Hamilton in *Federalist* No. 77. A small minority took a position even more extreme, insisting that executive officers could be removed only by impeachment.[54] That the majority in the 1789 debate were focused on countering two very extreme restrictions on presidential power counsels against reading a broad unity principle into the majority's objections to the same.[55] Indeed, several in the majority who spoke emphasized the functional intrusion on presidential power that a senatorial consent requirement would mark.[56] The debate and its result thus could be deemed to reflect functional reasoning rather than an absolute embrace of unity.

One additional fact-specific aspect of the debate is worth noting. Specifically, the representatives might have been motivated partly by their functional views on the control that the president should have over the secretary of foreign affairs in particular, as opposed to all executive officers. Indeed, James Madison—who voted with the majority regarding removal of the foreign affairs secretary—proposed, very shortly after the foreign affairs matter was resolved, imposing some restrictions on the president's ability to retain the comptroller general. Madison argued that the comptroller general was differently situated than the foreign affairs secretary, as the former's role was not "purely ... [e]xecutive." Madison eventually withdrew his proposal for reasons not reflected in the record.[57] This episode further highlights the difficulty of drawing categorical conclusions from the Debate of 1789.

The Role of Accountability in the Debate. If the 1789 debate supports a case-specific, functional analysis, it also offers guidance on how such analysis might be applied, and on why functional accountability concerns often will prove consistent with nonunitary measures. First, as with the presidential council debate, there was broad agreement on both sides that the executive must be accountable to the public and the other branches. And the accountability at issue was not mere formal accountability, but substantive accountability. Indeed, debate participants focused on how best to ensure that presidential misdeeds would not be hidden. Second, the two sides differed on whether unity helps or hinders substantive accountability. Much like the majority in the council debate, members of the 1789 minority warned that excessive presidential control of subordinates would enable the president to surround himself with loyalists who would hide his bad acts. While this position did not prevail in 1789, the rationales offered are instructive for functional analyses. Their significance is further bolstered by their similarity to the accountability-based arguments that did prevail in the preratification council debate.

Exemplifying the 1789 majority's accountability arguments, James Madison deemed "no principle . . . more clearly laid down in the Constitution than that of responsibility." "[S]o far . . . as we do not make the officers who are to aid [the president] . . . responsible to him," Madison concluded, "he is not responsible to his country."[58]

Those in the minority countered that unchecked removal power would enable the president to surround himself with loyal minions who could hide damaging information or otherwise enhance his power and shield him from accountability. For example, Representative Page argued:

> [T]he more power you give [the President], the more his responsibility is lessened. By making the heads of all the departments dependent upon the President, you enable him to swallow up all the powers of Government; you increase his influence, and every one will be studious to please him alone. . . .
>
> By this grant of [unilateral removal] power you secure the President against impeachment; you fence him round with a set of dependent officers, through whom alone it is probable you could come at the evidence of the President's guilt, in order to obtain his conviction on impeachment.[59]

Representative Jackson made the point with greater flair, warning: "Behold the baleful influence of the royal prerogative when officers hold their commission during the pleasure of the Crown!"[60]

THE OPINIONS CLAUSE.   The Constitution's Opinions Clause also reflects the facts that the founders did not embrace a unitary executive and that their concerns were predominantly functional ones centered on substantive accountability. The Opinions Clause empowers the president to "require the Opinion, in writing, of the principal Officer in each of the executive Departments, upon any Subject relating to the Duties of their respective Offices."[61] The clause was the sole surviving piece of the proposed provision for an executive council. As Martin Flaherty explains:

> The Opinions Clause is the lone surviving part of a plan put forward by Gouverneur Morris and Charles Pinckney on August 20 to create a Council of the State. The original proposal called for the Council to consist of the Chief Justice of the Supreme Court and Secretaries for Domestic Affairs, Commerce and Finance, Foreign Affairs, War, Marine, and State. Each of the Secretaries was to be appointed by the President alone and to hold his office "during pleasure." The plan further provided that the President "may require the written opinions of any one or more of the members: But he shall in all cases exercise his own judgment."
>
> Two days later the Committee of Detail returned the proposal with several changes. First, it expanded the roster of what it now called the President's "Privy Council" to include the President of the Senate and the Speaker of the House. In addition, it dropped the provisions specifying the President's appointment and removal authority over the Secretaries and provided simply that the Council would include "the principal Officer in the respective departments of foreign affairs, domestic affairs, War, Marine, and Finance, as such departments of office shall from time to time be established. . . ." Finally, the new version retained a slightly modified provision regarding opinions, stating that it would be the members' duty "to advise [the President] in matters respecting the execution of his Office, which he shall think proper to lay before them: But their advice shall not conclude him, nor affect his responsibility for the measures which he shall adopt." Despite this promising start, the Privy Council did not survive the Committee of Eleven, which scrapped the idea for the sole stated (but not necessarily only) reason that "it was judged that the Presidt. by persuading his Council—to concur in his wrong measures, would acquire their protection for them." All that remained was the Opinions Clause.[62]

Of course, the matter did not end there. As we saw above, the absence of a council remained an issue throughout the ratification debates.

The obvious question presented by this evolution from council to Opinions Clause is, what is the difference between the two? The draft council provisions made clear that the council's advice was to be just that, advice, and that it would not bind the president. And the proposed council was to be comprised largely of department heads. Had the inclusion of members of other branches been deemed a problem, it could have been remedied by simply subtracting those members from the council, rather than abandoning the council all together. It thus is not entirely plain, at first glance, what materially differs as between a council comprised largely of department heads whose role is to give nonbinding opinions to the president, versus a constitutional provision entitling the president to demand opinions from department heads.

The change begins to make sense, however, when viewed in light of the accountability concerns cryptically noted by the framing Committee of Eleven, and hashed out at length in the ratification debates. The perceived problem with the council was its grouping of members into a secretive cabal that the president could use as a shield, persuading them to offer "opinions" that he preordained. The founders feared this result despite the fact that the council's advice formally would not bind the president. Under the Opinions Clause, in contrast, department heads would not combine into a secretive entity with the president. Instead, they would issue opinions in their capacities as department heads, separate and apart from the presidential office. As Akhil Amar observes, this structure was geared to ensure accountability by the department heads and the president, respectively. Department heads would be accountable for their advice, the president for what he chose to do (or not to do) with the same. That the department heads' opinions were to be written (as they would also have been in the first draft of the Council plan) would further protect accountability. Indeed, James Iredell assured the North Carolina ratifying convention that "[t]he necessity of their opinions being in writing, will render them more cautious in giving them, and make them responsible should they give advice manifestly improper.... The opinion process is plain and open."[63]

The founders thus rejected a unitary entity (unitary insofar as the proposed council members would not have been able to bind the president with their advice) that they feared would undermine accountability through secrecy and obfuscation. In its place, they embraced a provision that retained relatively clear lines between the department heads and the president. This suggests again that the founders did not celebrate unity for its own sake, and that there is no clear, formalist unity directive embedded in the original meaning of the constitutional text. It also bolsters the notion that the founders sought whatever structures would further accountability, and that they understood that clear and transparent divisions of executive responsibility could serve this purpose by helping the public and other branches to trace a decision's origins.

Internal Checks and Substantive Accountability

Situating Internal Checks within the Substantive Accountability Framework

The Constitution thus does not demand unity as a matter of original meaning. Nor does unity follow from constitutional accountability principles. As we saw, the founders were not concerned with unity for its own sake. Nor were they determined to ensure merely formal accountability. Rather, they strove to develop mechanisms to protect substantive accountability and to contain executive energy.

When the specter of a categorical unity directive is stripped away, it becomes easy to see how internal checks fit within the substantive accountability framework. As we saw in chapter 3, the principle of substantive accountability and its corollary, contained energy, are reflected in constitutional text and structure. Chapter 3 focused predominantly on textual and structural features that relate to external checks, including the general rule of macro-transparency and the protections of the First Amendment. Yet text and structure also support internal checks that protect substantive accountability and contained energy. Constitutional mechanisms that facilitate internal checking include the Constitution's division of appointments responsibility between the president and Congress. They also include the Opinions Clause, with its provision for written exchanges between the president and department heads. Furthermore, aspects of text and structure bridge external and internal checking protections. For instance, Congress's enumerated lawmaking powers enable it to create macro-transparent statutory accountability tools to facilitate congressional and judicial oversight and other means of external checking. The same powers, particularly the provision enabling Congress to "[t]o make all Laws which shall be necessary and proper for carrying into Execution . . . Powers vested by this Constitution in the Government of the United States, or in any Department or Officer thereof,"[64] give Congress discretion to structure the administrative state. Absent a textual unity directive, this discretion naturally includes the imposition of internal checking mechanisms.

Commitments to substantive accountability and contained energy also are deeply evidenced by founding-era history, much of which centers on internal checking. Recall the many founding-era assurances that a single president without a council will be unable to hide his misdoings. Founding-era statements recounted earlier in this chapter help to flesh out the reasoning underlying these assurances. Federalists feared that a council would consist of a small, secretive band of sycophants behind whom the president could shield his misdeeds. In contrast, they predicted that a council-less president, assisted by appointees who would not "look[] up to the President alone as their master and benefactor," would have few places to hide from an inquiring Congress and public.

Substantive accountability and its corollary, contained energy, thus lie at the heart of internal and external checking mechanisms alike. The types of internal checks on which we are focused—those facilitated by legislation creating pockets of independence from presidential control in the administrative state—are accountability tools. Recall the three main components of the substantive accountability framework: the general rule of macro-transparency, extraordinary prerogative, and accountability tools. Internal checking mechanisms are among the statutory accountability tools that Congress has discretion to create. As with all legislation, of course, these mechanisms must go through the arduous legislative process, including presentment to the president and the possibility of a presidential veto. Internal checking mechanisms themselves thus are subject to the restraints of the legislative process, including those protective of the president's interests.

The Constitution Contains No Accountability-Based Unity Directive

EXISTING DEBATES.   Unity proponents argue, however, that unity furthers accountability and that breaches of unity undermine it. Indeed, they deem unity constitutionally required for this reason alone, independent of original meaning. Because the president is the sole nationally elected figure in American politics, unity proponents argue that unity gives the national electorate a clear object of blame or reward for federal law administration. In contrast, giving the final word in law execution to unelected bureaucrats leaves no avenue for political accountability. Even if power were deemed to rest not in unelected bureaucrats but in congresspersons—say, through their setting of the terms of bureaucratic employment or worse, through the influence of select congressional committee members—the undivided, national accountability of a president would be lacking. Even if power simply were deemed divided—for example, between Congress, the president, unelected bureaucrats, and the private interests that impact law execution—accountability again would suffer through the absence of a single, nationally responsive figure to blame or to reward.[65]

A number of scholars have criticized unity proponents' arguments from accountability. Critics observe, for one thing, that proponents assume an unduly simplistic version of accountability. Proponents equate accountability with the placing of thousands of administrative decisions— ranging from the high profile to the deeply technical and obscure—in the hands of a single person who is subject to reelection once. As critics point out, this vision of accountability is inconsistent with the far more complex accountability envisioned by the Constitution. The Constitution, say these critics, creates a web of accountability shared by multiple legislators representing multiple constituencies and by the president alike.[66] Furthermore, constitutional accountability mechanisms are not directed solely toward vindicating majority policy preferences (and certainly not toward doing so through the instrument of the presidency) but also toward guarding against abuse, incompetence, and majoritarian tyranny.[67] In the context of the administrative state, critics argue, constitutional accountability values demand not only multiple avenues for political accountability, but also intra-bureaucratic accountability mechanisms characterized by "complex chains of authority and expertise."[68]

These criticisms share a common set of insights that implicitly reflect the distinction between formal accountability and substantive accountability. The bare fact that the president formally controls a given decision or office does very little to ensure that executive branch activities will be known to courts, congresspersons, or the public, or that such parties will have means to respond to any information of which they do learn.

BUILDING ON EXISTING DEBATES: HOW UNITY CAN UNDERMINE, AND DIS-UNITY CAN FURTHER, SUBSTANTIVE ACCOUNTABILITY. Unfettered presidential control not only fails to guarantee accountability, it can positively undermine it. Much as members of the founding generation feared, unity can make the administrative decision-making chain less transparent by obfuscating responsibility. Perhaps most fundamentally, presidents can use the control that unity gives them to manipulate the very factual picture against which the public, Congress, and the courts can judge their decisions. For example, presidents or their proxies in a unitary system are well equipped to directly manipulate agencies' scientific or other findings, or to do so indirectly through unfettered control over all personnel who perform discretionary executive functions. Similarly, the White House may require government researchers or analysts to preclear any public statements, studies, press releases, or testimony with itself or with political appointees within an agency.

In addition to enabling the president to generate "expert" facts and analyses behind which he can cloak political judgments, unity can help the president and his proxies to obscure their involvement in such activity, or, for that matter, in any actions that prove controversial. There are at least three avenues through which such obfuscation can occur. First, unity and supremacy can join forces, with the White House invoking executive privilege and refusing to provide information to shed light on who, if anyone within the White House, was responsible for given actions or decisions. Second, the president can and does benefit from the entirely obvious fact that he cannot possibly know of every discretionary task performed within the executive branch. Even where he formally controls a decision, he can retain plausible deniability. For that matter, he often will be genuinely out of the loop. Third, presidential deniability is all the more viable in light of the nature of the modern executive branch. Formal presidential control today necessarily devolves into de facto control by any number of White House offices and persons. This enhances a president's ability to distance himself publicly from unpopular actions, while using unity's tools to exercise influence behind the scenes. It also raises the equally real possibility that White House officials will exert secret influence in the name of the president, even when the president himself remains uninformed.

While unity can undermine substantive accountability in the administrative state, internal checks can support it. To appreciate how internal checks can serve as accountability tools, consider the following hypothetical example involving the Federal Aviation Administration (FAA). Suppose that a statute required the FAA to assess particular crash risks, issue findings on the same, and propose new rules to address the risks. Suppose also that the White House fears alienating powerful political allies in the airline industry, and leans on top FAA officials to ensure that the findings and proposed rules are not unpalatable to the airlines. If the FAA heads do not serve at the president's pleasure but can be dismissed by the president only for cause, then structurally they are more likely to expose the

White House's request to public or congressional scrutiny, thus triggering immediate accountability for the White House's actions. Even if the FAA heads do not take so drastic a measure, they are better positioned to resist the White House's request if they have some tenure protection. Alternatively, if they do seek to comply with the White House's request but their inferiors have some tenure protection (for example, if the agency's scientists and other experts have statutory or constitutional protections against whistleblower retaliation and if the experts' immediate superiors can be terminated only for cause), then the request still might be foiled. If the White House were unsuccessful in altering the FAA's findings and proposed rule, it might still publicly disagree with the proposal and work to keep it from becoming final. It could no longer do so, however, under cover of "expert agreement" from within the FAA. Alternatively, if the White House does succeed in manipulating the record and proposed rule, rumors of its manipulation might still leak out. If that happens, and if Congress seeks to hold hearings, then agency officials and personnel might still serve as checks through their testimony. Candid testimony is more likely, however, if the White House cannot demand to review the written testimony before it is submitted to Congress. Similarly, the story of manipulation stands a better chance of leaking in the first place where statutory and constitutional whistleblower protections exist.

Functional Criteria for Assessing the Constitutionality of Internal Checks

As the above discussion demonstrates, strict categorical rules that grant the president unfettered discretion over all executive decisions and personnel do not necessarily further substantive accountability. To the contrary, such rules can be downright destructive to that end. It also is important to understand that one need not agree that unity plainly or always undermines substantive accountability to conclude that the accountability argument for an unyielding unity directive is flawed. To reject a categorical directive, it is enough that one can reasonably conclude that unity does not invariably further substantive accountability. So long as it is reasonably arguable that unity undermines, rather than bolsters, substantive accountability, then unity fails so plainly to further accountability as to justify a categorical rule.

This is not to say, however, that Congress has unbounded constitutional discretion to isolate the administrative state from presidential control or otherwise to structure agencies however it wishes. Rather, Congress must be constrained within functional limits so as to protect substantive account-ability. Those limits entail both a ceiling and a floor on internal checking mechanisms. A ceiling is required on the extent to which a statute may es-trange the president from administrative decision making. Congress may not detach the president from law implementation to a degree that func-tionally defeats his ability to "take Care that the Laws be faithfully exe-cuted" and to be held accountable—both formally and substantively—for the same. It is reasonably arguable, for example that the president at least must retain the power to remove for cause all agency heads.

At the same time, a floor of minimum procedural checks is necessary to maintain substantive accountability not only on the part of the presi-dent but on the part of Congress and unelected actors within the admin-istrative state. For example, without requirements ensuring a degree of transparency as to the bases for administrative decisions, it may be impos-sible to determine whether agencies are adhering to statutory and consti-tutional requirements, whether Congress's implementing statutes or over-sight efforts are adequate, and whether and how presidential involvement manifests itself. Given these functional boundaries and the arduous re-quirements of the Article I, § 7 legislative process, Congress does not pos-sess an unlimited license to impose or, for that matter, to forgo internal checks. Nonetheless, within these constraints, Congress maintains flexi-bility to determine what checks and procedures will best facilitate sub-stantive accountability.

The scheme just described coincides substantially with that embraced by the Supreme Court in its precedent. Through that precedent, then, we can see somewhat more concretely the contours of the functional boundaries within which Congress may impose internal checks.

Judicial Precedent

Two aspects of judicial precedent bear note. First, the most relevant body of precedent concerns the scope of the president's constitutional removal power. As we shall see, this body of precedent adopts a largely functional approach. An open question, particularly in light of the Court's most recent removal decision in 2010, is how far such functional analysis may tilt, in effect, toward unity. Nonetheless, the Court's rejection of a categor-ical unity directive gives supporters of nonunitary mechanisms leeway to argue, case by case, that particular mechanisms do not unduly undermine presidential oversight and thus are constitutional. Second, case law on the doctrine of nondelegation suggests the need for a minimum floor of internal procedural checks within the administrative state.

The Removal Power

The Supreme Court has evinced varying degrees of sympathy toward unitary executive theory in cases involving the removal power. Even at its most pro-unity, however, it has never embraced a full, categorical unity directive. On balance, its major cases embody a functional approach, largely consistent with the position advanced in this chapter.

The apex of any pro-unity bent on the Court's part is the 1926 case of *Myers v. United States*.[69] The *Myers* Court held unconstitutional a statute requiring senatorial consent before the president could remove a postmaster. The Court relied heavily on the Debate of 1789, and spoke in fairly sweeping terms of the president's need for an unencumbered removal power over all who execute the law. Even in *Myers,* however, the Court acknowledged, consistent with earlier precedent, that Congress could "limit and regulate" the removal of those inferior executive officers whose appointment it has vested in a department head.[70] The Court also observed that "there may be duties so peculiarly and specifically committed to the discretion of a particular officer as to raise a question whether the President may overrule or revise the officer's interpretation of his statutory duty in a particular instance."[71]

Just nine years after *Myers,* the Court in *Humphrey's Executor v. United States*[72] clarified that Congress retained leeway to impose some restrictions on the president's removal authority. The *Humphrey's* Court upheld a provision that allowed the president to remove a member of the Federal Trade Commission (FTC) only for "inefficiency, neglect of duty, or malfeasance in office."[73] The Court distinguished the case from *Myers* by explaining that FTC commissioners, unlike postmasters, do not play purely executive roles. Rather, the commissioners perform tasks both "quasi-legislative" and "quasi-judicial" in nature. The Court deemed it clear that Congress has the authority, "in creating quasi legislative or quasi judicial agencies, to require them to act in discharge of their duties independently of executive control."[74] The Court further expounded on the reasonableness of Congress's choice to impose a good-cause requirement, calling it "quite evident that one who holds his office only during the pleasure of another cannot be depended upon to maintain an attitude of independence against the latter's will."[75]

If *Humphrey's* implied that removal power inquiries entail functional, case-by-case assessments of factors including an office's nature, the Supreme Court confirmed the implication in 1986, in *Morrison v. Olson.* In *Morrison,* the Court upheld the independent counsel provisions of the Ethics in Government Act against a separation of powers challenge.[76] The provisions empowered the attorney general—an officer who serves by statute at the president's pleasure—to terminate the counsel only for "good cause."[77] Echoing *Myers,* the Court explained that Congress may not grant itself "a role in the removal of executive officials other than through its established powers of impeachment and conviction." Congress may, however, place internal restrictions—such as good-cause requirements—on the president's removal power, subject to a functional analysis. This is so even for purely executive officers. Indeed, the Court conceded that the independent counsel, while an inferior officer, played a purely executive role. Nonetheless, Congress could limit the attorney general's power to remove her so long as the limits do not "impede the President's ability to perform his constitutional duty."[78]

Finally, the Supreme Court in its 2010 opinion in *Free Enterprise Fund v. Public Company Accounting Oversight Board*[79] struck down a statutory provision that it deemed to impose too stringent a limit on the president's removal power. Under the provision, the Securities and Exchange Commission (SEC) could remove members of the PCAOB, which has regulatory enforcement powers over certain accounting firms, only "for good cause shown" and pursuant to statutory procedures.[80] The Court found that SEC members themselves can be removed by the president only for cause.[81] The Court made clear that it did "not . . . take issue with for-cause limitations in general. . . . The question here is far more modest. We deal with the unusual situation, never before addressed by the Court, of two layers of for-cause tenure." It concluded that the two layers at issue in *PCAOB*—the good-cause limit on the president's power to remove members of the SEC combined with the good-cause and procedural limits on the SEC's power to remove members of the PCAOB—too greatly burdened the president's ability to oversee the executive branch.[82]

Aspects of the *PCAOB* Court's analysis could pave the way for significant pro-unity inroads. For one thing, the Court's rhetoric at points suggests sympathy with unity and with the broad reasoning of *Myers.*[83] More concretely, if *PCAOB* is read to establish a categorical bar against two-layered good-cause protections for any agency employees who exercise discretionary executive power, it could severely disrupt civil service protections and other limits on presidential control throughout the administrative state. As Peter Strauss writes:

When the majority reasons that striking the "for cause" protection of PCAOB members renders them subject to the same level of presidential control as any inferior officer of the SEC, it elides the possibility that some of those inferior officers—for example, its Inspector General or its Administrative Law Judges—are themselves removable only "for cause," by an agency itself enjoying "for cause" protection. The members of the Nuclear Regulatory Commission and the Commissioner of the Social Security Administration are protected by "for cause" removal restrictions; and, as Justice Breyer details [in his dissent in *PCAOB*], so are a great many of the officials who head their various bureaus and subdivisions.[84]

Yet *PCAOB* does not mark a clear leap forward for unity. Although it plausibly can be read in the broad manner just indicated, it is equally consistent with a much narrower interpretation.[85] At its core, the opinion simply rests on the notion that the particular statutory scheme went too far in limiting presidential oversight. This notion itself is fully consistent with *Morrison*'s functional balancing assessment. Furthermore, the *PCAOB* Court consistently framed the constitutional powers at issue as those of presidential oversight and supervision, not direct control.[86] The Court also tied its reasoning to what it deemed the deeply unusual nature of the PCAOB framework. Indeed, the majority chides the dissent for deeming *PCAOB* a threat to well-established removal schemes throughout the administrative state.[87] The Court assures that "[n]othing in our opinion should be read to cast doubt on the use of what is colloquially known as the civil service system within independent agencies."[88] *PCAOB* thus can easily be read to hinge not on the notion that two levels of removal are invariably impermissible, but rather that this particular two-level scheme unduly compromised presidential oversight. The latter assessment could stem, as Strauss suggests, from the scheme's "virtually unique" housing of a "'for cause'—protected institution (the PCAOB) within another 'for cause'—protected institution (the SEC)."[89]

The Nondelegation Doctrine and a Minimum Floor of Procedural Checking

The Supreme Court's response to an additional concern about the structure of the administrative state—that Congress may shirk its legislative role and undermine its own accountability by delegating policymaking to administrators—also sheds some light on the unitary executive debate. Specifically, cases addressing "nondelegation" challenges to statutes support the notion that, in addition to any required ceiling on the extent to which Congress may limit the president's control of the administrative state, there is a procedural floor by which Congress must abide when it delegates power to the president. Congress may not delegate swaths of policymaking discretion so unchecked as to prevent Congress or the public from keeping watch over the use of that discretion. In other words, delegations must be accompanied by procedures sufficient to ensure substantive accountability within the administrative state and by the elected officials who oversee and delegate power to it.

In its nondelegation case-law, the Court accepts the legitimacy of broad policymaking delegations from Congress to the president and the administrative state. This reflects judicial recognition of the limits of bright-line, formalistic distinctions between legislating and executing. To say that only Congress may legislate is to suggest a sharp constitutional and practical boundary between creating and implementing law that does not exist. The Court instead has settled on a loose, deferential standard— Congress need only provide an "intelligible principle" to guide administrative policymaking.[90]

At the same time, there are hints in the Court's two 1935 cases striking down laws on nondelegation grounds—the only two Supreme Court cases to do so—of a functional concern with the processes by which delegated power is exercised.[91] In these early cases, decided before the Administrative Procedure Act (APA) imposed procedural discipline throughout much of the administrative state,[92] the Court expressed concern not only with the delegations' broad subject matters, but with the absence of transparency and procedural rigor. In *A. L. A. Schechter Poultry Corp. v. United States*, the Court objected that the president's statutory authority to approve or reject a code of fair competition was relatively unchecked. In contrast, the Court referred approvingly to other statutes delegating rulemaking power under prescribed, transparent procedures.[93] The Court voiced similar concerns in *Panama Refining Co. v. Ryan*, objecting among other things that executive orders promulgated under the statute were not required to state their grounds.[94] Notably, the Court in both *Schechter Poultry* and *Panama Refining Co.* observed that the respective statutes delegated excessive power to the president. Each contrasted the excessive delegation to the president with procedurally and substantively constrained, and hence proper, delegations made to administrative agencies.[95]

The Court in these cases recognized that excessive presidential discretion can undermine substantive accountability. Armed in the administrative state with both policymaking and policy-implementing powers, the president might act corruptly or incompetently. Regular and transparent procedures are necessary to protect against such abuses. Some floor of protective procedures thus is required when broad powers are delegated to the president.

CHAPTER EIGHT

How Unitary Executive Theory Undermines Substantive Accountability

Like supremacy, a central flaw of unitary executive theory is that it conflates substantive accountability and formal accountability. To unity's supporters, maximizing the president's power to execute the law necessarily enhances accountability. This view would make perfect sense were accountability comprised solely of one's being subject to election or defeat at the ballot box. By that measure, there is no downside to consolidating all executive power in the country's sole nationally elected figure, putting aside the fact that the president can be reelected only once. As we have seen, however, the accountability principle that the Constitution embodies is far more complex than that. Constitutional text, structure and history assume and demand multiple accountability mechanisms, including elections, press coverage, popular discourse, judicial review, congressional oversight, and impeachment. Those mechanisms cannot operate without a regular and reliable flow of information.

In chapter 7, we saw that a unitary executive can undermine, rather than further substantive accountability. It can do so by enabling the president and his proxies to control the flow of information from within the executive branch. This need not be true in every case, nor need it be true beyond reasonable doubts. So long as the point is reasonably arguable, then unity fails so definitively to support accountability as to justify a categorical unity directive. Nor is unity supported by alternative arguments from text, structure, and history. Indeed, the latter set of pro-unity arguments fail in part because proponents overlook the substantive nature of the accountability with which the founders were concerned. They also disregard founding fears that unfettered presidential control of subordinates will undermine substantive accountability.

This chapter demonstrates through examples how unity indeed can undermine substantive accountability while disunity can further it. It begins by discussing a major means by which presidents seek to enhance their power over the administrative state. That is, by charging offices within the Executive Office of the President (EOP)—particularly, though not exclusively the Office of Management and Budget (OMB)—with responsibilities to review and sign off on agency output, including proposed rules, public reports, and testimony. This approach amounts to what political scientist Terry Moe labels "centralization," whereby presidents seek to institutionalize top-down White House control over agencies.[1] The chapter explains that centralization is not invariably inconsistent with substantive accountability or synonymous with unity. It discusses what types of centralization manifest unity, and demonstrates that two forms of unity-based centralization—OMB clearance of agency testimony and reports and EOP control over rulemaking—can negatively impact substantive accountability.

The chapter also discusses the other major means, "politicization," by which presidents can enhance their control over the bureaucracy. Politicization, as coined by Moe, refers to the use of appointment and removal powers to create an administrative state more politically responsive to the White House.[2] The chapter explains that aspects of unity manifest themselves in arguments for heightened presidential control over administration through increases in politically appointed and removable personnel and through elimination of minimum qualification requirements for appointees. The chapter then demonstrates through examples how unity-driven politicization can undermine substantive accountability.

Creating an Infrastructure for Centralized White House Control

Forrest McDonald has observed that "[f]rom the point of view of administration, the history of the presidency in the twentieth century has been the history of presidents' attempts to gain control of the sprawling federal bureaucracy."[3] Early twentieth-century presidents sought to wrest control of the administrative state from Congress, which had come to dominate administration by the latter half of the nineteenth century.[4] A major focus of these presidential efforts was the budget. Prior to the passage of the Budget and Accounting Act of 1921,[5] there was no such thing as a centralized federal budget. Rather, a hodgepodge of statutory directives and informal practices dictated the terms through which the Treasury Department and individual agencies reported budgetary information to Congress, which in turn legislated expenditures through similarly disjointed processes. As President William Taft's Commission on Economy and Efficiency reported to Congress, no one in the administration, in Congress, or among the public or press could speak to the overall condition of the United States budget or to how different pieces of it complemented, duplicated, were inconsistent with, or otherwise related to one another.[6]

In 1912, President Taft presented the commission's findings to Congress, along with the commission's recommendations for a centralized federal budgetary process in which the president would play a prominent role. Under the proposed system, bureaucrats would report budgetary information and requests up the chain of command in the executive branch, ultimately reaching individual agency heads, the treasury secretary, and the president. Drawing from these reports, the treasury secretary would, under the president's oversight and direction, draw up a clear and detailed budget for congressional consideration. The commission also urged the creation of a high-level office to assist the president in this process.[7] While Congress initially rejected these proposals as presidential overreaching, it largely adopted them several years later in response to wartime deficits. "The Budget and Accounting Act of 1921 provided that the president, assisted by a new Bureau of the Budget (placed in the Treasury Department but understood to have a direct connection to the President), would oversee and coordinate all agencies' budget requests."[8]

The next major victory for White House administration occurred during Franklin Delano Roosevelt's presidency. With the New Deal having expanded an already broad administrative state, FDR sought to redirect concerns over a "headless 'fourth branch'" toward support for greater consolidation of federal agencies under presidential control. The Brownlow Commission, which FDR spearheaded, issued a report championing enhanced White House control and responsibility over the administrative state.[9] The report proposed, among other things, "six new assistants to be assigned at presidential discretion. It also recommended discretionary funds that would enable the president to acquire more help when needed." The report also "proposed a major organizational addition to the presidency, the Executive Office, with the Bureau of the Budget as its centerpiece."[10] The Brownlow Commission and FDR sought new legislation to implement these proposals. Their efforts, however, became caught in a political firestorm over fears of a dictatorial presidency. Such fears were compounded by FDR's simultaneous push to pack the Supreme Court.[11] Nonetheless, Congress partly relented in 1939, passing a Reorganization Act that gave the president some of the new authority that he sought. The act gave Roosevelt reorganization powers and authority to hire new staff. Roosevelt used the new authority to "create[] the Executive Office of the President." He moved the Bureau of the Budget, along with other central planning offices, into the EOP. He followed these changes with an executive order "designat[ing] the formal relationships in the Executive Office, the White House Office with its new assistants, the Bureau of the Budget, and the remaining components of the new presidential establishment."[12]

With the beginnings of a White House administrative infrastructure in place, and with the public increasingly accepting—even demanding—of presidential control over federal programs, the seeds of modern centralization were planted. The modern era, generally traced back to the Nixon administration, has been characterized by a large expansion of the EOP and increasingly aggressive efforts by presidents to shape, curtail, or spur specific agency actions.[13] Reflecting the modern approach, the Bureau of the Budget was renamed the Office of Management and Budget during the Nixon administration. The name change signaled the agency's new role as a clearinghouse not only for budgetary decisions but for broader policy actions.[14] Under President Nixon, the OMB was tasked with reviewing certain proposed agency rulemakings. The practice was continued and built upon under Presidents Gerald Ford and Jimmy Carter. Executive orders issued by Presidents Ronald Reagan, Bill Clinton, George W. Bush, and Barack Obama substantially expanded the OMB's review powers over agency rulemakings.[15]

Early Arguments for Substantive Accountability in Centralized Administration

Transparency and accountability were central topics in both the Taft and Brownlow Commission Reports. While both commissions were strongly oriented toward centralized administration, their reports evince some appreciation for the complex relationship between centralization, transparency, and accountability. Each report portrays the relationship between centralization and accountability as a positive one, explaining that the more control that the president wields over the administrative state, the more that Congress and the people will know who to blame or to credit for administrative actions. Yet neither report assumes that centralized presidential control alone is sufficient to create real accountability. Rather, each champions internal and external checking mechanisms to support and supplement presidential control. Both reports deem such mechanisms necessary to ensure a flow of accurate information to, within, and from the executive branch. Without this information flow, neither the president, nor Congress, nor the people could make well supported judgments or hold each other meaningfully to account.

The Taft Commission Report championed a presidentially prepared federal budget as a means to enhance accountability. President Taft echoed the report's reasoning in his message transmitting it to Congress. He explained:

> [T]here is at present no provision for reporting revenues, expenditures, and estimates for appropriations in such manner that the Executive, before submitting estimates, and each Member of Congress, and the people, after estimates have been submitted, may know what has been done by the Government or what the Government proposes to do.[16]

While the Taft Commission Report prescribed greater presidential control over appointments and administrative communications with Congress,[17] it also stressed the need to harness bureaucratic expertise to provide an accurate factual picture against which the president, Congress, and the public could make and judge decisions.[18] What is more, the report emphasized that the budgetary decision-making chain—from bureaucratic analyses and recommendations to presidential budget formation to legislative votes—should be transparent. The commission explained that "[o]ne of the most important features of [its] recommendation is that which requires that every plan to be executed be made an open book, to be read by the Congress, by officers of the administration, and by the public."[19]

The Brownlow Commission Report echoed and expanded on these themes. The commission famously observed that "[t]he President needs help." It envisioned some of this help taking the form of measures to "facilitate the flow upward to the President of information upon which he is to base his decisions and the flow downward from the President of the decisions once taken for execution by the department or departments affected."[20]

The commission also deemed the flow of information outside of the executive branch crucial. It urged:

> Nothing should be done that would diminish the importance of the work of the congressional committees in conducting hearings and pursuing investigations. Time and time again in our history investigations conducted by congressional committees have illumined [sic] dark places in the Government and in the affairs of the Nation and have resulted in the correction of abuses that otherwise might have been undetected for years and years. It is with full realization of the necessity of continuing and preserving this important function of the Congress and its committees that we suggest the necessity for improving the machinery of holding the Executive Branch more effectively accountable to the Congress.[21]

Indeed, while the commission supported the executive branch practice of centrally clearing agencies' legislative proposals, it also made plain its view that Congress must have access to truthful information from throughout the executive branch.[22]

The Brownlow Commission Report also criticized the structure of the Comptroller General's Office because the office performed both accounting and auditing functions but was not clearly accountable to either the president or Congress. While the commission deemed accounting an executive function that demands accountability to the president, it was equally emphatic in its view that auditors must be free from executive political controls to ensure the integrity of their work. The current system, said the commission,

> deprives the President of essential power needed to discharge his major executive responsibility. Equally important, it deprives the Congress of a really independent audit and review of the fiscal affairs of the Government by an official who has no voice in administrative determinations, which audit is necessary to hold the Administration accountable.[23]

Relatedly, the Brownlow Commission stressed the importance of neutral competence throughout the executive branch. It argued, for example, that "[t]he merit system should be extended upward, outward, and downward to include all positions in the Executive Branch of the Government except those which are policy-determining in character."[24]

Centralization, Politicization, and Unitary Executive Theory

Whatever the subjective intentions of the Taft and Brownlow Commission members, their analyses remind us that unity can undermine accountability. It is possible that the reports' authors meant only to suggest that administrations voluntarily adopt measures to ensure truthful budgetary reporting from within. They might also have meant to suggest that Congress strictly separate analytical and reporting functions from discretionary executive decision making so that the former functions, alone, could be independent from presidential control. Yet the reports' implications logically are not so confined. It follows from their analyses that substantive accountability will suffer should narrow measures consistent with unity fail to curtail presidential information control—should, for example, administrations fail to adopt or adhere to voluntary measures, should analysts or researchers be directly supervised by political officers, or should it prove infeasible to fully separate research and analysis from executive decision making and thus from political controls.

Furthermore, the fact that the Taft and Brownlow analyses could lend themselves to measures consistent or inconsistent with unity, and more likely to a mixture of the two, illuminates the fact that neither centralization nor politicization need be synonymous with unity. The president, in Straussian overseer fashion, may exercise substantial control through means including good-cause removals, extensive oversight and lobbying of administrators and Congress, and the presidential bully pulpit. Such measures need not include unfettered removal power, a power to step in and make decisions in lieu of administrators to whom the decisions are statutorily delegated, or a power to preclude administrators from speaking to the public or the Congress without White House approval.

Before turning to examples of unitary measures that undermine substantive accountability, then, it may be useful to recall what makes a measure or action unitary. Pro-unity scholars make clear that unity demands an unfettered presidential power to remove persons who exercise discretionary executive power. They also deem unity to require a presidential power to invalidate, or to substitute his own judgment for, decisions of the administrators to whom those decisions are statutorily delegated.[25]

Additionally, presidents have asserted, as a unity-based mandate, a right to control agency communications with Congress or the public, for example, by refusing to allow agency employees to submit unvetted testimony to Congress or to speak to the press without clearance.[26] Administrations and some scholars also have argued that unity demands that presidents not be restricted in their choice of nominees for executive offices. They have claimed, for example, that Congress may not impose a binding requirement that a presidential nominee have expertise in a particular field.[27]

Finally, modern manifestations of "presidential" control often take the form of control by OMB or other offices within the EOP, rather than by the president himself. At least one prominent unitary executive theorist has argued that unity only permits the president personally to make decisions that are statutorily delegated to others. It does not empower him to reassign decisions that are statutorily delegated to one officer to another officer of his choosing.[28] This is a potentially important limiting principle. Nonetheless, this chapter treats OMB review requirements and other presidential delegations to subordinates as aspects of unity. It does so for two reasons. First, when administrations exercise "presidential" control over decisions delegated by statute to agencies or over the dissemination of information by agencies, they typically do so by requiring review by the OMB, by another presidential office, or by agency political appointees who serve at the pleasure of the president or of another political appointee. As asserted and practiced by administrations, then, "unity" often entails control by presidential proxies rather than the president himself.

Second, a requirement that the president formally sign off on OMB actions or on other actions that the president delegated to someone other than the statutorily designated officer, would not resolve many of the substantive accountability problems posed by unity. As reflected in examples ranging from the dismissal of U.S. attorneys in the administration of George W. Bush to the Iran-Contra affair in the Reagan administration, presidential deniability for top-down political pressure is not difficult to maintain even when decisions formally belong to the president. This is a product of the practical and widely understood reality that the president cannot possibly be well acquainted with the nuances of every decision and its underlying reasoning, even where those decisions formally are his. Furthermore, the bare fact that a president claims entitlement to directly alter agency decisions or to fire executive personnel for any reason creates its own shadow effect, making it structurally easier for the president or his proxies to influence administrative actions behind the scenes. Through this shadow effect, unity enables the president or his proxies to influence agency action while leaving few if any fingerprints. It is instructive, therefore, to examine "unity" as it has been practiced through the OMB or other presidential proxies. At minimum, such examination provides a baseline from which one can extrapolate to consider how a narrower version of unity—whereby the OMB and other presidential proxies engage in the same work in which they now engage, while the president formally makes the final decision—would impact substantive accountability.

How Unity Can Undermine Substantive Accountability

OMB and Information Clearance Requirements

Administrations frequently assert a right to prohibit agency employees from speaking directly to the Congress, the press, or the public without first clearing their commentary with the OMB or another White House designated office. Administrations vary in the amount of detail with which they justify this position. The most comprehensive explanations cite both unity and executive privilege as independent rationales. Detailing the unity-based aspect of the claim, the Office of Legal Counsel in the Reagan administration wrote in 1988:

> The separation of powers *requires* that the President have ultimate control over subordinate officials who perform purely executive functions and assist him in the performance of his constitutional responsibilities. This power includes the right to supervise and review the work of such subordinate officials, *including reports issued* either *to the public* or to Congress. . . .
>
> Consistent with the preceding analysis, it matters not at all [whether] . . . information [is] . . . highly scientific in nature. The President's supervisory authority encompasses *all* of the activities of his executive branch subordinates, whether those activities be technical or non-technical in nature. This necessarily follows from the fact that the Constitution vests "[t]he entire executive Power," without subject matter limitation, in the President.[29]

During the Carter administration, the OLC launched a similar objection to provisions of the Inspector General Act. That act, passed in 1978, created the modern system of inspectors general (IGs). IGs are intra-agency watchdogs charged to investigate and to issue reports and recommendations on agency problems including inefficiency, fraud and abuse. IGs are not empowered to impose punishments or policy changes.[30] Despite IGs' purely investigative and reportorial functions, the Carter OLC objected to provisions of the act requiring IGs to supply information to Congress. The OLC argued:

> [T]he Inspector General's obligation to keep Congress fully and currently informed, taken with the mandatory requirement that he provide any additional information or documents requested by Congress, and the condition that his reports be transmitted to Congress without executive branch clearance or approval, and [sic] inconsistent with his status as an officer in the executive branch, reporting to and under the general supervision of the head of the agency. Article II vests the executive power of the United States in the President. This includes general administrative control over those executing the laws. *See,* Myers v. United States, 272 U.S. 52, 163–164 (1926). The President's power of control extends to the entire executive branch, and includes the right to coordinate and supervise all replies and comments from the executive branch to Congress.[31]

Similar examples can be found in the Obama administration. Like previous administrations, the Obama administration requires testimony and certain other statements by executive branch employees to be cleared by the OMB.[32] In a 2009 signing statement, President Obama flagged the narrow construction that he would accord a statutory provision that "prohibit[s] the use of appropriations to pay the salary of any Federal officer or employee who interferes with or prohibits certain communications between Federal employees and Members of Congress." The president indicated that he would "not interpret this provision to detract from [his] authority to direct the heads of executive departments to supervise, control, and correct employees' communications with the Congress in cases where such communications would be unlawful or would reveal information that is properly privileged or otherwise confidential."[33]

By definition, successful White House clearance efforts would remain in the shadows, with Congress and the public hearing or seeing only an administration's approved statements. From time to time, however, significant changes to statements or reports become known or alleged and trigger controversy. One recent such case involved British Petroleum's spring 2010 oil spill in the Gulf of Mexico. In an October 2010 working paper on the spill, the staff of the national commission investigating the incident (the National Commission on the BP Deepwater Horizon Oil Spill and Offshore Drilling) addressed the government's early estimates of the oil flow rate, which were found later to have been inaccurately low. The commission staff was informed that, shortly after the spill, "NOAA [the National Oceanic and Atmospheric administration] wanted to make public some of its long-term, worst-case discharge models for the . . . spill," but OMB denied its request to do so.[34]

The White House, OMB, and NOAA denied any improper interference.[35] Furthermore, the final commission report, released on January 11, 2011, neither repeats nor retracts the claim about OMB interference. The final report simply does not mention it. The final report does elaborate on the unrealistically low nature of the government's original public estimates. The report recounts a statement at a press conference by Admiral Mary Landry on April 28 that "'NOAA experts believe that the output could be as much as 5000 barrels [per day].'" The report notes that "5,000 barrels per day was a back-of-the-envelope estimate," but that it "remained the official government estimate of the spill size" for the next four weeks.[36] By the time that the final report was issued, the government's estimate had climbed to "about 60,000 barrels per day."[37]

Regardless of what actually transpired at OMB regarding flow-rate estimates, the controversy reminds us of the risk that scientific estimates or other analysis can become compromised in the process of political preclearance. Furthermore, the very fact that it remains unclear what occurred, even in this relatively high-profile case in which interference is publicly alleged, demonstrates the White House's capacity to cloak the nature of its influence over agencies in matters over which it asserts final decision-making authority.

Another striking example, this one from the Reagan administration, demonstrates both the risk that OMB review will compromise scientific reporting and the president's ability to distance himself from OMB interference should it become publicly known. In this instance, the OMB altered testimony that James Hansen—who served at NASA at the time and who is widely considered "the preeminent climate scientist of our time"—was to present to the Senate. The OMB "change[d] . . . the text, and the main point in particular, that the greenhouse effect was changing climate. The approved version stated that the cause was unknown." Less routine than the OMB's review was Hansen's response. Angered by the OMB's action and by similar reviews that he had undergone previously, Hansen "disavow[ed] his own written testimony in person before the [Senate] committee," "clarify[ing] the differences between his actual opinions and the text he had been forced to submit." Hansen's response was so unusual that it generated intense media interest, leading the White House to distance itself from what had occurred by blaming "a nameless OMB bureaucrat 'five levels down from the top.'"[38]

Interference with Rulemakings

Another way in which administrations manifest unity is by controlling agency rulemakings—either through implicit or explicit threats that the White House will directly displace agency decisions, through White House rulemaking review conducted in the shadow of such threats, or through pressure over agency officials who serve at the president's pleasure. Agencies engage in rulemaking when they promulgate regulatory policies pursuant to statutory directives. Under the constraints of the APA and other statutes, even so-called informal rulemaking processes entail protections of transparency and procedural regularity.[39] Under the APA, an agency must publish a notice of proposed rulemaking, give interested members of the public an opportunity to comment on the proposal in writing, and publish a "concise general statement of [the rule's] basis and purpose" with the final rule.[40] While the APA does not require an agency to rely exclusively on a designated legal record, it subjects the agency's informal rulemaking to judicial review.[41] Among other things, courts may review rulemakings for determinations that are "arbitrary, capricious" or "in excess of statutory jurisdiction, authority, or limitations."[42] While still a relatively lenient standard of review, it effectively requires agencies to rationally explain decisions and their evidentiary bases. It also puts them at risk of having their rules invalidated should they give insufficient attention to major objections made in the public comment process. They are at similar risk where it is evident that they relied on extra-statutory factors.[43] Some statutes go further and explicitly prohibit agencies from basing rules on information not in the public rulemaking record.[44]

Unity threatens to disrupt the layers of substantive accountability embedded in statutory rulemaking requirements by facilitating secretive White House influence over some rules and records while preventing others from seeing the light of day. It is intuitive that a president's capacity (or that of his proxies) for political influence over administrators will be greater where the president can terminate their employment for any reason. The president or his White House proxies can apply behind-the-scenes pressure not only as to final rulemaking determinations but as to the content of underlying factual findings and records. Knowing that the president has the power to step in and substitute his preferred rule for that formulated by administrators can have a similarly coercive effect on administrators, even if the president rarely exercises this power.

Furthermore, a president in a unitary regime remains at least as able as a president in a nonunitary setting to distance himself from agency actions and his own role in them. Even if the president were frequently to exercise his constitutional prerogatives to make final rulemaking decisions, the president is unlikely to do the grunt work of writing proposed rules, analyzing public comments, engaging in scientific or other technical analysis, or writing final rules. That being the case, the president remains well poised to distance himself publicly even from his own decisions should they prove unpopular. He can argue that the administrators below him failed him with flawed advice, flawed data, or the like. He can also distance himself from actions taken by administrators without firing them by explaining to the public that he maintains respect for an administrator but that they disagree on the issues at hand. The president can also claim that an administrator herself is not at fault for unpopular actions, that those below the administrator failed her with poor advice or incorrect data.[45]

Even where the president receives substantial political push-back in an unusually high-profile case, he can cite unity as a basis to prevent administrators from testifying or otherwise releasing information that would help Congress or the public determine who did what and when. Furthermore, while unity and executive privilege are separate arguments—indeed, at least one prominent unitary executive theorist argues that the president possesses no constitutional executive privilege[46]—as a practical matter, administrations also have made effective use of executive privilege and its shadow effect to forestall inquiries over White House involvement in rulemaking.[47] Furthermore, the Supreme Court has deemed the procedural requirements of the APA inapplicable to White House offices.[48] While Congress could, of course, amend the APA, such efforts would surely be met with resistance grounded in concerns over executive privilege and unity.

Of course, the more successful that secretive influence is, the less likely we are to learn of it. Still, secret influence attempts that have come to light provide examples of the phenomenon. One set of examples involves

President George H. W. Bush's Council on Competitiveness, chaired by Vice President Dan Quayle. The council's "modus operandi was to intervene quietly in rulemakings in an effort to persuade or coerce agencies to relax regulatory burdens on American businesses while 'leaving . . . no fingerprints' on the results of its interventions." Quayle's aides deemed the secrecy necessary "because many of these issues were 'political loser[s].'"[49] Efforts to keep the council's activities secret included

> resisting FOIA disclosure of documents belonging to President Reagan's Task Force on Regulatory Relief on the ground that the Task Force (and, by implication, the Council) was not a covered "agency"; resisting Congressional access to information about the Council beyond published fact sheets and the testimony of individuals who did not participate in Council deliberations; keeping decisions at staff level to shield them from the greater publicity that would likely follow cabinet level involvement.[50]

Another episode involved efforts by the George W. Bush administration to secretly shut down a proposed EPA rulemaking and to prevent disclosure of the EPA's related findings on greenhouse gases. The rulemaking proposal came about in response to a 2007 Supreme Court decision, *Massachusetts v. EPA*. The Court rejected the EPA's position in an earlier, 2003 rulemaking that it lacked statutory power to regulate greenhouse gas emissions from automobiles.[51] The Court also deemed the EPA's reasons for refusing to exercise such power inconsistent with statutory authority. The Court ordered the EPA either to regulate greenhouse gas emissions or to offer a sound statutory basis for not doing so. Such a basis would entail either a determination "'that greenhouse gases do not contribute to climate change,'" or "a good explanation why [the EPA] cannot or will not find out whether they do."[52]

The EPA's initial reaction to the ruling was quite vigorous. EPA administrator Stephen L. Johnson convened sixty to seventy EPA officials to respond to the Court's decision. The effort culminated in a December 2007 draft "endangerment finding" that greenhouse gases contribute to climate change and endanger public welfare.[53] The EPA also "used Energy Department data from 2007 to conclude that it would be cost effective to require the nation's motor vehicle fleet to average 37.7 miles per gallon in 2018."[54]

Rather than immediately initiating a public rulemaking process, the EPA comported with long-standing White House protocol by first sending the documents to the OMB.[55] Pursuant to executive order, the OMB has conducted pre-rulemaking review of proposed agency rules through its Office of Information and Regulatory Affairs (OIRA) since 1981.[56] In this case, upon receiving EPA's documents, OIRA refused to open them. It urged the EPA to retract them and to claim that they had been sent by mistake. OIRA warned that otherwise, the documents could become subject to disclosure rules.[57] This interchange was not revealed publicly until months after the fact, when it was leaked to the press.[58] Still, the Bush White House successfully resisted disclosing the documents to the public for the remainder of its tenure. The 2007 endangerment finding was not released until 2009, when the Obama administration released it and touted its overlap with findings of the Obama administration's EPA.[59]

As these episodes demonstrate, the OIRA review process creates opportunities for secretive pressure to alter records or proposed rules or to prevent them from becoming public at all. Research by Lisa Schultz Bressman and Michael P. Vandenberg further demonstrates the potential for OIRA, as well as other White House or EOP offices, secretly to influence rulemakings in the name of presidential control. It also demonstrates the fog in which such influence can occur, making it difficult if not impossible for outsiders and even many insiders to know what transpired and between whom. Bressman and Vandenberg studied White House influence over EPA rulemakings from 1989 to 2001, during the administrations of George H. W. Bush and Bill Clinton. They found that White House or EOP influence frequently occurs in secret and that it can threaten, among other things, to distort the scientific findings that the public and the other branches eventually will see. The study also found that presidents often are genuinely out of the loop—thus putting the "plausible" in plausible deniability—even as White House employees wield influence in their names.[60]

Based on their extensive interviews with top EPA officials across the two administrations, Bressman and Vandenberg conclude that

> [p]residential control is a "they," not an "it." ... EPA respondents did not merely confirm that both OIRA and other White House offices are involved in EPA rulemaking. Rather, they indicated that OIRA is not the primary source of influence on many major rulemakings, as scholars typically assume. OIRA often takes a back seat to other White House offices when both are involved. Although OIRA exerts influence on many day-to-day issues, other White House offices often wield more influence on high-profile or high-stakes matters.

EPA respondents also highlighted an ill-appreciated dynamic: White House offices form coalitions for or against the EPA. These coalitions frequently enlist OIRA to batter or shield the EPA rather than to avail themselves of the independent value of its regulatory review.[61]

Rulemaking review by this revolving cast of characters can blur politics and expertise and distort the factual records underlying rules. Foreshadowing the EPA greenhouse gases rulemaking controversy, some of the EPA officials interviewed by Bressman and Vanderberg noted:

> OIRA on occasion questioned whether the science really supported the results that the EPA had claimed. Whether or not OIRA actually had the authority to challenge agency scientific judgments, these respondents believed that it lacked the competence. One EPA respondent recalled asking an OIRA staffer, "[W]hen did [you] get a PhD in epidemiology? I must've missed that." These respondents suggested that OIRA challenged the science as a means to avoid regulation and reduce costs.[62]

The officials also cited a substantial lack of transparency in the OMB review process. As Bressman and Vanderberg report:

> According to 63% of EPA respondents, only rarely or sometimes were changes arising from White House involvement apparent in the record. This number actually understates the issue because a full 30% indicated that they had no knowledge of the contents of the record. Of the respondents who had awareness of the contents of the record, 90% stated that the record either rarely or sometimes did not contain evidence of White House involvement; the remaining 10% said it never did.[63]

Other studies document consistent failures, across administrations and parties, of adherence even to presidentially imposed transparency requirements for rulemaking oversight. For example, every administration since that of President Clinton has mandated, via executive order, that OIRA make publicly available "'all documents exchanged between OIRA and the agency during the [regulatory review process] by OIRA'" and that "all agencies ... 'identify for the public those changes in the regulatory action that were made at the suggestion or recommendation of OIRA.'"[64] A 2011 study by the Center for Progressive Reform concluded, however, that OIRA virtually never makes publicly available the most foundational of the documents exchanged between itself and the agency—namely, the agency's original proposed rule draft, documents suggesting or making changes to the draft, and the draft resulting from OIRA review.[65] As for agencies' own publication obligations, in the absence of "any government-wide guidance on what exactly to disclose, or monitoring of agency compliance, the transparency of agency disclosures has been wildly inconsistent."[66] The 2011 study also cited shortcomings and gaps in the executive order itself and in OIRA's interpretation of the same.[67] The General Accounting Office (GAO) found similar problems in the controlling executive order and in OIRA's interpretation of and compliance with the same. GAO conveyed these findings in its own reports issued in 2003 and 2009.[68] The holes in OIRA and agency reporting contrast with the wide volume of changes made to proposed rules in the OIRA review process, as signified by the "terse labels" that OIRA does publish to indicate whether rules were returned to agencies "with change" or "without change" or whether another outcome followed.[69] The 2011 study found, for example, that OIRA makes changes "to 84 percent of EPA and 65 percent of other agencies' submissions."[70]

Nina Mendelson reports her own very similar findings in a 2010 article:

> [D]espite the several hundred economically significant rules that were modified during the review process, the Bush Administration OMB posted only forty-two review and return letters that explain its problems with the agency rule under review. President Obama's OIRA appears to be even less committed to disclosure. As of January 20, 2010, it had posted no further review or return letters at all. . . . Between January 20, 2009 and January 20, 2010, Obama's OIRA reviewed 120 economically significant proposed or final rules. Of these, only 8 were issued without change; 46 were issued consistent with change; and 12 were withdrawn. In other words, over 90 percent of economically significant rules underwent some change or withdrawal during the OIRA review process. That figure remains stable even excluding economically significant rules that were submitted to the OMB prior to the change in administration. Again, no review or return letters of any sort appeared to have been posted electronically by Obama's OIRA during that time.[71]

In my own check of the relevant OIRA web page on October 28, 2013, I found only a single return letter and a single review letter posted at any point by the Obama administration.[72]

Finally, by creating and filling "advisory" positions within the EOP, presidents can give themselves new and opaque avenues through which to influence the administrative state. By statute, the president has substantial leeway to create such positions. Constitutionally, the persons appointed to them need not be confirmed by the Senate if their roles are purely advisory.[73] Yet these positions raise justifiable concerns precisely because they often have so little definition, are not subject to Senate confirmation, and their possessors at points have claimed immunity from testifying before Congress due to their close advisory relationships with the president.[74] Some of President Obama's so-called czar appointments raised additional concerns because the czars' portfolios overlapped substantially with those of Senate-confirmed agency heads. This led to suspicions that the czars were meant to serve as opaque shadow agencies, quietly displacing or supplementing the work of the formal agencies.[75] It did not help matters when the head of California's Air Resources Board said that negotiations on a national fuel economy standard held between her agency, President Obama's "climate czar" Carol Browner, and auto industry officials were successful partly because "'[w]e put nothing in writing, ever.'"[76]

Politicizing the Bureaucracy

The examples discussed thus far predominantly entail White House centralization. That is, White House efforts, through the OMB or other offices, to alter or suppress information—whether in the form of reports, testimony, proposed rules or rulemaking records—that agencies were otherwise prepared to make public. The examples also touch upon the risk that presidents will use EOP offices as shadow agencies to secretly pull the levers of non-EOP agencies. Yet a still more seamless approach—politicization—enables the White House to control information throughout the administrative state. Specifically, presidents can seek to staff agencies as thickly as possible with political appointees who serve at his pleasure and who can be chosen partly for their party affiliation or other indicia of loyalty to the administration. For ease of reference, I will refer to such appointees within agencies as "politicals," and to other agency employees as "nonpoliticals." As with centralization, the term and concept of politicization were coined by political scientist Terry Moe.[77]

By increasing the ratio of politicals to nonpoliticals, the president can enhance his ability to control agency messaging in two ways. First, where politicals themselves participate in creating reports, testimony, rules, or rulemaking records, they structurally are more likely than nonpoliticals to craft messages and to interpret and report facts in a manner compatible with administration politics. Second, when politicals are placed in supervisory roles over career scientists or other nonpolitical agency personnel, the former are well-situated to influence the latter's communications with the public and the other branches.

HOW UNITY CAN MANIFEST ITSELF IN A MORE POLITICIZED BUREAUCRACY. By putting concepts from unitary executive theory into practice, presidents indeed can impact the balance within agencies between politicals and nonpoliticals. First, unity can manifest itself in a presidential power to remove employees—at any time and for any reason—who exercise discretionary executive power. Precisely who that description encompasses is subject to case-by-case debate. Most alarming, from a substantive accountability perspective, would be an unfettered presidential power to remove scientists or other subject-specific experts from within agencies. These are the persons best situated, after all, to provide nonpolitically driven information and analyses against which the public and the other branches can assess the policy choices made by the president or agency politicals. A strong argument can be made that such persons do not exercise discretionary executive power and thus are outside of the category of those whom unity proponents deem fully removable. Yet given past administrations' suggestions that preparing information for public dissemination is a discretionary executive act that the president must control, and given the fact that some employees exercise research and analytical functions along with more clearly executive tasks, unity could be invoked to support their removability. Indeed, this notion is in keeping with the suggestion by some pro-unity scholars that a conflict may exist between unity and civil service protections.[78] It also is in keeping with presidential objections to the requirement that the president notify Congress of his reasons for removing an inspector general. Since the Carter administration, administrations have deemed this requirement inconsistent with Article II, despite the fact that IGs are empowered solely to gather information and issue reports and recommendations.[79]

Unity also can manifest itself in a presidential power to ignore statutory hiring criteria for those deemed to exercise discretionary executive power. Administrations and some scholars have argued that Congress constitutionally may not limit the pool from which the president chooses appointees by imposing minimum qualifications. For example,

President Clinton took the view, in a 1995 signing statement, that Congress may not forbid him from nominating "as United States Trade Representative or Deputy United States Trade Representative ... anyone who had ever 'directly represented, aided, or advised a foreign [government or political party] ... in any trade negotiation, or trade dispute with the United States.'"[80] In another signing statement, President Clinton objected to limits on who the transportation secretary could appoint to a committee that selects "entities to which certain historic lighthouses will be conveyed."[81] President George W. Bush also objected to statutory qualifications for executive nominations and appointments, including a requirement that nominees to head the Federal Emergency Management Agency have "demonstrated ability in and knowledge of emergency management and homeland security" and at least "5 years of executive leadership and management experience in the public or private sector."[82]

Unity thus demands a thickening of the ranks of politicals throughout the administrative state. Such thickening, in turn, has its own effects, creating opportunities for even formally "nonpolitical" parts of the administrative state to become politicized. Such effects are discernible not only as a matter of logic but through experience. Indeed, a variety of factors—including a political culture increasingly accepting of presidential control, presidential uses of reorganization and force reduction powers, and provisions of the Civil Service Reform Act of 1978 creating new political appointment opportunities—have substantially increased the ranks of agency politicals over the last several decades.[83] Furthermore, changes to the party and presidential nominating systems, as well as cultural and technological shifts enhancing direct presidential ties to ideological constituencies, have increased presidential incentives and opportunities to choose politicals predominantly for their ideological alignment with administrations.[84] Political scientists link these phenomena to yet further politicization within agencies' formally nonpolitical realms. Further politicization follows from, among other things, pressure on nonpoliticals by political supervisors, influence by politicals over the hiring of nonpoliticals, job reassignments or other changes to nonpoliticals' work to minimize their influence or encourage them to quit, and the use of shadow political staffs within agencies to bypass nonpolitical staffs.[85]

HOW A MORE POLITICIZED BUREAUCRACY CAN UNDERMINE SUBSTANTIVE ACCOUNTABILITY.   Studies in the political science literature support the intuition that excessive politicization has costs for agency competence and expertise. These studies find that politicals and nonpoliticals bring different skill sets to the table. Nonpoliticals generally have superior substantive expertise and public management skills, while politicals tend to be more politically responsive and adept at politics outside of bureaucratic confines. As such, a careful mix of politicals and nonpoliticals appears to be optimal for agency performance, with the exact balance varying by agency.[86] When agencies are stacked too heavily with politicals, competence and performance can suffer.[87]

It stands to reason that politicals' deficiencies will include shortcomings in subject-specific research, analysis, and reporting. These difficulties follow partly from politicals' relative substantive inexpertise and partly from their heightened propensity for political bias. One study found, for example, that state budget agencies with nonpolitical subordinates generated more accurate budget forecasts than did state budget offices staffed by political subordinates. The most accurate forecasts came from states with budget offices comprised of nonpolitical subordinates and political directors. The authors deemed the latter result to follow from the fact that nonpoliticals tended toward conservative biases while politicals tended toward optimistic biases, and the two biases helped to cancel one another out.[88] Nonetheless, the authors stressed that the single most important predictor of accurate forecasting was the employment of nonpolitical subordinates.[89] As the study demonstrates, the mix of politicals and nonpoliticals in an agency can impact the accuracy of information released to the public. Relatedly, it can impact the extent to which agency statements reflect the judgments of subject specific experts.[90]

One means through which nonpoliticals' judgments can be politicized is the use of intra-agency clearance processes run by politicals. Such processes essentially are in-house versions of OMB review. In-house political clearance requirements were used extensively for science reporting during the administration of George W. Bush. The administration enabled this system in part by increasing the use of political appointees, as opposed to career civil servants, to oversee the final vetting of reports within science agencies.[91] Indeed, the top three public affairs people at the National Aeronautics and Space Administration (NASA) were White House appointees during a now infamous period in the middle of the Bush administration.[92] In this period climate change reports and press releases routinely were edited—generally by nonscientists, and in one case by a twenty-four-year-old political appointee who lacked a college degree—to downplay scientists' conclusions on human-made global warming.[93] Also in this period, scientists for the first time since NASA's founding in 1958 were required to preclear media appearances with NASA's public affairs office.[94] According to journalist Andrew Revkin, White House interference with NASA's science reporting was particularly "intense in the run-up to the 2004 election."[95]

Another sharp example of intra-agency information control arose in the same administration's Justice Department. Specifically, it arose in the Voting Rights Section of the Department's Civil Rights Division. Under Section 5 of the Voting Rights Act of 1965, the division long had reviewed "preclearance" requests by "covered" jurisdictions. Until recently, covered jurisdictions were required to obtain preclearance to implement new voting procedures.[96] Preclearance was not to be granted if the new procedures would have the "purpose or the effect of denying or abridging the right to vote on account of race or membership in a language minority group."[97] As explained in 2007 by three former longtime career employees who had served in the Civil Rights Division across multiple administrations of both parties[98]:

> Historically, the Justice Department has avoided partisan application of the preclearance requirement in large part because of the well-established, bottom-up, process applied to Section 5 decision-making. Under this process, the nonpolitical career staff of the Civil Rights Division is solely responsible for investigating and making recommendations on all Section 5 submissions, and the staff's analyses frame each preclearance determination in terms of the law of Section 5 and the facts pertinent to the specific submitted change. This has had the effect of steering the political staff to make appropriate Section 5 decisions based upon the law and the facts, and not based upon partisan interests.
>
> ... In both Democratic and Republican administrations the political staff almost always has agreed with staff recommendations to interpose an objection. . . . In the few instances when staff recommendations to deny preclearance have been rejected by political appointees during past administrations, memoranda or written explanations of the reasons for such rejections were prepared by political decision-makers for career staff to provide the legal rationale for the decision and to make a complete record of the decision-making process to guide future Section 5 decisions. This longstanding deliberative process also has played an important role in ensuring that inappropriate political factors do not influence Section 5 decision-making.[99]

Yet as the three former division employees explained in the same report, the practice changed dramatically in the George W. Bush administration. Politicals' rejections of nonpoliticals' preclearance recommendations for

the first time became routine. More important, "political staff did not prepare any . . . explanation [again, in a sharp break from past practice,] for
their rejection of the staff recommendations."[100]

Most significant from the perspective of substantive accountability,
Voting Rights Section politicals forbid nonpoliticals from memorializing
their views on preclearance requests in writing.

> As reported in *The Washington Post* in December 2005, Voting Section leader-
> ship instituted a rule requiring that staff members who review Section 5 voting
> submissions limit their written analysis to the facts surrounding the matter and
> prohibited the career staff from making recommendations as to whether or not
> the Department should impose an objection to the voting change.[101]

This rule plainly "increase[d] the ability of political appointees to make
politically-motivated preclearance decisions without appearing to repu-
diate career staff directly."[102] It epitomizes the use of political decision
making to manipulate the very record—in this case of legal judgments
grounded in years of voting rights experience—against which final policy
decisions are made.

The Congressional–Presidential Struggle to Control
the Bureaucracy

Pro-unity scholars might respond to this chapter's analysis by arguing that
the alternative to presidential control is not neutral expertise and undis-
torted information flow, but rather congressional strong-arming of agency
personnel, often behind closed doors. As between these two choices, unitary executive theorists deem presidential control the surest path to accountability.[103] This, of course, returns us to unity's core functional arguments: The president alone represents the entire national electorate. He is
the nation's most visible political figure. He is an easily targeted object of
political blame or reward.

The premise that congressional control can take forms that undermine substantive accountability is sound. While the Constitution builds
important elements of dialogue and transparency into the legislative process, it is well known that much of Congress's work gets done behind the
scenes. Congressional committees and leadership can prevent legislation
from being introduced on the floor of either chamber and can dispropor-
tionately influence the content of legislation that is introduced. They can

do this through telephone calls, backdoor meetings, and staffer-to-staffer communications. A congressperson on a relevant committee thus is well positioned to influence the actions of agency officials and employees, and to do so behind closed doors. Agency personnel may have good reason to fear legislative changes—such as funding reductions—that negatively impact themselves or their agencies if they are insufficiently responsive to the concerns of key congresspersons.[104]

While these are important considerations, they in no way undermine the functional case for legislative flexibility and against a categorical unity directive. Indeed, the complicated nature of the factual picture only strengthens this case. Recall the point that functional reasoning alone cannot support an unyielding unity directive so long as it is reasonably arguable that unity sometimes undermines, rather than supports, substantive accountability. If some manifestations of unity undermine accountability, some enhance accountability, and some have neutral, fluctuating, or simply unpredictable relationships to accountability, then a categorical unity requirement cannot possibly follow from the constitutional principle of substantive accountability. Rather, Congress in crafting legislation, and the president in wielding his veto power or negotiating in its shadow, have substantial leeway to shape the administrative state. In so doing, they can and are well advised to consider how particular types of political controls may foster or undermine substantive accountability.

Furthermore, the alternative to unity is not unfettered congressional control. Indeed, the approach adopted by the Supreme Court and embraced in this book imposes functional boundaries on the extent to which statutes may estrange administrative actors from presidential control. As applied by the Supreme Court, these boundaries have been used with particular vigilance to prevent Congress from aggrandizing power to itself. As we saw in chapter 7, for example, while the Supreme Court generally has permitted statutes that impose "good-cause" limits on the president's removal power, it has deemed unconstitutional statutes that condition presidential removal on approval by the Senate. The built-in protections of the legislative process—including presidential participation through the veto power—combined with flexible, functionally defined constitutional limits and their shadow effect, thus comprise the alternative to a categorical unity directive. While this alternative is no panacea, it offers far better and more precise tools to respond and adapt over time to problems posed by excessive (or inadequate) congressional or presidential controls than does an unyielding, one-size-fits-all directive.

CHAPTER NINE

Where Do We Go from Here?

On occasion, I give talks to adult education classes, community groups, and university students about some of the issues raised in this book. Perhaps the most common question that I am asked in these settings is "what can we do?" This is no easy question, and attempting to answer it is always humbling. It is ironic, in a sense, that I find the question difficult. After all, my arguments center on the notion of government accountability, on the constitutional significance of maintaining a government that is "of the people, by the people, for the people." It seems intuitive that such arguments would conduce to ideas about fostering government responsiveness. Yet in another sense, the daunting nature of the question follows naturally from many of the problems described throughout this book. As we have seen, aspects of presidentialism and executive secrecy are well entrenched both inside and outside of the executive branch and prove formidable when challenged. They also tend to reinforce one another, making for moving targets.

Yet while gut reactions to the question "what can we do?" may be flecked with pessimism, there are hopeful notes from which to draw in reaching more considered answers. While the infrastructure of presidential power and secrecy runs deep—including the vast resources and longstanding norms and practices that make up the imperial presidency, the cultural phenomenon of the presidential mystique, and the legal trappings of presidentialism—there remain powerful counterforces in American government and society. The institutional components of the imperial presidency, while strong and far-reaching, nonetheless must contend with counterforces ranging from dedicated civil servants who push back against illegality and incompetence, to congressional oversight, to open government legislation, to a press willing to publish leaked information. Equally important, the presidential mystique has a formidable counterpart in Americans' investment in the notion that ours is and must remain an accountable government, one of "laws and not of men."[1] And of course, it is the thesis of this book that presidentialism's counterforce—substantive accountability—has been with us all along, in the U.S. Constitution.

The most basic answer to "what can we do?," then, is that we can seek to harness and support those aspects of American law, politics, and culture that advance substantive accountability. Of course, this deceptively simple answer encompasses an array of possible actions. This chapter will focus on five categories of action. The first and most intuitive entails public outreach. Just as the modern conservative legal movement has so successfully reached out in forums ranging from law schools to legal practice networks to popular media, so proponents of substantive accountability must reach out broadly, arguing the merits of their constitutional views. The second category involves bridging partisan and ideological divides in the course of such outreach and in the course of other efforts. As we have seen, presidentialism—despite its roots in the modern conservative legal movement—has crossed partisan and ideological borders. Yet so too, have concerns about its excesses. Alliances across partisan and ideological divides can prove important sources of strength for the cause of substantive accountability.

The third category entails putting existing accountability tools to work, or supporting groups and individuals who do the same. Consider the example of the Freedom of Information Act (FOIA). Some of the most important revelations about post-9/11 abuses stemmed directly from FOIA disclosures, or were confirmed or built on through such disclosures. Many of these revelations were facilitated through requests and litigation by the American Civil Liberties Union (ACLU). One way to help effectuate accountability tools is to support groups like the ACLU in such efforts. Persons with relevant skills and access to legal and institutional resources— such as lawyers and law school professors—can offer more than financial support. For instance, they might engage in pro bono FOIA work or help to create FOIA clinics. And FOIA, of course, is but one example of an accountability tool, and the ACLU but one example of an organization that makes effective use of such tools. Groups that use accountability tools serve substantive accountability directly by pushing the executive branch to articulate satisfactory rationales for keeping information secret and, of course, by uncovering information. They also protect the substantive accountability framework in a less direct respect. In using accountability tools to expose important information that was unjustifiably kept secret or manipulated, groups and individuals can bring the concept of substantive accountability to life for the public. It is one thing to argue in the abstract that our constitutional system can only function healthily if it includes the existence and active use of accountability tools. It is another thing to demonstrate through concrete examples that information control can undermine the checking functions of the other branches, the press, and the people, and that accountability tools can help Americans resist such control.

The fourth category entails working to improve accountability tools and to create new ones as needed, or to support groups who lobby for such changes. For example, concerned persons may wish to support groups like the Government Accountability Project (GAP) (disclosure: I am one of GAP's academic affiliates) that lobby for improved whistleblower protections. Lawyers and law professors might consider pro bono work with such groups or arranging for law school clinical students to work with them. Lawyers and law students may be well equipped, for example, to help such groups formulate legal arguments explaining that improved whistleblower protections or open government laws do not violate Article II of the Constitution.

The fifth and final category takes us back to the notion of conducting outreach in a variety of forums, across partisan and ideological borders. The category entails working—both separately and in tandem with presidentialists—to define the limits of presidentialism. In other words, even for those who subscribe to supremacy or to unitary executive theory, it is worth considering the limits of the respective theories. For example, unity proponents may conclude that the president may bypass statutorily designated power allotments only to exercise the allotted power himself, not to redelegate that power to the OMB. Such limits, in turn, can mitigate some of the tensions between presidentialism and substantive accountability.

Public Outreach

The first set of activities—public outreach—is perhaps the most intuitive one. It includes everything from books and other writings that make the case for substantive accountability and against presidentialism, to lectures and discussions with lawyering organizations, student and community groups, and college, law school, and adult education classes. In my own experiences of speaking to a range of groups on these issues, I have been somewhat surprised but always gratified by the deep interest and concerns expressed. More than anything, I have sensed a profound hunger to learn. This hunger seems borne partly of frustration over hearing terms like "executive privilege" and "unitary executive" bandied about on talk shows and in newspapers with little explanation. More so, many of the people with whom I have spoken—particularly in nonlawyer settings such as adult education classes and community group meetings—express a gut sense, grounded in notions of checks and balances and the rule of law, that presidentialist statements and defenses do not ring true. At the same time, they feel that they lack the knowledge and terminology with which to respond. Talk of presidentialism and substantive accountability may lack very wide appeal. But there is an audience out there, one that is engaged and highly motivated.

Apart from individual initiative, outreach efforts can benefit from organizational resources. As we saw in chapter 2, the conservative legal movement gave rise to, and has benefited enormously from, the broad and diversified outreach programs of the Federalist Society. The Federalist Society concerns itself with a host of issue areas under the broad label of legal conservatism. Progressives have created a counterpart organization—the American Constitution Society—that similarly engages a range of issues under the umbrella of legal progressivism. At some point, it may be valuable to create a legal organization with the mission of protecting substantive accountability, with public outreach among its agenda items. Apart from that possibility, however, substantive accountability proponents can join forces with existing organizations to conduct outreach. Indeed, a number of existing organizations work in one or more areas of interest to such proponents. These areas include, among many others, whistleblower protections, press protections, and open government legislation and litigation.

Furthermore, organizations not only can help to facilitate outreach, but in some cases can be targets of outreach. Some groups, for instance, may work in areas very closely related to substantive accountability, but may not yet have made the leap to supporting substantive accountability directly. Other groups may have taken positions at odds with substantive accountability at points, but may have evolved in a manner that suggests growing sympathy to substantive accountability. Alternatively, some groups may oppose aspects of substantive accountability yet embrace other aspects. Such groups themselves can be fruitful objects of outreach.

At minimum, such outreach can generate intergroup dialogue and debate. In some cases, dialogue and debate may lead to points of agreement and collaboration.

Reaching across Partisan and Ideological Borders

As the preceding section suggests, public and intergroup outreach should by no means be confined within traditional partisan or ideological enclaves. While presidentialism arose largely as a facet of the modern conservative legal movement, its appeal has expanded considerably since then. At the same time, concerns over presidentialism and its excesses also span partisan and ideological borders. In recent years, some prominent conservatives and progressives alike have expressed alarm over presidentialism in both Republican and Democratic administrations.

For example, Mickey Edwards—a former Republican congressman from Oklahoma, one of three founding trustees of the Heritage Foundation, and a former national chairman of the American Conservative Union[2]—railed against presidentialism in his 2008 book *Reclaiming Conservatism.* Referring to then president George W. Bush, Edwards wrote that

> the president, who called himself (and was called by others) a conservative, had
> become the very embodiment of everything conservatives had long feared and
> warned against. Operating almost unchecked by any other branch of govern-
> ment, he ordered wiretaps on citizens' phones, held prisoners without trial or
> charges, and refused to provide information to Congress even when federal law
> required him to do so.[3]

Edwards laid equal blame at the feet of the Congress, dominated by Republicans prior to 2006. "What had once been an attempt to strip power from Congress because it was controlled by Democrats," he observed, "had now become so much a part of the conservative litany that [Republican congresspersons] cheered at having *their own* power taken away."[4]

Other conservatives launched similar critiques of presidentialism during the Bush administration. For example, longtime conservative columnist George Will denounced as a "monarchical doctrine" the reasoning underlying the administration's position that the president could order warrantless wiretapping in violation of statutory provisions.[5] Bruce Fein, who held several high level appointments in the Reagan Justice Department, similarly lambasted the administration's warrantless wiretapping defenses as resting on "an imperial theory of inherent constitutional power."[6] Fein also criticized "Republicans in Congress [who] have bowed to the president's scorn for the rule of law and cravings for secret government."[7]

Some conservatives and progressives alike also have criticized presidentialism in the Obama administration. Bruce Fein, who had called for President Bush's impeachment, drafted articles of impeachment against President Obama for initiating military action without congressional approval.[8] And progressive reporter Glenn Greenwald has been among the most forceful and prolific critics of presidentialism in the Obama administration. In one column Greenwald facetiously congratulated Obama for being a "pioneer" in the realms of secrecy and presidentially ordered targeted killing. Greenwald explained that President Obama "did campaign on a promise of change, and vesting the President with the power to order the execution of citizens in secret and with no oversight certainly qualifies as that." What is more, wrote Greenwald, President Obama, "in another moment of trailblazing, has waged an unprecedented war on whistleblowers."[9]

As these examples reflect, many self-described conservatives and progressives can find common ground in concerns over presidentialism. While the nature and target of these concerns surely will vary—for instance, some conservatives have been highly critical of supremacy while embracing unity[10]—there clearly are points of existing and potential overlap. It thus is particularly important that public and intergroup outreach cross political and ideological barriers. Beyond the value of the resulting dialogue itself, avenues for collaboration may be discovered.

Putting Existing Accountability Tools to Work

Substantive accountability advocates also can seek out and assist in efforts to use existing accountability tools. At the start of this chapter, I cited the example of FOIA, explaining that advocates can support FOIA's use by providing legal assistance to FOIA requesters or by supporting groups that provide such assistance or who themselves rely on FOIA. I also cited some of the ACLU's important work in making and litigating FOIA requests. Of course, the ACLU is not alone in such work. Another prominent example is the National Security Archives at George Washington University. As the Archives notes on its website, it has, since its 1985 founding, made "40,000 targeted Freedom of Information and declassification requests to more than 200 offices and agencies of the U.S. gov-

ernment that have opened more than 10 million pages of previously secret U.S. government documents."[11] Citing these and other examples, Seth
Kreimer wrote in 2008 that "[t]he most effective [FOIA] requesters" with
respect to antiterrorism efforts "have included the National Security Archives, the ACLU, the Electronic Privacy Information Center, the Electronic Frontier Foundation, the Center for Constitutional Rights, Judicial
Watch, and the Center for National Security Studies."[12]

As we have seen, accountability tools extend well beyond FOIA. They
include other open government laws, free speech supportive statutes including whistleblower protection laws, statutes that create zones of independence in the administrative state, and constitutional protections
for free speech and congressional oversight. Such tools comprise what
Kreimer calls the "ecology of transparency."[13] Using FOIA as his focal
point, Kreimer demonstrates that FOIA requests often hinge on earlier disclosures facilitated by other accountability tools. He explains that
"[f]or FOIA requests to generate illuminating documents, they must be
precisely framed, and framing such requests requires knowledge regarding the activities to be illuminated."[14] Illumination can come from whistleblowers who leak information, from members of the press who publish the same, or from civil servants with some structural independence
from the White House who disclose politically inconvenient information
in the course of their duties.[15] These information sources are supported, in
turn, by constitutional and statutory free speech protections and by statutory zones of partial independence from political control within the administrative state. Once a FOIA request is made, success depends partly
on FOIA's administration by a "law-abiding civil service."[16] This condition, too, depends on the existence of some statutory zones of independence from political control. Finally, full or partial disclosures made in
response to FOIA requests—and in some cases, information revealed or
inferable from government refusals to disclose information—themselves
have "laid the groundwork for inquiry and disclosure by other institutions." These institutions include Congress, the courts, inspectors general,
and the media. Members of the public, too, may be moved to seek subsequent disclosures under FOIA or other open government laws.[17]

Using and defending any of the vast array of accountability tools is an
important step in which substantive accountability advocates can engage.
For example, attorneys can seek opportunities to engage in pro bono
work with organizations that litigate on behalf of whistleblowers' rights,
that make or support others' access requests, that defend press freedoms,
or that otherwise use or defend accountability tools. And individuals with

the means can donate money to such organizations. As Kreimer notes in discussing FOIA:

> The existence of an independent civil society sector ... backed up frequently by the litigation muscle of private law firms that have donated their services pro bono ... has proved to be the institutional matrix within which successful FOIA inquiries regarding [antiterrorism efforts] have been seeded.[18]

Using and protecting accountability tools serve at least three ends. First and most directly, such efforts can lead to important disclosures and can help to keep unnecessary secrecy in check. Second, in the course of responding to or anticipating government secrecy defenses, disclosure advocates can make the constitutional case for aspects of substantive accountability and against aspects of presidentialism. For example, in an amicus brief that I coauthored with Stephen Vladeck in 2007, we argued not only that Congress overrode the state secrets privilege for cases arising under FISA, but that Congress is constitutionally empowered to do so.[19]

Finally, in challenging government secrecy, demanding that the government justify disclosure refusals, and sometimes winning the release of information, advocates can bring the concept of substantive accountability to life for the public. It is one thing to argue, for example, that government frequently misuses the classification system and that persons who leak classified information can provide important checks against such abuse and warrant meaningful protections under the First Amendment. It is another thing to invoke real world examples of leaks that exposed government illegality or incompetence or betrayed the groundlessness of the information's classification. To this day, for example, courts and commentators invoke the Pentagon Papers leak as an example of a justified disclosure that confirmed government misdeeds and revealed unnecessary secrecy. In so doing, they implicitly undermine the case for deeming executive classification conclusive of a leak's illegality.[20]

Championing New Accountability Tools or Amendments to Existing Tools

Just as it is crucial to use and protect existing accountability tools, so vigilance is called for in detecting and responding to insufficiencies in existing tools. For example, a number of commentators have identified gaping holes in the statutory protections for national security whistleblowers.[21]

Advocates of substantive accountability can work with or support groups that lobby for improved accountability tools.

Many of the same organizations that use and defend existing accountability tools also monitor the adequacy of those tools and lobby for statutory or regulatory improvements. For example, the Reporter's Committee for Freedom of the Press (RCFP) provides and coordinates free legal assistance for journalists, and as such defends and invokes existing accountability tools including the First Amendment and FOIA.[22] It also serves as an educational resource to familiarize journalists and others with their constitutional and statutory free speech and press rights.[23] At the same time, RCFP has, through testimony and other means of advocacy and education, sought out legislative and regulatory changes to improve those existing tools.[24] Similarly, the Government Accountability Project (GAP) offers legal support to whistleblowers through existing constitutional and statutory avenues, while also helping to draft and lobby for new federal statutory protections.[25] Many other organizations similarly combine legislative and regulatory efforts with litigation and public outreach.[26]

Defining Presidentialism's Boundaries

In addition to critiquing supremacy and unity, it is important to define those concepts' boundaries. There are some points on which each theory's scope or application remains unexplored. On other points, proponents of a theory disagree among themselves as to the theory's reach. And in some cases, even where there is relative consensus on a question of scope or application, the consensus answer is sufficiently underdeveloped that it warrants rethinking. Where such areas of uncertainty exist, substantive accountability proponents should explain why adherents of unitary executive theory or supremacy should reject particular features and applications of the same.

Both unity proponents and supremacists already engage in some line-drawing in their respective analyses and debates. Among unity supporters, for instance, Saikrishna Prakash suggests a limit on the president's ability to reassign a power statutorily delegated to another executive branch officer or employee. Prakash takes the view that the president may exercise such power personally as a matter of constitutional right. He argues, however, that the president may not redelegate this power to another executive branch actor to whom the power is not statutorily granted.[27] And in the realm of supremacy, it is quite common—not surprisingly, given the number of doctrines that supremacy encompasses—to find commentators who believe that the Constitution extends to one or more aspects of supremacy but not to others. Perhaps the most obvious example of this phenomenon is that view that the First Amendment accords substantial protections to the press for publishing classified information, but not to government employees for leaking the same.

There also is a dispute between unity proponents and supremacists as to whether unity's textual, structural, and historical justifications extend to supremacy. Steven Calabresi and Christopher Yoo vigorously reject the contention that unity's rationales also support supremacy. During the administration of George W. Bush they wrote:

> Despite the current administration's attempt to tie claims of emergency presidential powers to the theory of the unitary executive, the inherent executive power that it seeks to assert has little to do with the framers' decision to vest the executive power in a single person rather than a plural body or with ensuring that the president possesses sufficient power to exercise supervisory authority over the entire executive branch.[28]

Calabresi and Yoo conclude that "[s]o long as the president possesses the power to remove and the power to direct all subordinates in their exercise of executive power, the classic theory of the unitary executive is quite agnostic on the question of whether the president possesses implied, inherent powers in foreign or domestic policy."[29]

John Yoo, on the other hand, argues that unitary executive theorists cannot escape the supremacist implications of unity's textual, structural, and historical underpinnings. He argues that the Vesting Clause thesis that underlies unity—that is, the notion that "the executive power" has a substantive original meaning—relies on founding-era understandings of "the executive power," and that those understandings were supremacist in nature. He also argues that the functional concerns that led to the founding decision to create a single president—that is, the desire to ensure presidential energy and accountability—lend themselves to supremacy just as to unity.[30]

My own view is that while unitary executive theory bears some slipperiness that makes it vulnerable to extensions unintended by its architects,[31] supremacy nonetheless need not follow from unity. It is logically consistent both to say that the president must control all of the executive power, and to contest supremacist definitions of that power. To the extent that unity proponents clarify this point, they help to fine-tune understandings of unity, which is a useful service in itself. Furthermore, such clarification can help to mitigate unity's impact on substantive accountability.

The remainder of this section focuses on four potential points for clarification or refinement—two with respect to the scope of unitary executive theory, and two with respect to the scope of supremacy. To be clear, these examples are by no means comprehensive. Indeed, supremacy in particular covers so many subtopics that it would be impossible to exhaust all points on which clarification can be sought. As for unitary executive theory, it has tended to be pitched at a level of abstraction that leaves open many questions of practical scope and application. Though not exhaustive, the examples that follow help to illuminate the theoretical and practical value in exploring points for clarification or refinement. The same is true of the two examples—that of the president's inability to redelegate unitary power to other officers and the distinction between punishing publishers versus leakers—cited briefly above.

Clarifying Supremacy's Boundaries

MINDING THE GAP BETWEEN INHERENT AND EXCLUSIVE POWERS.   The distinction between inherent or Jacksonian "zone two" power, whereby a president acts in the absence of statutory authority, and exclusive or Jacksonian "zone three" power, whereby a president acts in the face of statutory prohibition, is very important constitutionally. Yet presidentialists frequently elide the distinction between the two. As we have seen, for example, administrations and supremacist commentators often point to case law upholding zone two or zone one activity and cite examples of presidents acting without clear statutory authority. They cite these precedents as support for the constitutionality of zone three activity, or activity that violates statutes.

The distinction has begun to receive some attention of late, particularly by Barron and Lederman in their two-article series exploring the history of zone three actions and claims.[32] Nonetheless, those asserting or supporting ambiguous zone two/zone three claims should themselves be challenged to clarify the boundaries of their arguments. In some cases, advocates or commentators might agree that they support only zone two or even zone one claims, but might fall back on supremacist-infused arguments to the effect that statutes must be interpreted to permit presidential action wherever possible to avoid constitutional problems. Such clarification at least enables us to identify and to confront the zone three arguments at the heart of the asserted statutory interpretation claims. In other cases, advocates or commentators might assert a zone three claim more explicitly. This too, is valuable, as such framing places the zone three, or exclusivity claim front and center rather than obscuring it. Such reframing can highlight the fact that cited political or judicial precedents are inapposite to the exclusivity right asserted. Such reframing also may lead supremacists and others to directly confront another question too often elided. That is, what are the legitimate bounds of any constitutional exclusivity right?

DEFINING EXCLUSIVITY'S LIMITS.   Given the opacity and ambiguity in which exclusivity claims often are shrouded, it is not surprising that exclusivity's limits have received little sustained attention. Exclusivist claims tend to be accompanied by vague references to "emergency" and to the president's political accountability. Yet these references often confound rather than illuminate. The TSP's defenders insisted, for example, that the program's opponents were free to retaliate politically against the TSP and the president. They argued as well that the program, even if conducted in violation of statutory restrictions, was constitutionally warranted in light of a national security emergency. Yet pleas of emergency and assurances of accountability fly in the face of the fact that the program existed, and was shrouded in secrecy, for more than four years before it was revealed by the *New York Times*. Nonetheless, arguments that the TSP might have been constitutionally justified continue to have remarkable political resonance.[33]

Supremacists should be challenged to define what limits, if any, exclusivity contains. For example, to be constitutionally legitimate, must exclusivist actions be temporally limited? Must they be transparent? If led to confront these questions, some supremacists may identify limiting principles that could provide guidance for courts and administrations, and that might also impact public understandings of exclusivity. Other supremacists may argue that no constitutional limits exist, as exclusivity by definition hinges on subjective presidential judgments. The latter response, too, would be helpful in illuminating the expansiveness of some supremacist arguments.

Clarifying Unity's Boundaries

ARE INFORMATION-GATHERING, REPORTING, AND DISCLOSURE EXECUTIVE TASKS?   It is unclear whether unity proponents consider information-gathering, reporting, and disclosure—and jobs that consist solely of such activities—executive in nature. On the one hand, the Supreme Court, in a decision generally praised by unity supporters, implied that a pure research position is not executive in nature.[34] And at least one unity supporter has suggested that information dissemination may not be executive in nature, although he does not reach a firm conclusion on that point.[35] On the other hand, as we saw in chapters 7 and 8, presidential administrations of both parties have made unity-based claims to the effect that inspectors general must serve at the president's pleasure, despite their purely investigative and reporting functions. Administrations also regularly claim that unity demands White House control over any reports or testimony disseminated from within the executive branch to the public or Congress. Some unitary executive theorists cite these administration views with apparent approval.[36]

The status of information gathering, reporting, and disclosure warrant careful consideration. There is a strong argument to be made that these activities are not executive in nature, as they do not amount to making or carrying out policy. They are, however, crucial tools by which the public and the other branches can meaningfully judge law execution. White House control of these tools threatens to distort the very factual picture against which such judgments are made. Should unity proponents clarify that unity does not demand presidential control over mere investigating and reporting, or over positions that are solely investigative or reportorial in nature, this would go some way toward alleviating the tension between unity and substantive accountability. Alternatively, should proponents reach the opposite conclusion, their doing so explicitly would, at least, cast the tension in sharper relief.

UNITY AND RULEMAKING.   Unity proponents take the position that the president must have the power directly to make any and all executive decisions, including those statutorily delegated to others. While this view is simple conceptually, important uncertainties remain as to practical implementation. We have already seen some question, for example, as to whether unity entitles the president to redelegate power to an EOP office rather than to himself.

A particularly confounding question is how to reconcile unitary presidential control with statutory schemes that not only specify a nonpresidential decision maker, but that require that person to follow detailed procedures and subject their decision to judicial review. Under the Administrative Procedure Act and related case law, for example, rules issued by agencies must be accompanied by certain findings, must follow a public "notice and comment" period, and may be reviewed judicially for their basic soundness.[37] One possible interpretation of unity is that it demands a separate layer of presidential control on top of any statutorily mandated procedures. That is, it enables the president to step in and make a decision by fiat after or in lieu of any statutorily mandated procedures and "final" agency decisions. Alternatively, perhaps unity allows the president to make the final decision but requires him to abide by all other statutory constraints. Under this second approach, the president presumably would have to prepare any statutorily required records and statements or at least formally adopt those of the agency as his own.

The matter of judicial review adds another layer of complication. If unity demands presidential control by fiat, then what role, if any, is there for statutorily mandated judicial review of decisions' procedural and substantive fitness? On the other hand, if unity is compatible with the requirement that the president follow any statutorily mandated procedures and substantive requirements, then perhaps unity permits judicial review of the same. If the latter is the case, additional factors, including executive privilege, may still make presidential performance effectively unreviewable.

Clarification in this area would shed light on the line between unity and supremacy. As we have seen, some unity proponents distance themselves from supremacy. They explain that unity demands only that the president control the execution of all federal statutes; it does not license him to circumvent those statutes. Yet to prevent control from turning into statutory circumvention, it is necessary to ensure that even complicated procedural requirements dictated by statute be followed by the president when he purports to execute that statute. It also is necessary to ensure that he be subject to any judicial review dictated by statute. Indeed, scholars invested in unity's perceived legitimacy have an interest in challenging presidential circumvention of statutory requirements, even where the circumvention itself is supremacy-based, so long as the president's claimed right to execute the statute in the first place is grounded in unity. Ensuring that presidents adhere to statutory rulemaking requirements also can minimize the extent to which unity undermines substantive accountability.

Reclaiming Accountability

Reclaiming accountability is no single act. From internal challenges or external leaks by civil servants, to journalistic inquiries and reports, to congressional oversight, to FOIA requests, accountability is claimed and re-claimed every day by countless actors in myriad ways. This chapter has suggested some concrete ways in which people from a wide variety of backgrounds can participate in the ongoing project of claiming and re-claiming accountability. More broadly, this book has sought to illuminate the ways in which presidentialist arguments threaten substantive account-ability, to explain why those arguments are misguided, and to offer alter-native constitutional analyses that themselves can serve as legal tools in the never-ending fight for substantive accountability. Most fundamentally, this book has endeavored to explain how deeply the U.S. constitutional system depends on and assumes the existence of substantive accountabil-ity. Like liberty itself, the promise of the U.S. Constitution demands the "eternal vigilance" of the people.[38] Substantive accountability, in its multi-tudinous, ever-evolving manifestations, is an indispensable vehicle of that vigilance.

Notes

Chapter One

1. Clinton v. Jones, 520 U.S. 681, 682 (1997).

2. John Stuart Mill, *Of the Liberty of Thought and Discussion, in* THE PHILOSOPHY OF JOHN STUART MILL 225 (Marshall Cohen ed., Modern Library 1961).

3. Edward Rubin, *The Myth of Accountability and the Anti-Administrative Impulse,* 103 MICH. L. REV. 2073, 2119 (2005).

4. For further discussion on these points, see, for example, Heidi Kitrosser, *It Came from Beneath the Twilight Zone: Wiretapping and Article II Imperialism,* 88 TEX. L. REV. 1401, 1414–18 (2010); Neal Devins, *Presidential Unilateralism and Political Polarization: Why Today's Congress Lacks the Will and the Way to Stop Presidential Initiatives,* 45 WILLAMETTE L. REV. 395, 399 (2009); William P. Marshall, *Eleven Reasons Why Presidential Power Inevitably Expands and Why It Matters,* 88 B.U. L. REV. 505, 511–18 (2008); Mark Tushnet, *Controlling Executive Power in the War on Terrorism,* 118 HARV. L. REV. 2673, 2677 (2005); Terry M. Moe & William G. Howell, *Unilateral Action and Presidential Power: A Theory,* 29 PRES. STUD. Q. 850, 855–56, 860–62, 866–70 (1999).

5. *See generally* ARTHUR M. SCHLESINGER JR., THE IMPERIAL PRESIDENCY (1973). For more recent takes on the imperial presidency, *See generally,* for example, GARY WILLS, BOMB POWER: THE MODERN PRESIDENCY AND THE NATIONAL SECURITY STATE (2010); GENE HEALY, THE CULT OF THE PRESIDENCY (2008); CHARLIE SAVAGE, TAKEOVER: THE RETURN OF THE IMPERIAL PRESIDENCY (2007).

6. For an overview of the classification system and its history, see Heidi Kitrosser, *Classified Information Leaks and Free Speech,* 2008 U. ILL. L. REV. 881, 890–93.

7. Chapter 5 discusses the delegation of classification authority, and chapter 8 discusses delegation within the White House, the Executive Office of the President, and the broader administrative state.

8. Dahlia Lithwick, *Alberto Gonzales, Zen Master*, SLATE (May 10, 2007), http://www.slate.com/articles/news_and_politics/jurisprudence/2007/05/alberto_gonzales_zen_master.html.

9. THEODORE DRAPER, A VERY THIN LINE: THE IRAN-CONTRA AFFAIRS 275–76 (1991).

10. The examples discussed in this paragraph are elaborated on, with citations, in chapters 5 and 8.

11. *See* JACK GOLDSMITH, THE TERROR PRESIDENCY 32, 96–97 (2007); Trevor Morrison, *Stare Decisis in the Office of Legal Counsel*, 110 COLUM. L. REV. 1448, 1451 (2010).

12. *See, e.g.,* GOLDSMITH, *supra* note 11, at 34–39; Trevor Morrison, *Constitutional Alarmism*, 124 HARV. L. REV. 1688, 1713–18, 1721 (2011); Morrison, *supra* note 11, at 1501–3, 1521; Marshall, *supra* note 4, at 511–14.

13. See, for example, discussion in chapter 2 of such outreach by Attorney General Meese during the Reagan administration.

14. *See* Morrison, *supra* note 11, at 1468–69, 1497–1503.

15. *See* SAVAGE, *supra* note 5, at 232–37; Christopher S. Kelley, *A Matter of Direction: The Reagan Administration, the Signing Statement, and the 1986 Westlaw Decision*, 16 WM. & MARY BILL RTS. J. 283, 299–304 (2007).

16. *See* Heidi Kitrosser, *National Security and the Article II Shell Game*, 26 CONST. COMM. 483, 484, 499–500, 506–7 (2010); *id.* at 500 n.59 (citing John Hart Ely, *The American War in Indochina, Part I: The (Troubled) Constitutionality of the War They Told Us About*, 42 STAN. L. REV. 877, 878, 907 (1990)).

17. *See, e.g.,* THE FEDERALIST NO. 51, at 317–20 (James Madison) (Signet Classic 2003); Jack M. Balkin & Sanford Levinson, *The Processes of Constitutional Change: From Partisan Entrenchment to the National Surveillance State*, 75 FORDHAM L. REV. 489, 519 (2006).

18. *See* Daryl J. Levinson & Richard H. Pildes, *Separation of Parties, Not Powers*, 119 HARV. L. REV. 2311, 2313–14, 2323, 2344 (2006); *See also, e.g.,* Marshall, *supra* note 4, at 518–19; Neil Devins, *Presidential Unilateralism and Political Polarization: Why Today's Congress Lacks the Will and the Way to Stop Presidential Initiatives*, 45 WILLAMETTE L. REV. 395, 409 (2009); Balkin & Levinson, *supra* note 17, at 520; Tushnet, *supra* note 4, at 2678–79.

19. *See* Dana Milbank, *Bush's Fumbles Spur New Talk of Oversight on Hill*, WASH. POST, Dec. 18, 2005, at A7.

20. Cheney v. U.S. Dist. Ct., 542 U.S. 367, 381–91 (2004).

21. See chapter 5 for elaboration on the state secrets doctrine.

22. *See, e.g.,* HEALY, *supra* note 5, at 216; Balkin & Levinson, *supra* note 17, at 519, 528–29.

23. *See* SCHLESINGER, *supra* note 5, at 169. For similar descriptions of this mindset and its manifestations, see, for example, WILLS, *supra* note 5, at 45–53; HEALY, *supra* note 5, at 216; Alice Ristroph, *Professors Strangelove*, 11 GREEN BAG 2d 245,

246–47, 250–51, 253–54, 257–58 (2008). *Cf.* FORREST MCDONALD, THE AMERICAN PRESIDENCY 36–37 (1994) (referring to "an almost mystical quality that inheres in kingship and to some extent in any chief executive office.").

24. For references to these porous boundaries, see, for example, WILLS, *supra* note 5, at 3, 53; Balkin & Levinson, *supra* note 17, at 528.

25. THE FEDERALIST NO. 70, at 422–23 (Alexander Hamilton) (Clinton Rossiter ed., 2003).

26. This line of argument is detailed further in chapter 4.

27. *See* sources cited *supra* note 5 (detailing factors contributing to presidential imperialism); *See also, e.g.,* BARBARA HINCKLEY, THE SYMBOLIC PRESIDENCY (1990) (describing symbolism's role in heightening public expectations of and support for presidential power); JEFFREY K. TULIS, THE RHETORICAL PRESIDENCY (1987) (citing "rhetorical leadership" as the essential tool of the modern presidency); THEODORE J. LOWI, THE PERSONAL PRESIDENT (1985) (explaining the rise of what Lowi calls a "plesbicitary republic with a personal presidency").

28. For a recent, in-depth discussion of such arguments, *See generally* Curtis A. Bradley & Trevor W. Morrison, *Historical Gloss and the Separation of Powers,* 126 HARV. L. REV. 411 (2012).

29. For further discussion and evaluation of evolving history arguments, see chapters 2 and 4.

30. William P. Marshall, *Eleven Reasons Why Presidential Power Inevitably Expands and Why It Matters,* 88 B.U. L. REV. 505, 510–11 (2008) (emphasis added).

31. Josh Gerstein & Amie Parnes, *Obama: Truth Commission Is a Mistake,* POLITICO (Apr. 23, 2009), http://www.politico.com/news/stories/0409/21654.html.

32. *See* Kitrosser, *supra* note 16, at 517–18, 499 n.58 and accompanying text, 501 n.60 and accompanying text.

33. *See id.* at 506–7.

34. *See, e.g.,* Kitrosser, *supra* note 4, at 1401–2 (describing exclusivist reasoning); David J. Barron & Martin S. Lederman, *The Commander in Chief at the Lowest Ebb — Framing the Problem, Doctrine, and Original Understanding,* 121 HARV. L. REV. 689, 694 (2008) [hereinafter Barron & Lederman I] (describing exclusivist reasoning); David J. Barron & Martin S. Lederman, *The Commander in Chief at the Lowest Ebb — A Constitutional History,* 121 HARV. L. REV. 941, 1027 (2008) [hereinafter Barron & Lederman II] (invoking the term "presidential exclusivity" to describe this school of thought).

35. For further discussion on the accompanying paragraph's points, see chapters 4 and 5.

36. These points are discussed further in chapters 4 and 5.

37. Unitary executive theory and its foundations are detailed further in chapter 7.

38. Chapter 8 elaborates on unity's practical manifestations.

39. JOHN YOO, WAR BY OTHER MEANS 125 (2006).

40. *Id.*

41. *See generally* ERIC A. POSNER & ADRIAN VERMEULE, THE EXECUTIVE UNBOUND (2010).

42. *See, e.g.,* chapter 3, notes 21 & 47 and accompanying text (discussing and citing sources regarding such intertwined political and legal checks, or what Seth Kreimer labels "the ecology of transparency"); chapter 9, notes 13–18 and accompanying text (same).

43. THE FEDERALIST NO. 76, at 456 (Alexander Hamilton) (Clinton Rossiter ed., 2003).

44. *See supra* note 2, *quoting* John Stuart Mill, *Of the Liberty of Thought and Discussion, in* THE PHILOSOPHY OF JOHN STUART MILL 225 (Marshall Cohen ed., Modern Library 1961).

45. Edward Rubin, *The Myth of Accountability and the Anti-Administrative Impulse*, 103 MICH. L. REV. 2073, 2119 (2005).

46. U.S. CONST. art. I, § 8, cl. 18.

Chapter Two

1. Although largely beyond this book's scope, it is worth noting an important scholarly debate over whether the conventional premise of "judicial supremacy" in fact is warranted as a historical, textual, or normative matter. *See generally, e.g.,* LARRY D. KRAMER, THE PEOPLE THEMSELVES (2004); Mark Tushnet, *Non-Judicial Review*, 40 HARV. J. LEGIS. 453 (2003); Michael Stokes Paulsen, *The Most Dangerous Branch: Executive Power to Say What the Law Is*, 83 GEO. L.J. 217 (1994).

2. *See, e.g.,* KRAMER, *supra* note 1, at 83; Michael P. Riccards, *The Presidency and the Ratification Controversy*, 7 PRES. STUD. Q. 37, 38 (1977).

3. PAULINE MAIER, RATIFICATION ix (2010).

4. KRAMER, *supra* note 1, at 49, 108–14.

5. *Id.* For a discussion of early and mid-nineteenth-century efforts to channel constitutional debate through national political parties, *See id.* at 194–203.

6. *id.* at 229.

7. *See* Linda Greenhouse, *On the Wrong Side of 5 to 4, Liberals Talk Tactics*, N.Y. TIMES, July 8, 2007, at WK3.

8. *Id.*

9. *See, e.g.,* Reva B. Siegel, *Constitutional Culture, Social Movement Conflict and Constitutional Change: The Case of the De Facto ERA*, 94 CAL. L. REV. 1323, 1324–26 (2006).

10. JACK M. BALKIN, CONSTITUTIONAL REDEMPTION: POLITICAL FAITH IN AN UNJUST WORLD 184 (2011).

11. Thomas B. Colby, *The Sacrifice of the New Originalism*, 99 GEO. L.J. 713,

716 (2011); *See also, e.g.,* Steven M. Teles, *Transformative Bureaucracy: Reagan's Lawyers and the Dynamics of Political Investment,* 23 STUD. AM. POL. DEV. 61, 76 (2009); Robert Post & Reva Siegel, *Originalism as a Political Practice: The Right's Living Constitution,* 75 FORDHAM L. REV. 545, 552–57 (2006); Keith Whittington, *The New Originalism,* 2 GEO. L. & PUB. POL'Y 599, 599–601 (2004).

12. Colby, *supra* note 11, at 716 (quoting *Nominations of William H. Rehnquist and Lewis F. Powell Jr.: Hearings Before the S. Comm. on the Judiciary,* 92d Cong. 19 (1971) (question from Sen. John L. McClellan to William H. Rehnquist)).

13. Robert H. Bork, *Neutral Principles and Some First Amendment* Problems, 47 IND. L.J. 1, 1–4 (1971) (contrasting neutral principles–based approach with Warren Court activism); *See also id.* at 13 (noting that while the "words [of the Equal Protection Clause] are general surely that would not permit us to escape the framers' intent [on how to apply the clause] if it were clear.").

14. Teles, *supra* note 11, at 63.

15. *id.* at 63, 67–82.

16. Attorney General Edwin Meese III, Address before the American Bar Association, Washington, D.C. (July 9, 1985), *available at* http://www.fed-soc .org/resources/page/print/the-great-debate-attorney-general-ed-meese-iii-july -9-1985; *See also* Lawrence B. Solum, *Semantic Originalism* 13 (Ill. Public L. Research, Paper No. 07-24, Nov. 22, 2008), *available at* http://papers.ssrn.com /abstract=1120244 (observing that the ABA speech "put originalism on the political agenda"); Teles, *supra* note 11, at 75–78 (explaining that the department's "originalism project" started as a series of speeches, of which the ABA speech was the first).

17. Edwin Meese, *Toward a Jurisprudence of Original Intent,* 11 HARV. J.L. PUB. POL'Y 5, 5 (1987).

18. *id.* at 6; *See also* Colby, *supra* note 11, at 717 ("It would be difficult to overstate the extent to which the Old Originalism was characterized by its own proponents as a theory that could constrain judges and preclude them from reading their own policy preferences . . . into the Constitution.").

19. I discuss determinism and its relationship to originalism in depth in Heidi Kitrosser, Interpretive Modesty (article draft) (on file with author).

20. Meese, *supra* note 16 (emphasis added).

21. Meese, *supra* note 17, at 10.

22. Bork, *supra* note 13, at 7.

23. Vasan Kesavan & Michael Stokes Paulsen, *The Interpretive Force of the Constitution's Secret Drafting History,* 91 GEO. L.J. 1113, 1131 (2003).

24. *See, e.g.,* RANDY E. BARNETT, RESTORING THE LOST CONSTITUTION 92 (Kindle edition) ("Whereas 'original intent' originalism seeks the intentions or will of the lawmakers or ratifiers, 'original meaning' originalism seeks the public or objective meaning that a reasonable listener would place on the words used in the constitutional provision at the time of its enactment"); Gary Lawson & Guy Seid-

man, *The Jeffersonian Treaty Clause*, 2006 U. ILL. L. REV. 1, 7 ("original meaning represents hypothetical mental states of a legally constructed reasonable person rather than actual mental states held by concrete historical persons").

25. *See, e.g.*, Colby, *supra* note 11, at 719–26.

26. *See infra* notes 82–83.

27. *See* Kitrosser, *supra* note 19.

28. *See, e.g.*, Mitchell N. Berman, *Originalism Is Bunk*, 84 N.Y.U. L. REV. 1, 8 (2009) (citing originalism's "tendency to be deployed in the public square—on the campaign trail, on talk radio, in Senate confirmation hearings, even in Supreme Court opinions—to bolster the popular fable that constitutional adjudication can be practiced in something close to an objective and mechanical fashion.").

29. Rush Limbaugh, *Limbaugh Fundamentals: What Is Originalism?*, LIM-BAUGH LETTER (Dec. 5, 2005) (on file with author) (quoting a February 2001 speech by Justice Thomas to the American Enterprise Institute).

30. Jamal Greene, *Selling Originalism*, 97 GEO. L.J. 657, 672–73 (2009).

31. Jamal Greene, *On the Origins of Originalism*, 88 TEX. L. REV. 1, 11 (2009) (emphasis added).

32. Jamal Greene, Nathaniel Persily & Stephen Ansolabehere, *Profiling Originalism*, 111 COLUM. L. REV. 356, 359, 371, 385–411 (2011).

33. *See id.* at 387–91.

34. *See id.* at 401. The authors also include libertarianism and comfort with inequality in the cultural values bundle, and suggest similar ties between these views and an originalism steeped in original expected applications. *Id.* at 401–2.

35. *See id.* at 392.

36. *See id.* at 391–98.

37. *id.* at 416.

38. Antonin Scalia, *God's Justice and Ours*, FIRST THINGS (May 2002), http://www.firstthings.com/article/2007/01/gods-justice-and-ours.

39. Dahlia Lithwick, *Scaliapalooza*, SLATE (Oct. 30, 2003), http://www.slate.com/id/2090532/.

40. *See supra* note 29 and accompanying text.

41. *See* Thomas B. Colby & Peter J. Smith, *Living Originalism*, 59 DUKE L.J. 239, 304 (2009) (quoting Lewis v. Casey, 518 U.S. 343, 367 (1996) (Thomas, J., concurring)).

42. *See, e.g.*, JULIAN E. ZELIZER, ARSENAL OF DEMOCRACY 21–31, 52–59 (2010); Stephen Skowronek, *The Conservative Insurgency and Presidential Power: A Developmental Perspective on the Unitary Executive*, 122 HARV. L. REV. 2070, 2075, 2088–92 (2009); Jeffrey Hart, *The Presidency: Shifting Conservative Perspectives?*, NAT'L REV., Nov. 22, 1974, at 1351.

43. *See, e.g.*, Skowronek, *supra* note 42, at 2096–2100; Julian E. Zelizer, *The Conservative Embrace of Presidential Power*, 88 B.U. L. REV. 499, 500 (2008); Hart, *supra* note 42.

44. *See, e.g.,* Hart, *supra* note 42, at 1353.

45. *See, e.g.,* ZELIZER, *supra* note 42, at 5–7, 63–67, 74, 80.

46. *See The Need for a National Budget*, 62d Cong. 1–8, 140 (1912) (message from President William Howard Taft transmitting the Report of Commission on Economy & Efficiency on the subject of the need for a national budget); *See also* PERI ARNOLD, MAKING THE MANAGERIAL PRESIDENCY 32–51 (2d ed. 1988).

47. *See, e.g.,* FORREST MCDONALD, THE AMERICAN PRESIDENCY 338–39 (1994); Peter L. Strauss, *Overseer, or "The Decider"? The President in Administrative Law*, 75 GEO. WASH. L. REV. 696, 701–2, 719–20 (2007); Elena Kagan, *Presidential Administration*, 114 HARV. L. REV. 2245, 2275–82 (2001).

48. *See, e.g.,* STEVEN G. CALABRESI & CHRISTOPHER S. YOO, THE UNITARY EXECUTIVE 5, 99–101, 176 (2008).

49. *Id.* at 13; *See also* CHARLES FRIED, ORDER AND LAW (1991) (drawing from his experience as solicitor general during the Reagan administration, Fried recalls that "[t]he Reagan years were distinguished by the fact that [unitary executive theory] was made the subject of legal, rather than simply political, dispute.").

50. Statute Limiting the President's Authority to Supervise the Dir. of the Cent. for Disease Control in the Distribution of an AIDS Pamphlet, 12 Op. O.L.C. 47, 49 (1988).

51. Edwin Meese III, *Toward Increased Government Accountability*, Speech to Fed. Bar Ass'n, 32 FED. B. NEWS & J. 406, 408 (1985).

52. For example, two books from the late 1980s—one published by the Heritage Foundation in 1988 with a foreword penned by then representative Newt Gingrich, the other published by the American Enterprise Institute (AEI) in 1989 with a foreword by Robert Bork—argued that the presidency had become constrained in a way antithetical to founding intentions. The AEI book was entitled *The Fettered Presidency*, and the Heritage Foundation book was entitled *The Imperial Congress*. Among other topics, each book contained essays arguing that the founders had intended to create a unitary executive branch and that the United States had strayed far from that goal. *See generally* THE FETTERED PRESIDENCY: LEGAL CONSTRAINTS ON THE EXECUTIVE BRANCH (L. Gordon Crovitz & Jeremy A. Rabkin eds., 1989); THE IMPERIAL CONGRESS: CRISIS IN THE SEPARATION OF POWERS (Gordon S. Jones & John A. Marini eds., 1988).

53. *See, e.g.,* GARRY WILLS, BOMB POWER: THE MODERN PRESIDENCY AND THE NATIONAL SECURITY STATE 1–4, 57–59, 98–102, 237–40 (2010); Heidi Kitrosser, *Classified Information Leaks and Free Speech*, 2008 U. ILL. L. REV. 881, 890–93; Richard J. Barnet, *The Ideology of the National Security State*, 26 MASS. REV. 483, 485–88 (1985).

54. *See generally* sources cited *infra* note 53. *See also, e.g.,* Heidi Kitrosser, *It Came from Beneath the Twilight Zone: Wiretapping and Article II Imperialism*, 88 TEX. L. REV. 1401, 1410–11 (2010) (citing examples of fettered presidency narrative); Heidi Kitrosser, *Supremely Opaque? Accountability, Transparency, and Pres-*

idential Supremacy, 5 St. Thomas J.L. & Pub. Pol'y 62, 72 (2011) (discussing narrative of a post-Vietnam fettered presidency).

55. Barton Gellman, Angler: The Cheney Vice Presidency 100–101 (2008).

56. Minority Report, *in* Report of the Congressional Committees Investigating the Iran-Contra Affair, H.R. Rep. No. 100-433, S. Rep. No. 100-216, at 460 (1987).

57. *See* Frederick A. O. Schwarz Jr. & Aziz Z. Huq, Unchecked and Unbalanced: Presidential Power in a Time of Terror 154–55, 159–60, 200 (2007).

58. For more elaboration on this aspect of the Minority Report, see Kitrosser, *Supremely Opaque?*, *supra* note 54, at 73–74. *See also, e.g.,* Mariah Zeisberg, War Powers 191–92 (Kindle version) (discussing Oliver North's introduction of presidentialism to the Iran-Contra hearings, foreshadowing its prominence in the Minority Report).

59. *See, e.g.,* Gary J. Schmitt & Abram N. Shulsky, *The Theory and Practice of Separation of Powers: The Case of Covert Action,* in The Fettered Presidency, *supra* note 52, at 59: Lawrence J. Block & David B. Rivkin Jr., *The Battle to Control the Conduct of Foreign Intelligence and Covert Operations: The Ultra-Whig Counterrevolution Revisited,* 12 Harv. J.L. & Pub. Pol'y 303 (1989); Robert F. Turner, *The Constitution and the Iran-Contra Affair: Was Congress the Real Lawbreaker?,* 11 Hous. J. Int'l L. 83 (1988–89).

60. *See generally* The Fettered Presidency, *supra* note 52. *See also, e.g.,* The Imperial Congress, *supra* note 52; sources cited *supra* note 54.

61. *Compare* Edwin Meese III, *Constitutional Fidelity and Foreign Affairs,* 43 U. Miami L. Rev. 223 (1988) (citing original conceptions of executive power and founding emphases on presidential energy to support aspects of supremacy), *with* Memorandum from Stephen J. Markman, Assistant Attorney General, Office of Legal Policy, to Edwin Meese III, Attorney General, on Separation of Powers, at 2–3, 16–20, 33–34 (Apr. 30, 1986) (on file with author) (citing historical and textual points supportive of supremacy while cautioning against overreading the president's national security powers).

62. The constitutional politics of presidentialism call into question Posner and Vermeule's conclusion that elite opinion checks presidential power and that this is an adequate substitute for legal checks. *See generally* Eric A. Posner & Adrian Vermeule, The Executive Unbound (2010). As presidentialism's intellectual history demonstrates, elite opinion also can bolster presidential power and can do so partly through constitutional argument.

63. D.C. v. Heller, 554 U.S. 570, 576–77 (2008).

64. Quoted in Richard S. Kay, *Original Intention and Public Meaning in Constitutional Interpretation,* 103 Nw. U. L. Rev. 703, 722 (2009). Kay contrasts this characterization with Lawson and Seidman's own earlier, less elaborate conception of the original reader. *Id.*

65. Vasan Kesavan & Michael Stokes Paulsen, *The Interpretive Force of the Constitution's Secret Drafting History,* 91 Geo. L.J 1113, 1132 (2003).

66. Barnett, *supra* note 24, at 91.

67. *See, e.g.,* Block & Rivkin, *supra* note 59, at 307–13, 323–24; Charles J. Cooper, Orrin Hatch, Eugene V. Rostow & Michael Tigar, *Roundtable: What the Constitution Means by Executive Power,* 43 U. Miami L. Rev. 165, 166–68, 177 (1988–89) (comments of Charles J. Cooper). *Compare, e.g.,* Turner, *supra* note 59, at 92–94 (examining "Intent of the Founding Fathers") *with* Robert F. Turner, *Book Review: An Insider's Look at the War on Terrorism,* 93 Cornell L. Rev. 471, 474 (2008) (referring to the "original understanding of 'executive power'").

68. *Compare, e.g.,* John Yoo, Crisis and Command viii, xiv, 1, 47 (2010) (referring to intent and understandings of the framers), *with* John C. Yoo, *War and the Constitutional Text,* 69 U. Chi. L. Rev. 1639, 1660 (2002) (agreeing that "we should interpret the Constitution based on the meaning of its words as understood by its ratifiers"), *and* Ingrid Wuerth, *An Originalism for Foreign Affairs?,* 53 St. Louis U. L.J. 5, 5 n.2 (2008) (categorizing work of John Yoo and others as scholarship that "makes claims about the substance of the Constitution's original meaning"). *See also* Janet Cooper Alexander, *John Yoo's War Powers: The Law Review and the World,* 100 Cal. L. Rev. 331, 339 (2012) (citing Yoo's inconsistency with respect to the "meaning of [original] 'meaning'"). *Compare also, e.g.,* Michael S. Paulsen, *Youngstown Goes to War,* 19 Const. Comm. 215, 238 (2002) (describing supremacist version of the Vesting Clause thesis as following from how the term "executive power" was "understood at the time" of the founding), *with* Michael S. Paulsen, *Does the Constitution Prescribe Rules for Its Own Interpretation?,* 103 Nw. U. L. Rev. 857, 858 (2009) (describing appropriate interpretive inquiry as "[t]he search . . . for the objective, original meaning of the [Constitution's] language.").

69. *See infra* chapter 4.

70. *id.* For simplicity's sake, this book groups together supremacist arguments that effectively use the same reasoning as one another, regardless of whether that reasoning is couched in terms of framers' or ratifiers' intent or objective original meaning. And in describing such arguments, this book uses the language of original public or "objective" meaning as a default. For example, originalist supremacist arguments about the content of "executive power" generally will be described as arguments about the term's "original meaning."

71. This example is discussed in greater detail, with citations, in chapter 4.

72. The points made in this and the previous paragraph are elaborated on, with citations, in subsequent chapters.

73. *See generally* Curtis A. Bradley & Trevor W. Morrison, *Historical Gloss and the Separation of Powers,* 126 Harv. L. Rev. 411 (2012).

74. *See id.* at 453 (explaining that unitary executive theorists deem unity mandated by constitutional text, structure, and history, and that they examine evolving history only to establish that presidents have not acquiesced in disunity to such an extent as to undermine this constitutional mandate).

75. *See infra* chapter 4 at subsection entitled "Supremacist Reasoning from Constitutional Principles and Evolving History"; *See also* Kitrosser, *Twilight Zone, supra* note 54, at 1408–9.

76. *See infra* chapter 4 at subsection entitled "Supremacist Reasoning from Constitutional Principles and Evolving History"; *See also* Bradley & Morrison, *supra* note 73, at 414, 432–33; Kitrosser, *Twilight Zone, supra* note 54, at 1409–11.

77. *See* Bradley & Morrison, *supra* note 73, at 413 n.1 (citing Youngstown Sheet & Tube Co. v. Sawyer, 343 U.S. 579, 610–11 (1952) (Frankfurter, J., concurring)).

78. *See* Kitrosser, *Twilight Zone, supra* note 54, at 1411–21.

79. *See* Bradley & Morrison, *supra* note 73, at 414–15, 438–41; Kitrosser, *Twilight Zone, supra* note 54, at 1411, 1421–26, 1434.

80. Lawrence B. Solum, *Originalism and Constitutional Construction*, 82 FORDHAM L. REV. 453, 456 (2013).

81. Greene, *supra* note 31, at 8–9.

82. *See, e.g.,* Daniel A. Farber, *The Originalism Debate: A Guide for the Perplexed,* 49 OHIO ST. L.J. 1085, 1089, 1105 (1989); *cf.* Paul Brest, The Misconceived Quest for Original Understanding, 60 B.U. L. REV. 204, 221 (1980) ("When the interpreter engages in . . . [originalist] projection, she is in a fantasy world more of her own than of the adopters' making").

83. *See, e.g.,* ANTONIN SCALIA, A MATTER OF INTERPRETATION 17 (1997) ("[I]t is simply incompatible with democratic government . . . to have the meaning of a law determined by what the lawgiver meant, rather than by what the lawgiver promulgated."); ROBERT H. BORK, THE TEMPTING OF AMERICA 143–44 (Kindle version) (embracing "public meaning" originalism rather than original intent in part because "law is a public act" whereas intentions can be secretive); *cf.* Vasan Kesavan & Michael Stokes Paulsen, *The Interpretive Force of the Constitution's Secret Drafting History,* 91 GEO. L.J. 1113, 1115–20 (2003) (citing conventional wariness of reliance on Constitution's secret drafting history but arguing that that history can be used as a legitimate tool in seeking out objective meaning).

84. *See, e.g.,* BARNETT, *supra* note 24, at 91–92; Solum, *supra* note 80, at 459, 464–66.

85. *See infra* text accompanying notes 63–66 (citing malleability of originalism's hypothetical original reader); *See also, e.g.,* Jack N. Rakove, *Joe the Ploughman Reads the Constitution, or, the Poverty of Public Meaning Originalism,* 48 SAN DIEGO L. REV. 575, 586 (2011) (criticizing as intrinsically arbitrary the creation and use of hypothetical founding-era interpreters); Saul Cornell, *The People's Constitution vs. The Lawyer's Constitution: Popular Constitutionalism and the Original Debate Over Originalism,* 23 YALE J.L. & HUMAN. 295, 296, 298–301, 334–36 (2011) (criticizing new originalists on grounds including their assuming a founding-era consensus on interpretive methodologies and interpretive results, their misunderstanding of the nature of founding-era dictionaries, and the manipulability of their approach); Kay, *supra* note 64, at 722–23 (citing malleability of

hypothetical original reader); *id.* at 725 ("relying on an artificial concept instead of an actual historical event inevitably enlarges the field of . . . imaginative reconstructions"); Larry Alexander, *Simple-Minded Originalism* (San Diego Legal Studies, Paper No. 08-067, Aug. 18, 2008), *available at* http://ssrn.com/abstract=1235722 (also citing malleability of hypothetical original reader).

86. *See, e.g.,* Cornell, *supra* note 85, at 299–301 ("Ignoring the real voices of eighteenth century Americans . . . enables some New Originalists to side step dealing with the actual beliefs of Americans and substitute the beliefs of a fictive reader, effectively turning constitutional interpretation into an act of historical ventriloquism."); Kay, *supra* note 64, at 723 (making roughly the same point).

87. *See* Rakove, *supra* note 85, at 588–91 (explaining that the Constitution-making process exemplifies "how political concepts . . . acquire whatever meaning they may obtain through processes of collective deliberation that themselves subject prior understandings of terms to further refinement," and that this is true of "the key word constitution itself," which cannot adequately be defined "independently of the political discussions and developments that took place after 1765").

88. *See, e.g.,* Rakove, *supra* note 85, at 588–93; Cornell, *supra* note 85, at 296, 301; Saul Cornell, *Originalism on Trial: The Use and Abuse of Law Office History in* District of Columbia v. Heller, 69 Ohio St. L.J. 625, 631 (2008); Gordon S. Wood, *The Fundamentalists and the Constitution,* N.Y. Rev. Bks., Feb. 18, 1988 (see especially pt. 4).

89. For a more elaborate discussion of my approach to constitutional interpretation, see Heidi Kitrosser, Interpretive Modesty (article draft) (on file with author). There, I explain that where more than one original meaning can plausibly be supported by the evidence assessed through new and old originalist approaches, interpreters should deem only the thinnest of the meanings locked in by constitutional text. The thinnest meaning is the one that leaves most room to be built upon, or thickened, through factors beyond linguistic meaning. These factors include normative considerations and, most centrally, the constitutional principles underlying the relevant text. Choosing the thinnest interpretation in the first instance (that is, as a matter of identifying the "correct" linguistic meaning) leaves room for thicker meanings to prevail when these additional factors are considered. In other words, the thicker meaning still may prevail in the "construction" phase if not in the "interpretation" phase, terms that are described in the next text paragraph and discussed at length in "Interpretive Modesty." In this book, for simplicity's sake, I gloss over the notion of an explicit preference for thin meanings, largely collapsing it into the notions that meanings on which there were no positive founding-era consensuses should be viewed very skeptically and that meanings must be formulated in light of relevant constitutional principles.

90. *See, e.g.,* Jack Balkin, Living Originalism 2–3 (2011); Solum, *supra* note 16, at 69; Whittington, *supra* note 11, at 611–12.

91. Balkin, *supra* note 90, at 3.

Chapter Three

1. *See, e.g.*, 1 THE RECORDS OF THE FEDERAL CONVENTION OF 1787, at 64–65 (Max Farrand ed., 1911) [hereinafter RECORDS, vol. 1] (quoted in Curtis A. Bradley & Martin S. Flaherty, *Executive Power Essentialism and Foreign Affairs*, 102 MICH. L. REV. 545, 593 (2004)); *See also infra* chapter 4, note 47 and accompanying text.

2. U.S. CONST. art. I, § 7, cl. 2.

3. *Id.* § 8.

4. For arguments that Congress has broad powers to control executive operations and procedures, including executive privilege claims, *See generally*, e.g., Saikrishna Bangalore Prakash, *A Critical Commentary on the Constitutionality of Executive Privilege*, 83 MINN. L. REV. 1143 (1999); William W. Van Alstyne, *The Role of Congress in Determining Incidental Powers of the President and of the Federal Courts: A Comment on the Horizontal Effect of the Sweeping Clause*, 40 LAW & CONTEMP. PROBS. 102 (1976).

5. THE FEDERALIST NO. 70, at 423 (Alexander Hamilton) (Clinton Rossiter ed., 1961) [hereinafter FEDERALIST NO. 70].

6. *Id.*

7. U.S. CONST., art. I, § 5, cl. 3.

8. *Id.* § 6, cl. 1.

9. DANIEL N. HOFFMAN, GOVERNMENTAL SECRECY AND THE FOUNDING FATHERS: A STUDY OF CONSTITUTIONAL CONTROLS 14 (1981).

10. *Id.* at 37.

11. James M. Landis, *Constitutional Limitations on the Congressional Power of Investigation*, 40 HARV. L. REV. 153, 159 (1926).

12. *See, e.g.*, Josh Chafetz, *Executive Branch Contempt of Congress*, 76 U. CHI. L. REV. 1083, 1116–19 (2009); Landis, *supra* note 11, at 162–64.

13. Chafetz, *supra* note 12, at 1126–27; *See also* Landis, *supra* note 11, at 165–67; C. S. Potts, *Power of Legislative Bodies to Punish for Contempt*, 74 U. PA. L. REV. 691, 708–13 (1926).

14. U.S. CONST. art. I, § 8, cl. 18.

15. *Id.* § 5, cl. 2.

16. I have introduced and discussed the concepts of "macro" and "micro" secrecy elsewhere. *See, e.g.*, Heidi Kitrosser, *"Macro-Transparency" as Structural Directive: A Look at the NSA Surveillance Controversy*, 91 MINN. L. REV. 1163 (2007).

17. *See, e.g.*, Doug Gross, *Digital Monkeys with Typewriters Recreate Shakespeare*, CNN.COM (Sept. 26, 2011) (citing infinite monkey theorem), http://www.cnn.com/2011/09/26/tech/web/monkeys-typewriters-shakespeare/.

18. U.S. CONST. art. II, § 2, cl. 2.

19. *Id.* art. I, § 2, cl. 5; art. I, § 3 cl. 6–7; art. II, § 4.

20. *Id.* art. I, § 6, cl. 1.

21. Seth Kreimer very aptly labels this cycle and its many component parts and players "the ecology of transparency." *See generally* Seth F. Kreimer, *The Freedom of Information Act and the Ecology of Transparency*, 10 U. PA. J. CONST. L. 1011 (2008).

22. FEDERALIST NO. 70, *supra* note 5, at 423.

23. *Id.* at 428.

24. *Id.* at 427.

25. 3 THE RECORDS OF THE FEDERAL CONVENTION OF 1787, at 347 (Max Farrand ed., 1911) [hereinafter RECORDS, vol. 3].

26. 5 THE DOCUMENTARY HISTORY OF THE RATIFICATION OF THE CONSTITUTION 738–39 (John P. Kaminski & Gaspare J. Saladino eds., 1998) [hereinafter DOCUMENTARY HISTORY, vol. 5].

27. 8 THE DOCUMENTARY HISTORY OF THE RATIFICATION OF THE CONSTITUTION 245 (John P. Kaminski & Gaspare J. Saladino eds., 1988) [hereinafter DOCUMENTARY HISTORY, vol. 8].

28. 2 THE DOCUMENTARY HISTORY OF THE RATIFICATION OF THE CONSTITUTION 141 (John P. Kaminski & Gaspare J. Saladino eds., 1976) [hereinafter DOCUMENTARY HISTORY, vol. 2].

29. DOCUMENTARY HISTORY, vol. 8, *supra* note 27, at 203.

30. 9 THE DOCUMENTARY HISTORY OF THE RATIFICATION OF THE CONSTITUTION 865 (John P. Kaminski, Gaspare J. Saladino eds., 1990) [hereinafter DOCUMENTARY HISTORY, vol. 9].

31. DOCUMENTARY HISTORY, vol. 2, *supra* note 28, at 495.

32. THE FEDERALIST NO. 66, at 404–5 (Alexander Hamilton) (Clinton Rossiter ed., 1961) [hereinafter FEDERALIST NO. 66].

33. GORDON S. WOOD, THE CREATION OF THE AMERICAN REPUBLIC 393, 407–9, 430–46 (1998); JACK N. RAKOVE, ORIGINAL MEANINGS 250–56 (1997); FORREST MCDONALD, THE AMERICAN PRESIDENCY 148–53 (1994).

34. WOOD, *supra* note 33, at 33–34, 135–37, 157–58, 437; RAKOVE, *supra* note 33, at 244–57; MCDONALD, *supra* note 33, at 12–66, 99, 104, 110–11, 124, 126, 157, 171–72; EDMUND S. MORGAN, THE BIRTH OF THE REPUBLIC 12, 53–54, 71–76 (1977).

35. MCDONALD, *supra* note 33, at 157.

36. FEDERALIST NO. 70, *supra* note 5, at 423.

37. In a recent book, Rahul Sagar observes that the founders supported both executive secrecy and executive accountability. He adds that while the founders had some ideas as to mechanisms that would mitigate tensions between these two goals—such as congressional inquiries—for the most part they were silent, even confused, as to how these competing values might be reconciled. RAHUL SAGAR, SECRETS AND LEAKS 16–30 (2013) (Kindle edition). Sagar is correct, certainly, that the founders supported both secrecy and openness and that they did not fully

resolve the obvious tensions between the two. Yet he reads too much into the historical evidence to the extent that he implicitly equates clear federalist support for presidential secret-keeping capacity with consensus support for a presidential legal prerogative to keep secrets. *See id.* To put the point in terms used throughout this book, there was no historical consensus sufficient to lock in legal secret-keeping prerogatives as a matter of original textual meaning. And in terms of constitutional principle, founding support for both secrecy and openness is most logically manifest in the principle of contained executive energy—including a contained, not unfettered, executive secret-keeping capacity.

38. *See, e.g.*, McDonald, *supra* note 33, at 173 (recounting arguments made by Madison and Gerry at the Constitutional Convention that the executive must be empowered to "repel sudden attacks").

39. John Locke, Two Treatises of Government 421–27 (Peter Laslett ed., Cambridge Univ. Press 1963) (1690); *See also* Benjamin A. Kleinerman, The Discretionary President: The Promise and Peril of Executive Power 67 (2009) (explaining Locke's view that if the executive exercises prerogative outside of "the standing laws for the public good," "a properly designed Constitution should seek that the 'Legislative' soon 'be Assembled to provide for it'").

40. *See, e.g.*, Oren Gross, *Chaos and Rules: Should Responses to Violent Crises Always Be Constitutional?*, 112 Yale L.J. 1011, 1099–1100, 1111–15 (2003); Lucius Wilmerding Jr., *The President and the Law*, 67 Pol. Sci. Q. 321, 321–24, 329–30 (1952).

41. *See* Jules Lobel, *Emergency Power and the Decline of Liberalism*, 98 Yale L.J. 1385, 1392–97 (1989); Wilmerding, *supra* note 40, at 323–29, 338.

42. See Kleinerman, *supra* note 39, at 9–10.

43. *See* examples cited in chapter 5.

44. *See* Heidi Kitrosser, *Secrecy and Separated Powers: Executive Privilege Revisited*, 92 Iowa L. Rev. 489, 493–94, 514–15 (2007). *See generally* David E. Pozen, *Deep Secrecy*, 62 Stan. L. Rev. 257 (2010) (elaborating on concepts of deep and shallow government secrets and their implications for law and policy).

45. Pozen, *supra* note 44, at 260–61, 266–68; Kitrosser, *supra* note 44, at 514–15.

46. U.S. Const. art. I, § 7, cl. 2.

47. *See* Senate Select Comm. on Presidential Campaign Activities v. Nixon, 498 F.2d 725, 726–29 (D.C. Cir. 1974); *See also, e.g.*, Jack Goldsmith, Power and Constraint 118–21 (2012) (citing examples of discoveries of executive branch secrets that led to further discoveries and so on); Kreimer, *supra* note 21, at 1030–51, 1056–59 (citing such examples as part of larger phenomenon of the "ecology of transparency").

48. This point parallels criticisms made of the Bush administration for grounding national security decisions in what it believed it had a legal right to do, rather than the decisions' policy wisdom. *See, e.g.*, Jack Goldsmith, The Terror Presidency: Law and Judgment Inside the Bush Administration 131 (2009)

("[T]he question 'What should we do?' so often collapsed into the question 'What can we lawfully do?'").

49. For a very good summary of the current state of affairs and its problems, see EMILY BERMAN, BRENNAN CTR. FOR JUSTICE, EXECUTIVE PRIVILEGE: A LEGISLATIVE REMEDY 16–25 (2009).

50. William P. Marshall, *The Limits on Congress's Authority to Investigate the President*, 2004 U. ILL. L. REV. 781.

51. Daryl J. Levinson & Richard H. Pildes, *Separation of Parties, Not Powers*, 119 HARV. L. REV. 2311, 2345, 2368–75 (2006).

52. BERMAN, *supra* note 49.

53. U.S. CONST. art. I, § 5, cl. 2.

54. As we shall see in subsequent chapters, courts generally take the view that the political branches ideally should resolve such disputes on their own, but that if and when courts do step in, they should apply a balancing test with a presumption favoring executive privilege. (As we shall also see, courts apply this approach to all executive privilege disputes, whether or not grounded in statutory access claims). Some commentators suggest that courts should intervene rarely if at all in such disputes. *See, e.g.*, Neal Devins, *Congressional-Executive Information Access Disputes: A Modest Proposal—Do Nothing*, 48 ADMIN. L. REV. 109, 110, 130–33 (1996); Todd D. Peterson, *Prosecuting Executive Branch Officials for Contempt of Congress*, 66 N.Y.U. L. REV. 563, 625–31 (1991); Gary J. Schmitt, *Executive Privilege: Presidential Power to Withhold Information from Congress*, in THE PRESIDENCY IN THE CONSTITUTIONAL ORDER 154, 178, 181–82 (Joseph M. Bessette & Jeffrey Tulis eds., 1981). At least one contemporary commentator argues that a congressional body, following its internal procedures, should have the final say as to whether its inherent contempt and enforcement powers may be invoked in any given case. *See* Chafetz, *supra* note 12, at 1143–55.

55. *See* Todd David Peterson, 14 U. PA. J. CONST. L. 77, 110 (2011) (citing longstanding executive branch policy against prosecuting executive branch officials who assert executive privilege claims supported by the president).

56. *Id.* at 86–90 (discussing cases in which Congress imprisoned persons, including executive branch officials, pursuant to its inherent contempt powers); Chafetz, *supra* note 12, at 1135–39, 1146–48 (same).

57. Chafetz, *supra* note 12, at 1145.

58. For discussions of the close and interdependent nature of external and internal checks on executive power generally, see, e.g., Kathleen Clark, *The Architecture of Accountability: A Case Study of the Warrantless Surveillance Program*, 2010 BYU L. REV. 357, 362–64, 376–89; Kreimer, *supra* note 21, at 1016–21, 1033, 1045–46, 1056–59; Gillian E. Metzger, *The Interdependent Relationship Between Internal and External Separation of Powers*, 59 EMORY L.J. 423, 425–26, 439–52 (2009).

59. The literature is vast. A small but eclectic sampling of works in this area in-

cludes, e.g., STEVEN H. SHIFFRIN, THE FIRST AMENDMENT, DEMOCRACY, AND ROMANCE (1990); FREDERICK SCHAUER, FREE SPEECH: A PHILOSOPHICAL ENQUIRY (1982); ALEXANDER MEIKLEJOHN, FREE SPEECH AND ITS RELATION TO SELF-GOVERNMENT (1948); Seana Valentine Shiffrin, *A Thinker-Based Approach to Freedom of Speech*, 27 CONST. COMMENT. 283 (2011); Susan H. Williams, *Feminist Jurisprudence and Free Speech Theory*, 68 TUL. L. REV. 1563 (1994); Martin H. Redish, *The Value of Free Speech*, 130 U. PA. L. REV. 591 (1982); Vincent Blasi, *The Checking Value in First Amendment Theory*, 1977 AM. B. FOUND. RES. J. 521; Robert H. Bork, *Neutral Principles and Some First Amendment Problems*, 47 IND. L.J. 1 (1971); Thomas I. Emerson, *Toward a General Theory of the First Amendment*, 72 YALE L.J. 877 (1963).

60. One such notable exception is found in a recent dissenting opinion by Justice Thomas. There, he invoked the founders' child-rearing practices to conclude that the First Amendment today protects neither the right of minors to see or hear speech that their parents do not wish for them to observe nor the right of speakers to convey such speech to minors. *See* Brown v. Entm't Merchs. Ass'n, 131 S. Ct. 2729, 2751–61 (2011) (Thomas, J., dissenting).

61. For a statement of this conventional view, see Near v. Minnesota, 283 U.S. 697, 713–14 (1931). For description and rejection of the strongest version of this view—that the Free Press Clause "meant freedom only from ... prior restraint[]," see JEFFREY A. SMITH, PRINTERS AND PRESS FREEDOM: THE IDEOLOGY OF EARLY AMERICAN JOURNALISM 164 (1988); *See also id.* at 4–13.

62. To the extent that the view influences doctrine, it does so by contributing to the very strong presumption against prior restraints on speech. *See Near*, 283 U.S. at 713–16. It has not, however, resulted directly in limits on protections against other types of restrictions.

63. See sources cited in note 59, *supra*. Each of these works deems such speech either central to the First Amendment's purpose or encompassed in a broader free speech value or set of values.

64. The seminal work on "The Checking Value in First Amendment Theory" is Vincent Blasi's article of that title. *See* Blasi, *supra* note 59. In addition to detailing the checking value, the article explores the value's relationship to other major theories of free speech value. *Id.* at 548, 553–54, 557–65.

65. This would be true in any event, but it is particularly so in light of the historical backdrop against which the First Amendment was created. Federalists had issued assurances that Congress lacked the power, under Article I of the original Constitution, to regulate speech or the press. Anti-Federalists disputed that these freedoms were adequately protected by Article I and insisted that the Constitution be revised to protect them explicitly. There thus was a consensus in debates on the original document that the document either did or must protect speech and press. *See, e.g.*, David A. Anderson, *The Origins of the Press Clause*, 30 UCLA L. REV. 455, 467–75 (1983).

66. DOCUMENTARY HISTORY, vol. 8, *supra* note 27, at 245 (emphasis added).

67. *See supra* note 65.

68. Blasi, *supra* note 59, at 530.

69. Some recent scholarship concludes that as a matter of original meaning, "the press" referred to the printing press, which was the only technology of the time whereby the written word could be disseminated en masse. In England, control of this technology had been an extremely effective form of censorship. *See, e.g.*, Eugene Volokh, *Freedom for the Press as an Industry, or for the Press as a Technology? From the Framing to Today*, 160 U. PA. L. REV. 459, 462–64 (2011); Edward Lee, *Freedom of the Press 2.0*, 42 GA. L. REV. 309, 316, 328–30, 339–52 (2008).

70. For reference to American uses of the "bulwark of liberty" language, see, e.g., Anderson, *supra* note 65, at 463, 473, 478, 491–93.

71. *See, e.g.*, Blasi, *supra* note 59, at 530–35.

72. Anderson, *supra* note 65, at 463–64.

73. *See* Anderson, *supra* note 65, at 467–75, 490–91.

74. Blasi, *supra* note 59, at 527.

75. *See infra* chapter 7 at text accompanying notes 36–46.

76. *See, e.g.*, DANIEL PATRICK MOYNIHAN, REPORT OF THE COMMISSION ON PROTECTING AND REDUCING GOVERNMENT SECRECY, S. DOC. NO. 105-2, at xxxviii, 5, 11–13 (1997) [hereinafter MOYNIHAN REPORT]; HAROLD C. RELYEA, SECURITY CLASSIFIED AND CONTROLLED INFORMATION: HISTORY, STATUS AND EMERGING MANAGEMENT ISSUES 2–5 (2007); ARTHUR M. SCHLESINGER JR., THE IMPERIAL PRESIDENCY 338–41 (1973). A few discrete categories of information are classified by statute. *See, e.g.*, NATHAN BROOKS, CONG. RESEARCH SERV. REP., THE PROTECTION OF CLASSIFIED INFORMATION: THE LEGAL FRAMEWORK 2 n.7 (2004), *available at* http://www.au.af.mil/au/awc/awcgate/crs/rs21900.pdf; MOYNIHAN REPORT, at 5, 15, 23–24.

77. INFO. SEC. OVERSIGHT OFFICE, 2012 ANNUAL REPORT TO THE PRESIDENT 1–2 (2013) [hereinafter ISOO 2012 REPORT].

78. INFO. SEC. OVERSIGHT OFFICE, 2009 ANNUAL REPORT TO THE PRESIDENT 4 (2010) [hereinafter ISOO 2009 REPORT]; *See also* ISOO 2012 REPORT, *supra* note 77, at 2–3 (describing a recent downward trend in the number of original classification authorities).

79. ISOO 2012 REPORT, *supra* note 77, at 2.

80. ISOO 2012 REPORT, *supra* note 77, at 7.

81. Precise numbers of derivative classifiers are not recorded given the fluid means by which they are designated. A 1997 Report of the Commission on Protecting and Reducing Government Secrecy estimated that "three million government and industry employees … have the ability to mark information as classified." MOYNIHAN REPORT, *supra* note 76, at 31.

82. ISOO 2012 REPORT, *supra* note 77, at 7.

83. Scott Shane, *Since 2001, Sharp Increase in the Number of Documents Classified by the Government*, N.Y. TIMES, July 3, 2005, at A1; *See also* Steven Aftergood, *Former Secrecy Czar Asks Court to Release NSA Document*, SECRECY NEWS, May 23, 2012 (explaining the ISOO director's role and noting the "classification czar" term).

84. *Espionage Act and the Legal and Constitutional Issues Raised by Wikileaks: Hearing Before the H. Comm. on the Judiciary*, 111th Cong. 27 (2010) [hereinafter *Espionage Act Hearing*] (statement of Abbe D. Lowell, Partner, McDermott Will & Emery LLP) (emphasis in original) (citing *Too Many Secrets: Overclassification as a Barrier to Critical Information Sharing: Hearing Before the Subcomm. on Nat'l Sec., Emerging Threats & Int'l Relations, Comm. on Gov't Reform*, 108th Cong. 82–83 (2004)).

85. *id.* at 84 (statement of Thomas S. Blanton, National Security Archive, George Washington University) (citing statement of Rodney McDaniel).

86. 108 CONG. REC. S9714 (2004).

87. MOYNIHAN REPORT, *supra* note 76, at xxi.

88. Erwin N. Griswold, *Secrets Not Worth Keeping*, WASH. POST, Feb. 15, 1989, at A25.

89. PUB. INTEREST DECLASSIFICATION BD., TRANSFORMING THE SECURITY CLASSIFICATION SYSTEM: REPORT TO THE PRESIDENT FROM THE PUBLIC INTEREST DECLASSIFICATION BOARD, at iv (Nov. 2012); *See also id.* at 2, 9–10, 42–43.

90. ISOO 2009 REPORT, *supra* note 78, at 9. For both original and derivative classification statistics from FY 2012 and comparisons between them and earlier years' numbers, see ISOO 2012 REPORT, *supra* note 77, at 4–8.

91. *See, e.g.*, *Espionage Act Hearing*, *supra* note 84, at 51 (testimony of Gabriel Schoenfeld, PhD, Senior Fellow, Hudson Institute) (discussing common practice of authorized leaking); *See also The Espionage Statutes: A Look Back and a Look Forward: Hearing Before the Subcomm. on Terrorism & Homeland Sec.*, 111th Cong. 7, 10–11, 14 (2010) [hereinafter *Espionage Statutes Hearing*] (statement and testimony of Jeffrey H. Smith, Partner, Arnold & Porter) (same).

92. This quote has been attributed to journalist James Reston. *See* David E. Rosenbaum, *First a Leak, Then a Predictable Pattern*, N.Y. TIMES, Oct. 3, 2003, http://www.nytimes.com/2003/10/03/world/debating-a-leak-political-memo-first -a-leak-then-a-predictable-pattern.html?ref=david_e_rosenbaum.

93. Richard B. Kielbowicz, *The Role of News Leaks in Governance and the Law of Journalists' Confidentiality, 1795–2005*, 43 SAN DIEGO L. REV. 425, 444 (2006) (describing Theodore Roosevelt's use of this strategy); *See also* Mary-Rose Papandrea, *Lapdogs, Watchdogs and Scapegoats: The Press and National Security Information*, 83 IND. L.J. 233, 251–52 (2008) (describing the ubiquity of and strategies behind authorized leaks from the top); William E. Lee, *Deep Background: Journalists, Sources, and the Perils of Leaking*, 57 AM. U. L. REV. 1453, 1469–70 (2008) (same).

94. *See, e.g.,* Kielbowicz, *supra* note 93, at 444; Papandrea, *supra* note 93, at 236.

95. Jane Mayer, *The Secret Sharer,* NEW YORKER, May 23, 2011 (quoting Jack Goldsmith); *See also* Michael Isikoff, *"Double Standard" in White House Leak Inquiries?,* NBCNEWS.COM (Oct. 18, 2010), http://www.nbcnews.com/id/39693850/ns/us_news-security#/; Jack Goldsmith, *Classified Information in Woodward's "Obama's Wars,"* LAWFARE BLOG (Sept. 29, 2010, 7:50 AM), http://www.lawfare blog.com/2010/09/classified-information-in-woodwards-obama%E2%80%99s-wars/.

96. Papandrea, *supra* note 93, at 236.

97. In his recent book, Rahul Sagar argues that overclassification is no reason to tolerate unauthorized leaks of classified information. He explains that we cannot "be sure that the ensuing unauthorized disclosures of classified information will not harm national security," SAGAR, *supra* note 37, at 112, and that neither leakers, publishers, nor judges are well equipped to determine the gravity or likelihood of national security harm. *Id.* at 112, 119–25. He adds that "[i]f we allow private actors to ignore classification markings, then we ought to ask ourselves why we have established a classification system in the first place." *Id.* at 113. This reasoning fails to accord any weight to the fact of overclassification, a fact about which there is widespread, cross-ideological, and cross-partisan consensus. This consensus does not tell us precisely what to do, nor does it suggest that classification markings should be deemed meaningless. It does, however, offer strong reasons against deferring fully to classifiers' judgments. This is particularly so where there are constitutional (First Amendment) and policy interests to be weighed against the constitutional (Article II–based) and national security interests invoked in favor of deference.

98. I say "akin" to the incitement standard to acknowledge the possibility that slightly different standards should apply to speech that incites violence through advocacy versus speech that enables violence by disclosing information. Such variance may be appropriate in light of the different mechanisms and different timeframes through which the respective types of speech may cause harm. *See* Heidi Kitrosser, *Classified Information Leaks and Free Speech,* 2008 U. ILL. L. REV. 881, 927–28.

99. One might object to the very notion of calibrating First Amendment protections by the nature of the penalty that the government seeks to impose. An objector might point out that First Amendment protections typically hinge on what a restriction targets—whether, for instance, a law targets speech on the basis of its content, and whether that content falls into an unprotected speech category—rather than the type of penalty imposed. He or she might deem it unwise to stray from this approach. I address these objections in depth in Heidi Kitrosser, *Free Speech Aboard the Leaky Ship of State: Calibrating First Amendment Protections for Leakers of Classified Information,* 6 J. NAT'L SEC. L. & POL'Y 409 (2013). Chapter 6 of this book also offers some case law support for this position. For another, very recent academic take on the notion that First Amendment protec-

tions ought to be "penalty sensitive," *See generally* Michael Coenen, *Of Speech and Sanctions: Toward a Penalty-Sensitive Approach to the First Amendment*, 112 COLUM. L. REV. 991 (2012).

100. *See, e.g.,* Heidi Kitrosser, *National Security and the Article II Shell Game*, 26 CONST. COMMENT. 483 (2010) (citing influence and ubiquity of such "exclusivity" arguments).

Chapter Four

1. These four claim types are discussed and illustrated in much greater detail in chapter 5.

2. U.S. CONST. art. II, § 1, cl. 1.

3. See Gary Lawson, *What Lurks Beneath: NSA Surveillance and Executive Power*, 88 B.U. L. Rev. 375, 376 (2008) (referring to the "Article II Vesting Clause thesis" as "one of the most hotly debated propositions in modern constitutional law").

4. U.S. CONST. art. II, § 2, cl. 2.

5. JOHN C. YOO, CRISIS & COMMAND 35, 43–47 (2009); Lawson, *supra* note 3, at 389–91. For earlier supremacist uses of the Vesting Clause thesis, see, e.g., Lawrence J. Block & David B. Rivkin Jr., *The Battle to Control the Conduct of Foreign Intelligence and Covert Operations: The Ultra-Whig Counterrevolution Revisited*, 12 HARV. J.L. & PUB. POL'Y 303, 307–20 (1989); Robert F. Turner, *The Constitution and the Iran-Contra Affair: Was Congress the Real Lawbreaker?*, 11 HOUS. J. INT'L L. 83, 91–99 (1988).

6. U.S. CONST. art. I, § 1 (emphasis added).

7. *See, e.g.*, Lawson, *supra* note 3, at 390. Supporters also cite the plain language of the Vesting Clause, the etymology of the word "vest," the analogy between its uses in Article II and Article III, and the fact that it is used to signify a substantive grant of power elsewhere in the Constitution. *Id.* at 386–88 (summarizing arguments made elsewhere by Lawson, Guy Seidman, Christopher Moore, Steven Calabresi, and Kevin Rhodes).

8. *See* Gary Lawson & Guy Seidman, *The Jeffersonian Treaty Clause*, 2006 U. ILL. L. REV. 1, 38 ("The content of the 'executive Power' granted to the President by the Vesting Clause is an issue separate from whether the Article II Vesting Clause grants power."); Curtis A. Bradley & Martin S. Flaherty, *Executive Power Essentialism and Foreign Affairs*, 102 MICH. L. REV. 545, 553 (2004) ("[E]ven if the Article II Vesting Clause were read as a power-conferring provision, the argument would not tell us which powers the Clause encompasses.").

9. *See, e.g.*, Henry P. Monaghan, *The Protective Power of the Presidency*, 93 COLUM. L. REV. 1, 22–24, 31–32, 38, 65–66, 69–74 (1993) (deeming the executive power to include a limited protective power to act absent statutory authority,

but not to act against statutory authority); *See also, e.g.*, Lawson & Seidman, *supra* note 8, at 41–42, 45–62 (describing a residual executive power over foreign affairs that is not clearly or necessarily supremacist in nature); Saikrishna B. Prakash & Michael D. Ramsey, *The Executive Power Over Foreign Affairs*, III YALE L.J. 231, 234–35, 253–56, 262–65 (2001) (describing residual executive foreign affairs powers that do not preclude roles for Congress, though reading some important limits into the latter); *id.* at 238–40 (criticizing theories of "presidential primacy" in foreign affairs).

10. *See* STEVEN G. CALABRESI & CHRISTOPHER S. YOO, THE UNITARY EXECUTIVE 18–21 (2008) ("The classic vision of the unitary executive . . . had absolutely nothing to do with claims of implied, inherent presidential domestic and foreign policy power of the kind asserted by the [George W. Bush] administration"). *But see* Julian G. Ku, *Unitary Executive Theory and Exclusive Presidential Powers*, 12 U. PA. J. CONST. L. 615, 615–16, 621 (2010) (arguing that unitary executive theory itself is a form of presidential exclusivity); John C. Yoo, *Unitary, Executive, or Both?*, 76 U. CHI. L. REV. 1935, 1937–38, 1965–66, 1976–85 (2009) (positing that the reasoning underlying unitary executive theory also supports supremacy).

11. See sources cited in note 5, *supra.*

12. *See, e.g.*, Yoo, *supra* note 10, at 1984–85.

13. For a brief description of TSP, see chapter 1 at text accompanying notes 39–40.

14. *See* Lawson, *supra* note 3, at 389–93; *See also id.* at 389–90 n.93 and accompanying text (citing John C. Eastman, *Listening to the Enemy: The President's Power to Conduct Surveillance of Enemy Communications During Time of War*, 13 ILSA J. INT'L & COMP. L. 49, 57 (2006)); *See also* Eastman, *supra*, at 55–57 ("FISA . . . may well be unconstitutional" if it restricts the president's power of surveying "communications with enemies of the [United States] and people he reasonably believes to be working with them").

15. Turner, *supra* note 5, at 92.

16. U.S. CONST. art. II, § 2, cl. 1.

17. *See, e.g.*, U.S. DEP'T OF JUSTICE, LEGAL AUTHORITIES SUPPORTING THE ACTIVITIES OF THE NATIONAL SECURITY AGENCY DESCRIBED BY THE PRESIDENT 6–7, 29–35 (2006) [hereinafter DOJ Whitepaper] (positing an exclusivist argument by reference to the Commander-in-Chief Clause); JOHN C. YOO, WAR BY OTHER MEANS 103, 114, 119–22 (2006) (describing justifications for wartime exclusivity grounded partly in the Commander-in-Chief Clause); *See also, e.g., From the Department of Justice to Guantanamo Bay: Administration Lawyers and Administration Interrogation Rules: Hearing Before the Subcomm. on Admin. Oversight & the Courts of the S. Judiciary Comm.*, 110th Cong. 4 (2008) (written testimony of Michael Stokes Paulsen) (identifying a large realm of exclusivist presidential power regarding military and foreign affairs under the Commander-in-Chief Clause and executive power); Lawson, *supra* note 3, at 384 ("[A]lthough the [DOJ White-

paper] does not articulate the Vesting Clause thesis with clarity, it seems clear that the Vesting Clause thesis lurks beneath the argument and provides it with substance."); Yoo, *supra*, at 103 (combining Vesting Clause and Commander-in-Chief arguments); Eastman, *supra* note 14, at 53 (underscoring supremacist argument by reference to Commander-in-Chief Clause, executive power, and the president's "inherent power as the organ of U.S. sovereignty on the world stage.").

18. *See* Saikrishna B. Prakash, *The Separation and Overlap of War and Military Powers*, 87 Tex. L. Rev. 299, 350–51, 364 (2008) (describing such arguments); David J. Barron & Martin S. Lederman, *The Commander-in-Chief at the Lowest Ebb — Framing the Problem, Doctrine, and Original Understanding*, 121 Harv. L. Rev. 689, 694–95, 705, 750–52 (2008) (same); *See also, e.g.*, Michael Stokes Paulsen, *The War Power*, 33 Harv. J.L. & Pub. Pol'y 113, 124–27 (2010) (making such an argument); Turner, *supra* note 5, at 118–19 (same).

19. DOJ Whitepaper, *supra* note 17, at 28–35.

20. *See, e.g.*, *infra* note 64 and accompanying text; *See also* Barron & Lederman, *supra* note 18, at 694 (deeming this notion part of a "dense fog of half-developed and largely unexamined intuitions").

21. *See, e.g.*, DOJ Whitepaper, *supra* note 17, at 7, 18; Minority Report, *in* Report of the Congressional Committees Investigating the Iran-Contra Affair, H.R. Rep. No. 100-433, S. Rep. No. 100-216, at 460 (1987); Yoo, *supra* note 17, at 119–20.

22. *See, e.g.*, DOJ Whitepaper, *supra* note 17, at 7, 28–29, 31, 34–35; Yoo, *supra* note 17, at 119–22.

23. 2 The Records of the Federal Convention of 1787, at 318–19 (Max Farrand ed., Yale Univ. Press 1966) (1911); *See also, e.g.*, Forrest McDonald, The American Presidency 173 (1994).

24. *See, e.g.*, John C. Yoo, *The Terrorist Surveillance Program and the Constitution*, 14 Geo. Mason L. Rev. 565, 593 n. 202 (2007) (taking broad view of the "repel sudden attacks" rationale and of the implications for presidential power of the linguistic change from "make" to "declare"); *cf. id.* at 595–99 (defending TSP's legality by citing presidential duty and power to stave off attacks); Block & Rivkin, *supra* note 5, at 321 (inferring broad preemptive powers from Commander-in-Chief Clause).

25. *See supra* note 18 and accompanying text.

26. Minority Report, *supra* note 21, at 460.

27. *Id.* at 463–69 (quoting Gary Schmitt, *Jefferson and Executive Power: Revisionism and the "Revolution of 1800,"* 17 Publius 7, 23 n.29 (1987)).

28. Gary J. Schmitt & Abram N. Shulsky, *The Theory and Practice of Separation of Powers: The Case of Covert Action*, *in* The Fettered Presidency: Legal Constraints on the Executive Branch 62–65, 71–75 (L. Gordon Crovitz & Jeremy A. Rabkin eds., 1989).

29. Minority Report, *supra* note 21, at 467, 469.

30. *See, e.g.*, YOO, *supra* note 5, at 3–7, 32–51; Michael S. Paulsen, *Youngstown Goes to War*, 19 CONST. COMMENT. 215, 237–38 (2002); Block & Rivkin, *supra* note 5, at 307–15; Turner, *supra* note 5, at 91–95; Charles J. Cooper, Orrin Hatch, Eugene V. Rostow & Michael Tigar, *Roundtable: What the Constitution Means by Executive Power*, 43 U. MIAMI L. REV. 165, 167–68, 177 (1988) (comments of Charles J. Cooper); *id.* at 191–93 (comments of Eugene V. Rostow).

31. Turner, *supra* note 5, at 92–93; *See also, e.g.*, Block & Rivkin, *supra* note 5, at 307–9 nn.14–16.

32. *See* sources cited *supra* note 30.

33. *See* chapter 2, notes 67–68 and accompanying text.

34. *See* JOHN LOCKE, *Second Treatise of Government*, *in* TWO TREATISES OF GOVERNMENT 410–12 (1960 ed. reprt. with amendments, Cambridge Univ. Press 1963) (1690); *See also* JACK N. RAKOVE, ORIGINAL MEANINGS 247 (1997); Bradley & Flaherty, *supra* note 8, at 560–61.

35. *See* 11 CHARLES DE SECONDAT BARON DE MONTESQUIEU, THE SPIRIT OF LAWS: OF THE LAWS WHICH ESTABLISH POLITICAL LIBERTY, WITH REGARD TO THE CONSTITUTION (1748), *reprinted in* 38 BRITTANICA GREAT BOOKS OF THE WESTERN WORLD: MONTESQUIEU & ROSSEAU 69–75 (Robert Maynard Hutchins & Mortimer J. Adler eds., 1952); *See also* RAKOVE, *supra* note 34, at 248; Bradley &Flaherty, *supra* note 8, at 563–65; M. J. C. VILE, CONSTITUTIONALISM AND THE SEPARATION OF POWERS 94–96 (2d ed. Liberty Fund 1998).

36. Bradley & Flaherty, *supra* note 8, at 561–62; *See also* RAKOVE, *supra* note 34, at 245–46; VILE, *supra* note 35, at 114–15. Montesquieu's discussion, too, had been influenced partly by the concept of mixed government. *See* VILE, *supra* note 35, at 99, 102.

37. VILE, *supra* note 35, at 123.

38. RAKOVE, *supra* note 34, at 245; *See also, e.g.*, GORDON S. WOOD, THE CREATION OF THE AMERICAN REPUBLIC 151–53 (1998); McDONALD, *supra* note 23, at 4; VILE, *supra* note 35, at 36–38, 59, 81–82, 134–35.

39. WOOD, *supra* note 38, at 136.

40. *Id.* at 149.

41. *id.* at 149–50.

42. *See also, e.g.*, RAKOVE, *supra* note 34, at 249–50 (discussing postindependence state constitutions and noting that "executive authority became merely that, the obligation to carry out the legislative will."); VILE, *supra* note 35, at 145 (explaining that "[i]n the revolutionary period . . . the colonists' approach to the office of Governor was to strip it of all prerogatives, and to turn it into a purely executive position"); WOOD, *supra* note 38, at 148 (making the same point). For a discussion of the extent to which the concept of a "purely executive" leader also had roots in French and British experience, see WOOD, *supra* note 38, at 42, 46–47, 107–8.

43. *See, e.g.*, WOOD, *supra* note 38, at 393–96, 432–38; *cf.* Julian Davis Mortenson, *Executive Power and the Discipline of History*, 78 U. CHI. L. REV. 377, 396

(2011) (criticizing, in a review of John Yoo's work, the fact that "Yoo repeatedly returns to the English understanding of kingship, as if the Founders' developing unease with a headless state meant that they wiped post-Revolutionary history clean and began afresh with a neat chalkboard exercise in subtraction from the very king they had cast off less than fifteen years before.").

44. RAKOVE, *supra* note 34, at 257.

45. Bradley & Flaherty *supra* note 8, at 593.

46. RAKOVE, *supra* note 34, at 257.

47. Bradley & Flaherty, *supra* note 8, at 593.

48. 3 THE DOCUMENTARY HISTORY OF THE CONSTITUTION 571 (John P. Kaminski & Gaspare J. Saladino eds., 1978) [hereinafter DOCUMENTARY HISTORY, vol. 3].

49. 9 THE DOCUMENTARY HISTORY OF THE RATIFICATION OF THE CONSTITUTION 1097–98 (John P. Kaminski & Gaspare J. Saladino eds., 1990) [hereinafter DOCUMENTARY HISTORY, vol. 9].

50. *See generally, e.g.*, THE FEDERALIST NO. 67, at 405–9 (Alexander Hamilton) (Clinton Rossiter ed., 1961) [hereinafter FEDERALIST NO. 67].

51. THE FEDERALIST NO. 77, at 458–63 (Alexander Hamilton) (Clinton Rossiter ed., 1961). For reference to a recent debate about the meaning of Hamilton's statement in *Federalist* No. 77, see chapter 7, note 19.

52. *See* chapter 3, notes 28–31 and accompanying text; *See also, e.g.*, 2 THE DOCUMENTARY HISTORY OF THE RATIFICATION OF THE CONSTITUTION 495 (John P. Kaminski & Gaspare J. Saladino eds., 1976) [hereinafter DOCUMENTARY HISTORY, vol. 2] (citing absence of presidential privileges, presidential vulnerability to punishment); DOCUMENTARY HISTORY, vol. 9, *supra* note 49, at 723 (commentary in the *Virginia Independent Chronicle* by A Freeholder, citing numerous means to check and punish the president, noting that he "can by no means be compared to Kings, even the most limited we read of in history.").

53. PACIFICUS NUMBER I, *reprinted in* THE PACIFICUS—HELVIDIUS DEBATES OF 1793–1794 (Morton J. Frisch ed., Liberty Fund ed. 2007). For examples of supremacist works citing these Hamiltonian arguments, see, e.g., Block & Rivkin, *supra* note 5, at 314–15; Turner, *supra* note 5, at 96–97. *See also* Thomas S. Langston & Michael E. Lind, *John Locke and the Limits of Presidential Prerogative*, 24 POLITY 49, 53–54 (1991) (citing scholarship that invokes Pacificus I toward supremacist ends).

54. After reading Hamilton's defense of President Washington's Neutrality Proclamation, Jefferson urged Madison: "For God's sake, my dear Sir, take up your pen, select the most striking heresies, and cut him to pieces in the face of the public." Letter from Thomas Jefferson to James Madison (July 7, 1793) reprinted in THE PACIFICUS—HELVIDIUS DEBATES OF 1793–1794, *supra* note 53, at 54.

55. HELVIDIUS I, reprinted in THE PACIFICUS—HELVIDIUS DEBATES OF 1793–1794, *supra* note 53, at 63 (emphasis in original). Madison also helpfully ex-

plained that Pacificus's writings were "read with singular pleasure and applause, by the foreigners and degenerate citizens among us." Id. at 55.

56. See, e.g., Turner, *supra* note 5, at 97–99, 97 n.52; Block & Rivkin, *supra* note 5, at 314 n.41.

57. See, e.g., Turner, *supra* note 5, at 98–99; Block & Rivkin, *supra* note 5, at 314 n.41.

58. See, e.g., Turner, *supra* note 5, at 95, 97 n.52.

59. See, e.g., Yoo, *supra* note 5, at 102, 121–22 ; Block & Rivkin, *supra* note 5, at 313 n.39.

60. See, e.g., Yoo, *supra* note 5, at 48–49 (noting that the Federalists "downplayed comparisons of the President's powers with those of the British Crown" in the ratification period, and that Hamilton's anti-monarchist rhetoric in Federalist No. 69 "got the better of him"); cf., e.g., Lawson & Seidman, *supra* note 8, at 35 (agreeing that Hamilton likely downplayed his personal beliefs about the presidency in the Federalist and observing that "[t]he Federalist was campaign literature, and it needs to be viewed as such.").

61. See chapter 7 at text accompanying note 57.

62. PACIFICUS NUMBER I, *supra* note 53; cf. Mortenson, *supra* note 43, at 419–20 (noting that President Washington, too, explicitly acknowledged that Congress had the power to "correct, improve, or enforce" the Neutrality Proclamation).

63. See, e.g., Jeremy David Bailey, Executive Prerogative and the "Good Officer" in Thomas Jefferson's Letter to John B. Colvin, 34 PRESIDENTIAL STUDIES Q. 732, 736–40, 747–49 (2004); Lucius Wilmerding Jr., The President and the Law, 67 POL. SCI. Q. 321, 328–29 (1952).

64. Michael Stokes Paulsen, The Constitutional Power to Interpret International Law, 118 YALE L.J. 1762, 1840 (2009).

65. Id. at 1839–40; *See also* Paulsen, *supra* note 18, at 126.

66. Michael Stokes Paulsen, The Emancipation Proclamation and the Commander in Chief Power, 40 GA. L. REV. 807, 825–26, 826 n.51 (2006).

67. See Prakash, *supra* note 18, at 350; Barron & Lederman, *supra* note 18, at 696, 769–70.

68. Prakash, *supra* note 18, at 352–53, 368.

69. Id. at 368–70.

70. See Barron & Lederman, *supra* note 18, at 772–800.

71. See David J. Barron & Martin S. Lederman, The Commander in Chief at the Lowest Ebb—A Constitutional History, 121 HARV. L. REV. 941, 951–52 (2008); Prakash, *supra* note 18, at 370–71.

72. Prakash, *supra* note 18, at 372.

73. DOJ Whitepaper, *supra* note 17, at 7–8, 16–17.

74. Yoo, *supra* note 17, at 114–15.

75. THE FEDERALIST NO. 48, at 308 (James Madison) (Clinton Rossiter ed., 1961).

76. *See* Curtis A. Bradley & Trevor W. Morrison, *Historical Gloss and the Separation of Powers*, 126 HARV. L. REV. 411, 414–15, 432–33, 448–51 (2012); Heidi Kitrosser, *It Came from Beneath the Twilight Zone: Wiretapping and Article II Imperialism,* 88 TEX. L. REV. 1401, 1411, 1421–26, 1434 (2010).

77. DOJ Whitepaper, *supra* note 17, at 7.

78. *See* Kitrosser, *supra* note 76, at 1405, 1421–26 and sources cited therein.

Chapter Five

1. *See* OFFICES OF INSPECTORS GEN. OF THE DEP'T OF DEF. ET AL., (U) UNCLASSIFIED REPORT ON THE PRESIDENT'S SURVEILLANCE PROGRAM 10–12 (2009), *available at* http://www.fas.org/irp/eprint/psp.pdf.

2. Indeed, critics derided the FAA as essentially codifying the TSP. See, e.g., Patrick Radden Keefe, *Legislating in the Dark*, 34 INDEX ON CENSORSHIP 14, 26 (2008); Samantha Fredrickson, *Tapping into the Reporter's Notebook*, 32 NEWS MEDIA & L. 10, 11 (2008).

3. *FISA Amendments: How to Protect Americans' Security and Privacy and Preserve the Rule of Law and Government Accountability: Hearing Before the S. Comm. on the Judiciary*, 110th Cong. 16 (2007) (statement of Kenneth L. Wainstein, Ass't Att'y Gen. for Nat'l Sec., U.S. Dep't of Justice).

4. MARK J. ROZELL, EXECUTIVE PRIVILEGE 39 (Univ. Press of Kan. rev. 2d ed. 2002).

5. *Id.* at 29–30; DANIEL N. HOFFMAN, GOVERNMENTAL SECRECY AND THE FOUNDING FATHERS 235 (1981); Saikrishna B. Prakash, *A Critical Comment on the Constitutionality of Executive Privilege*, 83 MINN. L. REV. 1143, 1177–79 (1999); Archibald Cox, *Executive Privilege*, 122 U. PA. L. REV. 1383, 1391–92 (1974); William P. Rogers, *The Papers of the Executive Branch*, 44 A.B.A. J. 941, 943–44 (1958).

6. ROZELL, *supra* note 4, at 30; *See also id.* at 30–31; HOFFMAN, *supra* note 5, at 236–37; Prakash, *supra* note 5, at 1179–80.

7. ROZELL, *supra* note 4, at 31; Prakash, *supra* note 5, at 1181–83.

8. Prakash, *supra* note 5, at 1183–84.

9. *Id.* at 1184.

10. *Id.* at 1180; *See also* Abraham D. Sofaer, *Executive Privilege: An Historical Note*, 75 COLUM. L. REV. 1318, 1321 (1975).

11. HOFFMAN, *supra* note 5, at 237; *See also supra* note 8 and accompanying text.

12. HOFFMAN, *supra* note 5, at 193–94, 238.

13. *See, e.g.*, Rozell, *supra* note 4, at 32–39 (describing executive privilege claims in the Adams to Eisenhower administrations); Cox, *supra* note 5, 1395–1405 (discussing executive privilege claims from the Washington through Truman administrations).

14. *See, e.g.*, Rozell, supra note 4, at 28–32 (supporting a qualified executive privilege based partly on this history).

15. *See, e.g., id.* at 24–25 (citing two such passages from the *Federalist* to support a qualified executive privilege).

16. *Texts of Eisenhower Letter and Brownell Memorandum on Testimony in Senate Inquiry*, N.Y. TIMES, May 17, 1954, at 24.

17. Cox, *supra* note 5, at 1433.

18. *See, e.g.*, Gia B. Lee, *The President's Secrets*, 76 GEO. WASH. L. REV. 197, 198–202, 205–13 (2008).

19. The episode also demonstrates the shadow effect of the privilege, as the administration alluded to, but did not explicitly invoke the privilege in that case. *Compare* Michael D. Shear, *Government Openness Is Tested by Salahi Case*, WASH. POST, Dec. 4, 2009, at C7 (citing White House to the effect that it was not, in that case, "formally invoking an executive privilege claim, but rather speaking broadly to the fact that previous presidents had resisted having their top advisers give testimony about internal deliberations and discussions"), *with* Charlie Savage, *House Panel's Vote Steps Up Partisan Fight on Gun Inquiry*, N.Y. TIMES (June 20, 2012), http://www.nytimes.com/2012/06/21/us/obama-claims-executive-privilege-in-gun-case.html?_r=0 (deeming a different dispute that arose more than two years later to occasion President Obama's first invocation of executive privilege).

20. Shear, *supra* note 19.

21. 418 U.S. 683 (1974).

22. *Id.* at 686–90.

23. *Id.* at 705–9.

24. *Id.* at 710–11.

25. *See, e.g.*, *The Whistleblower Protection Enhancement Act of 2009: Hearing on H.R. 1507 Before the H. Comm. on Oversight and Gov't Reform*, 111th Cong. 66–67 (2009) (statement of Ragish De, Deputy Ass't Att'y Gen., Office of Legal Policy, Dep't of Justice) [hereinafter *Hearing on H.R. 1507*]; Assertion of Exec. Privilege Concerning the Special Counsel's Interviews of the Vice President & Senior White House Staff, 32 Op. Att'y Gen. 1, 2–3 (2008) [hereinafter Vice President & Senior White House Staff]; Assertion of Exec. Privilege for Documents Concerning Conduct of Foreign Affairs with Respect to Haiti, 1996 WL 34386606, at *1–2 (Sept. 20, 1996) [hereinafter Foreign Affairs with Respect to Haiti]; Applicability of Executive Privilege to the Recommendations of Independent Agencies Regarding Presidential Approval or Veto of Legislation, 10 Op. O.L.C. 176, 177–78 (1986).

26. Senate Select Comm. on Presidential Campaign Activities v. Nixon, 498 F.2d 725, 731 (D.C. Cir. 1974).

27. *See, e.g.*, Letter from Attorney Gen. Holder, to President Obama 5, 8 (June 19, 2012); Vice President & Senior White House Staff, *supra* note 25, at 4–6; Foreign Affairs with Respect to Haiti, *supra* note 25, at *2–3; Applicability of Execu-

tive Privilege to the Recommendations of Independent Agencies Regarding Presidential Approval or Veto of Legislation, 10 Op. O.L.C. 176, 177 (1986).

28. *See, e.g.*, EMILY BERMAN, EXECUTIVE PRIVILEGE: A LEGISLATIVE REMEDY 2–4, 7–13, 16–23 (2009); Lee, *supra* note 18, at 198–99, 209–13; Heidi Kitrosser, *Secrecy and Separated Powers: Executive Privilege Revisited*, 92 IOWA L. REV. 489, 496–501 (2007).

29. The President's Compliance with the "Timely Notification" Requirement of Section 501(B) of the Nat'l Sec. Act, 10 Op. O.L.C. 159 (1986) [hereinafter "Timely Notification" Memo].

30. 50 U.S.C. § 413(b) (1988) (repealed 1991).

31. "Timely Notification" Memo, *supra* note 29, at 173–74.

32. *Id.* at 165 (emphasis omitted).

33. 542 U.S. 367 (2004).

34. *Id.* at 375, 388–90.

35. *See In re* Cheney, 406 F.3d 723, 725, 727, 731 (D.C. Cir. 2005) (discussing separation of powers issues, ordering case dismissed on remand).

36. President Barack Obama, Statement of Administration Policy: H.R. 2701—Intelligence Authorization Act for Fiscal Year 2010 (July 8, 2009) [hereinafter Policy Statement on Intelligence Authorization Act for Fiscal Year 2010]; *See also, e.g.*, Scott Shane, *CIA Reviewing Its Process for Briefing Congress*, N.Y. TIMES, July 10, 2009, at A16.

37. Policy Statement on Intelligence Authorization Act for Fiscal Year 2010, *supra* note 36.

38. *See* Letter from Peter R. Orszag, Director, Office of Mgmt. & Budget, to Diane Feinstein, Chairwoman, Select Comm. on Intelligence (Mar. 15, 2010); *See also, e.g.*, Walter Pincus, *White House Threatens Veto on Intelligence Activities Bill*, WASH. POST, Mar. 16, 2010, at A4.

39. *See, e.g., Hearing on H.R. 1507, supra* note 25, at 65–67; Auth. of Agency Officials to Prohibit Emps. from Providing Info. to Cong., 2004 WL 3554702, at *1–4 (May 21, 2004); Access to Classified Information, 20 U.S. Op. Off. Legal Counsel 402, *2–3 (1996); Constitutionality of Statute Requiring Exec. Agency to Report Directly to Cong., 6 Op. O.L.C. 632, 637–38, 641–42 (1982).

40. Heidi Kitrosser, *Supremely Opaque? Accountability, Transparency, and Presidential Supremacy*, 5 U. ST. THOMAS J.L. & PUB. POL'Y 62 (2010) (addressing this uncertainty at text accompanying notes 89–91).

41. See Amanda Frost, *The State Secrets Privilege and Separation of Powers*, 75 FORDHAM L. REV. 1931, 1935–37 (2007).

42. *See, e.g.*, Laura K. Donohue, *The Shadow of State Secrets*, 159 U. PA. L. REV. 77, 82–83 & 83 n.17 (2010); Robert M. Chesney, *State Secrets and the Limits of National Security Litigation*, 75 GEO. WASH. L. REV. 1249, 1270–71 (2007).

43. 345 U.S. 1 (1953).

44. Donohue, *supra* note 42, at 82–83, 82 n.9 (explaining that the roots of state

secrets privilege run deeper than *Reynolds*, but acknowledging that *Reynolds* "created historical precedent in recognizing the state secrets doctrine"); Chesney, *supra* note 42, at 1270–83 (tracing privilege's pre-*Reynolds* route and noting that *Reynolds* "entrenched the state secrets privilege in its modern form").

45. U.S. v. Reynolds, 345 U.S. 1, 1–2 (1953); *See also* LOUIS FISHER, IN THE NAME OF NATIONAL SECURITY 3, 29 (2006).

46. *Reynolds*, 345 U.S. at 3.

47. *Id.* at 3–4, 6; *See also* FISHER, *supra* note 45, at 96–99.

48. FISHER, *supra* note 45, at 53 (quoting statement of Secretary of the Air Force Thomas K. Finletter, filed Oct. 10, 1950, Civil Action No. 10142 (E.D. Pa. 1950)); *See also* U.S. v. Reynolds, 345 U.S. 1, 4–5 (1953).

49. *Reynolds*, 345 U.S. at 6; *See also* FISHER, *supra* note 45, at 102.

50. *Reynolds*, 345 U.S. at 6–7.

51. *Id.* at 7–8.

52. *id.* at 8.

53. *id.* at 9–10.

54. *id.* at 10.

55. *Id.* at 11.

56. *Id.*

57. *id.* at 11–12.

58. *id.* at 8 n.21 (internal citation omitted).

59. James Zagel, *The State Secrets Privilege*, 50 MINN. L. REV. 875, 891 (1966).

60. FISHER, *supra* note 45, at 116.

61. *Id.*

62. *Id.*

63. *Id.* at 117.

64. *Id.* at 167.

65. Timothy Lynch, *An Injustice Wrapped in a Pretense*, WASH. POST, June 22, 2003, at B3; *See also* FISHER, *supra* note 45, at 167–68; Warren Richey, *Security or Coverup? How a Murky Case Became Precedent*, CHRISTIAN SCI. MONITOR, June 8, 2006, at 1, *available at* http://www.csmonitor.com/2006/0608/p01s02-usju .html.

66. ROBERT M. PALLITTO & WILLIAM G. WEAVER, PRESIDENTIAL SECRECY AND THE LAW 107 (2007); Meredith Fuchs, *Judging Secrets: The Role that Courts Should Play in Preventing Unnecessary Secrecy*, 58 ADMIN. L. REV. 131, 167–68 (2006); Neil Kinkopf, *The State Secrets Problem: Can Congress Fix It?*, 80 TEMP. L. REV. 489, 490 (2007); Carrie Newton Lyons, *The State Secrets Privilege: Expanding its Scope Through Government Misuse*, 11 LEWIS & CLARK L. REV. 99, 107–8, 119 (2007); *Restoring the Rule of Law: Hearing Before the Constitution Subcomm. of the S. Judiciary Comm.*, 110th Cong. 14 (2008) (written testimony of Amanda Frost and Justin Florence on reforming the state secrets privilege) [hereinafter Frost and Florence testimony]; *Examining the State Secrets Privilege: Protecting National Se-*

curity While Preserving Accountability: Hearing Before the S. Comm. on the Judiciary, 110th Cong. 2–3 (2008) (written testimony of Louis Fisher); THE CONSTITUTION PROJECT, REFORMING THE STATE SECRETS PRIVILEGE 3–7 (2007), *available at* http://www.constitutionproject.org/manage/file/52.pdf.

67. *See* Edmonds v. U.S. Dep't of Justice, 323 F. Supp. 2d 65, 76–77 (D.D.C. 2004), *aff'd*, 161 F. App'x 6 (D.C. Cir. 2005); *See also* David Vladeck, *Litigating National Security Cases in the Aftermath of 9/11*, 2 J. NAT'L SEC. L. & POL'Y 165, 167–71, 186–92 (2006) (discussing *Edmonds* case).

68. PALLITTO & WEAVER, *supra* note 66, at 110–12.

69. Christina Wells, CIA v. Sims: *Mosaic Theory and Government Attitude*, 58 ADMIN. L. REV. 845, 846 (2006); *See also* David E. Pozen, *The Mosaic Theory, National Security, and the Freedom of Information Act*, 115 YALE L.J. 628, 630–31 (2005).

70. Chesney, *supra* note 42, at 1307.

71. Government Defendants' Notice of Motion and Motion to Dismiss and for Summary Judgment, at 12 n.9, Jewel v. Nat'l Sec. Agency, 2010 WL 235075 (N.D. Cal. Apr. 3, 2009) (No. C:08-cv-4373-VRW) [hereinafter Jewel MTD]; *See also infra* notes 83–85 and accompanying text.

72. Frost and Florence testimony, *supra* note 66, at 14.

73. El-Masri v. Tenet (*El-Masri II*), 479 F.3d 296 (4th Cir. 2007).

74. El-Masri v. Tenet (*El-Masri I*), 437 F. Supp. 2d 530, 532–34 (E.D. Va. 2006); Complaint at ¶¶ 1–3, 15, 27–54, *El-Masri I*, 437 F. Supp. 2d 530 (No. 1:05cv1417).

75. *El Masri II*, 479 F.3d at 301, 311.

76. *Id.* at 303.

77. *Id.* at 303–4 (quoting Chi. & S. Air Lines, Inc. v. Waterman S.S. Corp., 333 U.S. 103, 111 (1948)).

78. *Id.* at 304 (quoting Dep't of the Navy v. Egan, 484 U.S. 518, 527 (1988)).

79. *Id.* at 305.

80. Donohue, *supra* note 42, at 87.

81. *Id.* at 99.

82. *Id.* at 213.

83. Jewel MTD, *supra* note 71, at 24–25.

84. *id.* at 25 n.25 (citing to briefs filed in Al-Haramain Islamic Found. v. Bush, 2008 WL 5552047 (N.D. Cal. Mar. 14, 2008)).

85. Defendants' Notice of Motion and Second Motion to Dismiss in or, in the Alternative, for Summary Judgment at 14, *Al-Haramain*, 2008 WL 5552047 (No. M:06-CV-01791-VRW); *See also* Defendants' Reply in Support of Second Motion to Dismiss or, in the Alternative, for Summary Judgment, Al-Haramain Islamic Found. v. Bush, 2008 WL 1956160 (N.D. Cal. Apr. 14, 2008) (No. M:06-CV-01791-VRW).

86. *See* Letter from Michael Mukasey, U.S. Attorney Gen., to Patrick Leahy, U.S. Senator (Mar. 31, 2008).

87. *See, e.g.*, Christina E. Wells, *State Secrets and Executive Accountability*, 26 CONST. COMMENT. 625, 630 (2010).

88. *See, e.g., From the Department of Justice to Guantanamo Bay: Administration Lawyers and Administration Interrogation Rules: Hearing Before the Subcomm. on Administrative Oversight and the Courts of the S. Judiciary Comm.*, 110th Cong. 4 (2008) (written testimony of Michael Stokes Paulsen) (referring to broad areas of military and foreign affairs in which the president's judgment is constitutionally exclusive); John C. Eastman, *Listening to the Enemy: The President's Power to Conduct Surveillance of Enemy Communications During Time of War*, 13 ILSA J. INT'L & COMP. L. 49, 55 (2006) ("Congress cannot by mere statute restrict powers that the President holds directly from the Constitution itself," including his ability to make decisions as commander-in-chief or chief executive).

89. *See* FREDERICK A. O. SCHWARZ JR. & AZIZ Z. HUQ, UNCHECKED AND UNBALANCED: PRESIDENTIAL POWER IN A TIME OF TERROR 155–56 (2007) (quoting Richard Nixon and linking this sentiment to modern exclusivity claims). Nixon similarly told a congressional committee in 1976 that "any action a president might authorize in the interest of national security," including setting aside statutes, "would be lawful." *Id.* at 155.

90. Some may contest the accuracy of the label "secret law." On the one hand, some may argue that the types of activities described here constitute clear violations of the law as opposed to the creation or operation of new, secret laws. Yet this argument misses the point, which is that the executive branch itself deems such actions lawful based on secret constitutional reasoning. Alternatively, some may argue that the activities described here constitute the dispensing of legal advice, not the formulation of new law. Such an argument mischaracterizes both the content and the consequences of the legal advice at issue, which is to secretly authorize executive branch conduct that could reasonably be deemed to contradict existing, public statutory law. *Compare, e.g., Secret Law and the Threat to Democratic and Accountable Government: Hearing Before the Subcomm. on the Constitution of the S. Comm. on the Judiciary*, 110th Cong. 3–4 (2008) (opening statement of Sen. Sam Brownback) (contesting use of term "secret law" to describe secret OLC opinions), *and id.* at 6–7 (testimony of John P. Elwood, Deputy Ass't Att'y Gen., Office of Legal Counsel) (same), *and id.* at 9–10 (testimony of Bradford A. Berenson, Partner, Sidley & Austin, LLP) (same), *with id.* at 7–8 (testimony of Dawn E. Johnsen, Former Acting Ass't Att'y Gen., Office of Legal Counsel) (explaining why "secret law" is an accurate term for some secret OLC opinions), *and id.* at 15 (testimony of Heidi Kitrosser, Associate Professor, Univ. of Minn. Law School) (same), *and id.* at 18 (Sen. Russell D. Feingold) (same).

91. *See, e.g.*, Sudha Setty, *No More Secret Laws: How Transparency of Executive Branch Legal Policy Doesn't Let the Terrorists Win*, 57 U. KAN. L. REV. 579, 579–80, 588–94 (2009). For arguments to the effect that internal legal opinions do not constitute secret law and responses thereto, *See supra* note 90.

92. JACK GOLDSMITH, THE TERROR PRESIDENCY: LAW AND JUDGMENT IN-
SIDE THE BUSH ADMINISTRATION 18–19 (2007) (citing DOUGLAS W. KMIEC,
THE ATTORNEY GENERAL'S LAWYER: INSIDE THE MEESE JUSTICE DEPARTMENT
(1992)).

93. *See supra* chapter 1 at note 11 and accompanying text; *See also* GOLDSMITH,
supra note 92, at 32; Dawn Johnsen, *Faithfully Executing the Laws: Internal Legal
Constraints on Executive Power*, 54 UCLA L. REV. 1559, 1576–77 (2007).

94. GOLDSMITH, *supra* note 92, at 32.

95. *Id.* at 96.

96. *Id.* at 97.

97. JANE MAYER, THE DARK SIDE 66 (2008); GOLDSMITH, *supra* note 92, at
22–23, 98.

98. See MAYER, *supra* note 97, at 66 (quoting colleague of Addington and Yoo
who said, "It's incredible, but John Yoo and David Addington were running the
war on terror almost on their own."); *See also* MAJORITY STAFF OF H. COMM. ON
THE JUDICIARY, 111TH CONG., REINING IN THE IMPERIAL PRESIDENCY: LES-
SONS AND RECOMMENDATIONS RELATING TO THE PRESIDENCY OF GEORGE W.
BUSH 147 (2009) [hereinafter "Staff Report"] (citing "extraordinary line of com-
munication . . . between Mr. Yoo and Mr. Addington").

99. *See* GOLDSMITH, *supra* note 92, at 27, 76–79, 170; MAYER, *supra* note 97, at
63–64.

100. GOLDSMITH, *supra* note 92, at 23.

101. *Id.* at 98.

102. *Id.* at 166–67, 205–6.

103. Memorandum from John Yoo, Deputy Ass't Att'y Gen., Office of Legal
Counsel, U.S. Dep't of Justice, to William J. Haynes II, Gen. Counsel of the Dep't
of Defense 5 (Mar. 14, 2003); *See also id.* at 1, 11–13, 18–19.

104. Setty, *supra* note 91, at 592.

105. *Id.*

106. *Secret Law and the Threat to Democratic and Accountable Government:
Hearing Before the Subcomm. on the Constitution of the S. Comm. on the Judiciary*,
110th Cong. 2 (2008) (written testimony of J. William Leonard, Former Director,
Information Security Oversight Office) (internal citation omitted).

107. *Id.* at 8.

108. Trevor W. Morrison, *Executive Branch Avoidance and the Need for Congressional Notification*, COLUM. L. REV. SIDEBAR, Feb. 15, 2007, at 2.

109. *See generally* 149 CONG. REC. S8858–62 (daily ed. Sept. 16, 2008).

110. *Id.*

111. Constitutionality of the OLC Reporting Act of 2008, 32 Op. Att'y Gen. 1,
3 (2008).

112. *Id.* at 5.

113. *Id.*

114. Complaint at ¶ 37, 44, New York Times Co. v. U.S. Dep't of Justice, 915 F. Supp. 2d 508 (S.D.N.Y. 2013) (No. 11 CIV 9336).

115. Request Under Freedom of Information Act from ACLU 5 (Oct. 19, 2011).

116. *Id.* The ACLU also seeks materials relating to the factual basis for targeted killings. Id. at 5–6.

117. *New York Times*, 915 F. Supp. 2d at 516–19; Brief for Defendants-Appellees at 9–11, 14–18, 26–28, 32, New York Times Co. v. U.S. Dep't of Justice, No. 13–445 (2d Cir. June 14, 2013); Memorandum of Law in Support of Motion for Summary Judgment at 2–8, New York Times v. U.S. Dep't of Justice, 915 F. Supp. 2d 508 (S.D.N.Y. 2013) (No. 1:12-cv;00794-CM) [hereinafter Memorandum of Law, *New York Times v. U.S. Dep't of Justice*]; Brief for Defendant-Appellee at 11–12, 29–30, 43, ACLU v. CIA, 710 F.3d 422 (D.C. Cir. 2013) (No. 11–5320).

118. For references to some of these disclosures, see, for example, New York Times, 915 F. Supp. 2d at 524–31 (summarizing a number of public statements by administration officials including the president).

119. ACLU v. CIA, 710 F.3d 422, 431–32 (D.C. Cir. 2013); *New York Times*, 915 F. Supp. 2d at 518–19; Brief for Defendants-Appellees, *supra* note 117, at 11–18, 23–26, 32, 39–40, 46–48; Memorandum of Law, *New York Times v. U.S. Dep't of Justice*, *supra* note 117, at 7–8, 14–22.

120. *See, e.g.*, Brief for Defendants-Appellees, *supra* note 117, at 26–31; Memorandum of Law, *New York Times v. U.S. Dep't of Justice*, *supra* note 117, at 9, 15–22.

121. Brief for Defendants-Appellees, *supra* note 117, at 33, 35; Memorandum of Law, *New York Times v. U.S. Dep't of Justice*, *supra* note 117, at 10–11.

122. See, e.g., Meredith Fuchs, *Judging Secrets: The Role Courts Should Play in Preventing Unnecessary Secrecy*, 58 ADMIN. L. REV. 131, 159–67 (2006).

123. The most recent opinions as of this writing are *New York Times Co. v. U.S. Dep't of Justice*, 915 F. Supp. 2d 508 (S.D.N.Y. 2013) from January 2013, and *ACLU v. CIA*, 710 F.3d 422 (D.C. Cir. 2013) from March 2013.

124. *New York Times*, 915 F. Supp. 2d at 535. While the court indeed relies on a tradition of judicial deference that arguably flies in the face of the language and history of FOIA's classification exemption, the court also suggests that Congress could impose tougher disclosure requirements on the executive if it so wished. *id.* at 538.

125. *Id.* at 536 (citations omitted). In *ACLU v. CIA*, the U.S. Court of Appeals for the D.C. Circuit did find waiver on the CIA's part of its right to refuse to confirm or deny whether it possessed materials responsive to the FOIA requests. The D.C. Circuit acknowledged that courts are deferential in evaluating FOIA exemption claims, whether direct claims or refusals to confirm or deny the existence of responsive materials. The court concluded, however, that the CIA had waived any right to assert a need to avoid revealing whether it has an interest in the topic of drone strikes. The court explained that many official administration disclosures had already rendered obvious the CIA's interest in the topic. The court also cited

the CIA's recent acknowledgment, in the separate litigation in the U.S. District Court in New York, that it possessed some responsive materials. *ACLU*, 710 F.3d at 427–32.

126. *New York Times*, 915 F. Supp. 2d at 537 (emphasis in original).

127. *Id.* at 538.

128. Chapter 6 elaborates on these aspects of free speech doctrine in greater detail.

129. Government's Response to Defendant's Motion to Dismiss at 2, U.S. v. Drake, No. 10 CR 00181 RDB (D. Md. Mar. 11, 2011).

130. *Id.*

131. Supplemental Brief in Support of Defendants' Motion to Dismiss Count III at 22, 29–30, U.S. v. Rosen, 445 F. Supp. 2d 602 (E.D. Va. 2006) (No. 1:05 cr225).

132. *Id.* at 34.

133. *See* U.S. v. Morison, 844 F.2d 1057, 1068–70 (4th Cir. 1988); U.S. v. Morison, 604 F. Supp. 655, 664 (D. Md. 1985).

134. *See, e.g.*, Scott Shane, *Administration Takes a Hard Line Against Leaks to the Press*, N.Y. TIMES, June 10, 2010, at A1; Eli J. Lake, *Trouble for Journalists: Low Clearance*, NEW REPUBLIC, Oct. 10, 2005, at 13, available at http://www.tnr.com /article/politics/steve-rosen-keith-weissman-journalism.

135. *See* Heidi Kitrosser, *What if Daniel Ellsberg Hadn't Bothered?*, 45 IND. L. REV. 89, 111 nn.142–43 and accompanying text (2011); Heidi Kitrosser, *Supremely Opaque?, Accountability, Transparency, and Presidential Supremacy*, 5 U. ST. THOMAS J.L. & PUB. POL'Y 62, 105–06 (2010).

136. Leonard Downie Jr., *The Obama Administration and the Press*, COMM. TO PROTECT JOURNALISTS, Oct. 10, 2013, at 1, *available at* http://www.cpj.org /reports/2013/10/obama-and-the-press-us-leaks-surveillance-post-911.php (citing eight prosecutions under the Espionage Act); *See also, e.g.,* Richard Moberly, *Whistleblowers and the Obama Presidency: The National Security Dilemma*, 16 EMPL. RTS. & EMPLOY. POL'Y J. 51, 75–76 (2012) (discussing Obama administration's tough stances toward national security leakers).

137. *Id.* at 3.

138. *Id.* at 5.

139. Chapter 6 discusses *Morison* in greater detail.

140. Josh Gerstein, *Justice Dept. Cracks Down on Leaks*, POLITICO (May 25, 2010, 04:44 AM), http://www.politico.com/news/stories/0510/37721.html.

141. *See* Indictment at 2–3, U.S. v. Drake, 818 F. Supp. 2d 909 (D. Md. 2011) (No. ROB 10 CR 0181); Jane Mayer, *The Secret Sharer*, NEW YORKER (May 23, 2011), http://www.newyorker.com/reporting/2011/05/23/110523fa_fact_mayer.

142. *See* Mayer, *supra* note 141; *The Espionage Act: Why Tom Drake Was Indicted*, CBS NEWS (May 22, 2011, 8:20 PM), http://www.cbsnews.com/news /the-espionage-act-why-tom-drake-was-indicted-22-05-2011/.

143. Mayer, *supra* note 141; *The Espionage Act*, *supra* note 142; Shaun Water-

man, *Government's Espionage Case Against NSA Official Stumbles*, WASH. TIMES, June 10, 2011, at A5.

144. Mayer, *supra* note 141.

145. *Id.*; Indictment, *supra* note 141.

146. Drake Sentencing Transcript, July 15, 2011, at 2, 7, 15–18, 21–30, 41–46; *See also, e.g.*, Josh Gerstein, *Ex-NSA Official Thomas Drake Takes Plea Deal*, POLITICO (June 9, 2010, 7:33 PM), http://www.politico.com/news/stories/0611/56665 .html (quoting government secrecy expert Steven Aftergood: "The outcome pales in comparison to the opening thunder of the indictment and that shows that the government miscalculated both the severity of the offense and the quality of its own evidence."); Tricia Bishop, *NSA Espionage Case Closes Quietly*, BALT. SUN, June 11, 2011, at 2A (citing Jesselyn Radack, who consulted on Drake's case for the Government Accountability Project, to the effect that Drake's career, life, and finances remain deeply harmed by the case).

147. *See, e.g.*, Michael Isikoff, *Justice Case Against Alleged Leaker Collapses*, NBC NEWS (June 9, 2011, 11:03 PM), http://www.today.com/id/43349086/ns/us_ news-security/#.Unh8gBC7FXg; Jean Marbella, *Charges Dropped in NSA Leak Case*, BALT. SUN, June 10, 2011, at A1; *cf.* Downie, *supra* note 136, at 11 (noting that even former NSA director Michael Hayden believes that Drake should not have been prosecuted under the Espionage Act. Hayden said that Drake "should have been fired for unauthorized meetings with the press.... Prosecutorial overreach was so great that it collapsed under its own weight.").

148. Scott Shane, *Complaint Seeks Punishment for Classification of Documents*, N.Y. TIMES, Aug. 2, 2011, at A16; *See also Secret Law and the Threat to Democratic and Accountable Government: Hearing Before the Subcomm. on the Constitution of the S. Comm. on the Judiciary*, 110th Cong. 2 (2008) (written testimony of J. William Leonard, Former Director, Information Security Oversight Office) (citing his extensive access to classified information while serving as ISOO); J. William Leonard, *When Secrecy Gets Out of Hand*, L.A. TIMES (Aug. 10, 2011), http://articles .latimes.com/2011/aug/10/opinion/la-oe-leonard-classified-information-20110810.

149. *See* Mayer, *supra* note 141.

150. DEPUTY INSPECTOR GENERAL FOR INTELLIGENCE, No. 05-INTEL-03, OFFICE OF THE INSPECTOR GENERAL OF THE DEP'T OF DEFENSE ii (2004); *See also Inspector General's Report Backs NSA Whistleblower's Allegations of Waste*, PROJECT ON GOV'T OVERSIGHT (June 22, 2011), http://www.pogo.org/about /press-room/releases/2011/wi-20110622.html (discussing report and its declassification).

151. Downie, *supra* note 136, at 2.

152. *See* 28 C.F.R. § 50.10 (1980); *The Department of Justice Guidelines on Subpoenas*, REPORTER'S COMM. (July 11, 2013), http://www.rcfp.org/browse-media -law-resources/digital-journalists-legal-guide/department-justice-guidelines -subpoenas#sthash.PLVP4W1Q.dpuf (explaining that the regulations have been in

effect since 1970 with respect to subpoenas to journalists and that they have been in effect since 1980 with respect to subpoenas issued to telephone companies for journalists' telephone records).

153. Downie, *supra* note 136, at 18 (summarizing and quoting parts of 20 C.F.R. § 50.10); 20 C.F.R. § 50.10.

154. Downie, *supra* note 136, at 17.

155. *Id.*

156. *See, e.g.*, *id.* at 9, 14; Adam Liptak, *A High-Tech War on Leaks*, N.Y. TIMES, Feb. 12, 2012, at SR5; Michael Isikoff, *DOJ Gets Reporter's Phone, Credit Card Records in Leak Probe*, NBC NEWS (Feb. 25, 2011, 7:11 PM), http://www.nbcnews .com/id/41787944/#.UniBlBC7FXg; Fredrickson, *supra* note 2, at 10–11.

157. Downie, *supra* note 136, at 21.

158. *Id.* at 22.

159. See Yochai Benkler, *A Free Irresponsible Press: Wikileaks and the Battle Over the Soul of the Networked Fourth Estate*, 46 HARV. C.R.-C.L. L. REV. 311, 313–14, 338–42 (2011); Mark Townsend, *Paypal Joins Internet Backlash Against WikiLeaks*, GUARDIAN (Dec. 4, 2010), http://www.guardian.co.uk/media/2010 /dec/04/paypal-internet-backlash-wikileaks; Dan Gillmor, *Online, the Censors Are Scoring Big Wins*, SALON (Dec. 3, 2010, 01:45 PM), http://www.salon .com/2010/12/03/the_net_s_soft_underbelly/; Charles Arthur, *WikiLeaks Cables Visualization Pulled After Pressure from Joe Lieberman*, GUARDIAN (Dec. 2, 2010, 07:01 EST), http://www.theguardian.com/world/blog/2010/dec/03/wikileaks -tableau-visualisation-joe-lieberman; Glenn Greenwald, *More Joe Lieberman-Caused Internet Censorship*, SALON (Dec. 2, 2010, 04:03 PM), http://www.salon .com/news/opinion/glenn_greenwald/2010/12/02/censorship/index.html.

Chapter Six

1. Senate Select Comm. on Presidential Campaign Activities v. Nixon, 498 F.2d 725, 731 (D.C. Cir. 1974).

2. Cheney v. U.S. Dist. Ct., 542 U.S. 367, 384–85 (2004).

3. U.S. v. AT&T (*AT&T I*), 419 F. Supp. 454, 458–61 (D.D.C. 1976).

4. U.S. v. AT&T (*AT&T II*), 551 F.2d 384, 392 (D.C. Cir. 1976).

5. *Id.* at 390–95. The appeals court reviewed the negotiations in a subsequent opinion. It acknowledged that the negotiations had not resolved all matters and directed the parties to take steps designed to approach a rough middle ground between their respective positions. U.S. v. AT&T (*AT&T III*), 567 F.2d 121, 123, 130–33 (D.C. Cir. 1977).

6. Comm. on the Judiciary v. Miers, 558 F. Supp. 2d 53, 103 (D.D.C. 2008).

7. *id.* at 106 n.38.

8. The U.S. District Court for the District of Columbia recently cited both *Miers*

and *AT&T* for the yet more elemental proposition that courts have jurisdiction to decide, and need not abstain from deciding for prudential reasons, lawsuits brought by congressional committees challenging assertions of executive privilege. Comm. on Oversight & Gov't Reform v. Holder, No. 12-1332, slip op. at 3–5 (D.D.C. Sept. 30, 2013).

9. Nixon v. Adm'r of Gen. Serv., 433 U.S. 425, 433–36, 443–44, 448–52, 455 (1977).

10. *id.* at 453.

11. *id.* at 453–54.

12. Comm. on the Judiciary v. Miers, 558 F. Supp. 2d 53, 102–3 (D.D.C. 2008).

13. *Comm. on Oversight & Gov't Reform*, slip op. at 17–18.

14. U.S. v. Reynolds, 345 U.S. 1, 9–10 (1953).

15. Mohamed v. Jeppesen Dataplan, Inc., 614 F.3d 1070, 1079 (9th Cir. 2010) (en banc); *See also id.* at 1082–83.

16. *Id.* at 1073–76.

17. *Id.* at 1088.

18. Gen. Dynamics Corp. v. U.S., 131 S. Ct. 1900, 1906 (2011).

19. Tenet v. Doe, 544 U.S. 1, 8 (2005).

20. *See* Weinberger v. Catholic Action of Haw., 545 U.S. 139, 146–47 (1981); *See also Mohamed*, 614 F.3d at 1084.

21. Al-Haramain Islamic Found., Inc. v. Bush, 507 F.3d 1190, 1197 (9th Cir. 2007).

22. *Gen. Dynamics*, 131 S. Ct. at 1910; *See also, e.g., Mohamed*, 614 F.3d at 1084, 1089–90.

23. *See generally Tenet*, 544 U.S. 1; Totten v. U.S., 92 U.S. 105 (1875).

24. *See generally Gen. Dynamics*, 131 S. Ct. 1900.

25. *Id.* at 1906.

26. *Id.*

27. *id.* at 1909.

28. Weinberger v. Catholic Action of Haw., 545 U.S. 139, 146–47 (1981).

29. *id.* at 146.

30. *id.* at 149–50 (Blackmun, J., concurring).

31. *See infra* chapter 5 at notes 66–67 and accompanying text.

32. U.S. v. Reynolds, 345 U.S. 1, 9–10 (1953).

33. *See* Gen. Dynamics Corp. v. U.S., 131 S. Ct 1900, 1906 (2011) (citing Totten v. U.S., 92 U.S. 105, 107 (1875); Tenet v. Doe, 544 U.S. 1, 3 (2005)).

34. *Gen. Dynamics*, 131 S. Ct. at 1906.

35. *Tenet*, 544 U.S. at 11 (Steven, J., concurring).

36. Mohamed v. Jeppesen Dataplan, Inc., 614 F.3d 1070, 1073 (9th Cir. 2010) (en banc).

37. *id.* at 1091.

38. *id.* at 1092 (quoting Halkin v. Helms, 690 F.2d 977, 1001 (D.C. Cir. (1982)).

39. *In re* Nat'l Sec. Agency Telecomms. Records Litig., 564 F. Supp. 2d 1109, 1111, 1118 (N.D. Cal. 2008).

40. *Id.* at 1123.

41. *id.* at 1123–24 (internal citation omitted).

42. *id.* at 1121 (internal citations omitted) (emphasis in original).

43. For consideration of arguments that such phenomena do not constitute "secret law," *See infra* chapter 5 at note 90.

44. *See, e.g.*, Heidi Kitrosser, *National Security and the Article II Shell Game*, 26 CONST. COMMENT. 483, 501–20 (2010).

45. Youngstown Sheet & Tube Co. v. Sawyer, 343 U.S. 579, 582–89 (1952).

46. *See* David J. Barron & Martin S. Lederman, *The Commander in Chief at the Lowest Ebb — A Constitutional History*, 121 HARV. L. REV. 941, 1059–60 (2008).

47. *Youngstown*, 343 U.S. at 701–4, 709–10 (Vinson, C.J., dissenting).

48. *Id.* at 635 (Jackson, J., concurring); *See also* David Cole, Youngstown v. Curtiss-Wright, 99 YALE L.J. 2063, 2081 (1990) (citing Mistretta v. United States, 109 S. Ct. 647, 659 (1989); Dames & Moore v. Regan, 453 U.S. 654, 661–62, 668–69, 674 (1981)).

49. *Youngstown*, 343 U.S. at 635–38 (Jackson, J., concurring).

50. *id.* at 640–47.

51. 6 U.S. 170 (1804).

52. *id.* at 176–79.

53. Barron & Lederman, *supra* note 46, at 970.

54. Hamdan v. Rumsfeld, 548 U.S. 557, 593 n.23 (2006); *See also* David J. Barron & Martin S. Lederman, *The Commander-in-Chief at the Lowest Ebb — Framing the Problem, Doctrine, and Original Understanding*, 121 HARV. L. REV. 689, 762–63 (2008); *Youngstown*, 343 U.S. at 635 n.2 (Jackson, J., concurring).

55. See Barron & Lederman, *supra* note 54, at 761 nn.211–13 and accompanying text.

56. 299 U.S. 304 (1936).

57. *Id.* at 320.

58. HAROLD KOH, THE NATIONAL SECURITY CONSTITUTION 94 (1990). For more recent observations to the effect that government attorneys frequently cite to *Curtiss-Wright*'s "sole organ" discussion to support presidentialism, see, for example, Michael P. Van Alstyne, *Taking Care of John Marshall's Political Ghost*, 53 ST. LOUIS U. L.J. 93, 101 (2008); Martin S. Flaherty, *Organs Misused and Used: A Comment on the Sole Organ Problem*, 53 ST. LOUIS U. L.J. 137, 138, 143 (2008); Louis Fisher, *A Series of Studies on Presidential Power in Foreign Relations: No. 1: The "Sole Organ" Doctrine*, L. LIBR. CONG. 1, 1–2 (2006).

59. For such criticisms or references to the same, see, for example, KOH, *supra* note 58, at 94; Van Alstyne, *supra* note 58, at 94–95, 119–35; Flaherty, *supra* note 58, at 141–43; Fisher, *supra* note 58 at 2, 7–11, 21–23.

60. *See Curtiss-Wright*, 299 U.S. at 311–15.

61. *See, e.g.*, Fisher, *supra* note 58, at 9.

62. *See Curtiss-Wright*, 299 U.S. at 321–22.

63. *See, e.g.*, Heidi Kitrosser, *It Came from Beneath the Twilight Zone: Warrantless Wiretapping and Article II Imperialism*, 88 TEX. L. REV. 1401, 1421–25 (2010); *id.* at 1421 (citing Barron & Lederman, *supra* note 46, at 948–49, 952, 993–94, 999–1004, 1007–9, 1015–16, 1027, 1034–35, 1057–58; Barron & Lederman, *supra* note 54, at 697, 718–20, 763–64). Even Justice Sutherland's own pre-judicial writings, while reflecting an attraction to strong presidential powers, were inconsistent in the nature and extent of their support for exclusivity. *See* Fisher, *supra* note 58, at 15–17.

64. Fisher, *supra* note 58, at 14–15.

65. *See* Barron & Lederman, *supra* note 54, at 741–43, 761 n.212 (describing recent examples of this confusion).

66. In addition to the cases cited in the accompanying text, *See also*, for example, Dames & Moore v. Regan, 453 U.S. 654, 675, 686–87 (1981) (upholding president's order transferring Iranian assets pursuant to hostage crisis negotiations as authorized by statute, also upholding presidential suspension of pending claims on such assets because Congress implicitly authorized the latter and, "[j]ust as importantly, Congress [did] not disapprove[] of the action taken").

67. *See, e.g.*, Chi. & S. Air Lines, Inc. v. Waterman, 333 U.S. 103, 111 (1948) (deeming foreign policy questions political matters that "should be undertaken only by those directly responsible to the people whose welfare they advance or imperil").

68. *See infra* chapter 5 at notes 129–33 and accompanying text and *infra* this chapter at notes 69–95 and accompanying text; *See also* Heidi Kitrosser, *Free Speech Aboard the Leaky Ship of State: Calibrating First Amendment Protections for Leakers of Classified Information*, 6 J. NAT'L SEC. L. & POL'Y 409, 413–21 (2013).

69. N.Y. Times Co. v. U.S., 403 U.S. 713, 714 (1971) (per curiam opinion denying government request for prior restraint); *id.* at 730–31, 733 (concurring—in an opinion by Justice White joined by Justice Stewart—"only because of the concededly extraordinary protection against prior restraints." and noting that newspapers will not be "immune from criminal action" if they proceed to publish the documents that the government sought to restrain) (White, J., concurring); *id.* at 743 (noting that "we are not faced with a situation where Congress has failed to provide the Executive with broad power to protect the Nation from disclosure of damaging state secrets," as statutes provide for postpublication criminal penalties) (Marshall, J., concurring); *id.* at 752, 755–59 (dissenting—in an opinion by Justice Harlan joined by Chief Justice Burger and Justice Blackmun—from the Court's denial of the prior restraint sought by the government).

70. *id.* at 756 (Harlan, J., dissenting).

71. Snepp v. U.S., 444 U.S. 507, 513 n.8, 515–16 (1980).

72. *Id.* at 512.

73. Wilson v. CIA, 586 F.3d 171, 185 (2d Cir. 2009) (quoting McGehee v. Casey, 718 F.2d 1137, 1141 (D.C. Cir. 1983), and citing *Snepp*, 444 U.S. at 513 n.8 for proposition that "[i]f in fact information is unclassified or in the public domain, neither the CIA nor foreign agencies would be concerned."); *See also Snepp*, 444 U.S. at 511 ("the government does not deny—as a general principle—Snepp's right to publish unclassified information"); *McGehee*, 718 F.2d at 1141 (quoting U.S. v. Marchetti, 466 F.2d 1309, 1313 (4th Cir. 1972), and citing *Snepp*, 444 U.S. at 513 n.8 for proposition that unclassified information may not be restricted by contract or otherwise); *cf.* Weaver v. U.S. Info. Agency, 87 F.3d 1429, 1435–36, 1442 n.4 (D.C. Cir. 1996) (deeming review requirement for unclassified information acceptable because it does not entail punishments for unapproved publications; indicating that serious First Amendment problems would exist were punishments imposed).

74. U.S. v. Morison, 844 F.2d 1057, 1068–70 (4th Cir. 1988).

75. *Id.* at 1069–70.

76. *Marchetti*, 466 F.2d at 1312, 1315–18.

77. *Id.* at 1313; *See also id.* at 1317 ("[w]e would decline enforcement of the secrecy oath ... to the extent that it purports to prevent disclosure of unclassified information").

78. U.S. v. Drake, 818 F. Supp. 2d 909, 919–21 (D. Md. 2011).

79. *See* Heidi Kitrosser, *Classified Information Leaks and Free Speech*, 2008 U. ILL. L. REV. 881, 902–3 (citing U.S. v. Rosen, 445 F. Supp. 2d 602 (E.D. Va. 2006)).

80. U.S. v. Rosen, 599 F. Supp. 2d 690, 695 (E.D. Va. 2009).

81. *Id.*

82. *See* Brandenburg v. Ohio, 395 U.S. 444, 447 (1969).

83. U.S. v. Morison, 844 F.2d 1057, 1068–69 (4th Cir. 1988).

84. Snepp v. U.S., 444 U.S. 507, 510 (1980).

85. *Id.* at 510–11.

86. *Id.* at 515–16.

87. Wilson v. CIA, 586 F.3d 171, 174 (2d Cir. 2009).

88. U.S. v. Aguilar, 515 U.S. 593, 595, 605–6 (1995).

89. *Wilson*, 586 F.3d at 183.

90. U.S. v. Kim, 808 F. Supp. 2d 44, 56–57 (D.D.C. 2011) (quoting Boehner v. McDermott, 484 F.3d 573, 579 (D.C. Cir. 2007)).

91. Connick v. Myers, 461 U.S. 138, 140 (1983) (quoting Pickering v. Bd. of Educ., 391 U.S. 563, 568 (1968)).

92. Garcetti v. Ceballos, 547 U.S. 410, 413 (2006); *See also id.* at 418–23.

93. Stephen I. Vladeck, *The Espionage Act and National Security Whistleblowing After* Garcetti, 57 AM. U. L. REV. 1531, 1534–35, 1540–41 (2006).

94. Geoffrey R. Stone, *Secrecy and Self-Governance*, 56 N.Y.L. SCH. L. REV. 81, 87–90 (2011).

95. *id.* at 91 ("Applying the *Pickering* standard, the government has no legiti-

mate interest in keeping secret its own illegality, and the public has a compelling interest in the disclosure of such information."). Similarly, some lower court opinions deem *Snepp* to have implicitly applied *Pickering* balancing to classified information leaks. *See, e.g.*, Weaver v. U.S. Info. Agency, 87 F.3d 1429, 1439–43 (D.C. Cir. 1996); *id.* at 1439–40 (citing Zook v. Brown, 865 F.2d 887 (7th Cir. 1989)).

96. U.S. v. Morison, 844 F.2d 1057, 1083 (4th Cir. 1988) (Wilkinson, J., concurring).

97. *Id.* at 1084.

98. *Id.* at 1085 (Phillips, J., concurring).

99. *Id.* at 1086 (Phillips, J., concurring).

100. N.Y. Times Co. v. U.S., 403 U.S. 713, 753 (1971) (Harlan, J., dissenting).

101. *Cf.* Harold Edgar & Benno C. Schmidt Jr., Curtiss-Wright *Comes Home: Executive Power and National Security Secrecy*, 21 HARV. C.R.-C.L. L. REV. 349, 361 (1986) ("A number of the Justices volunteered readings of the espionage statutes in relation to hypothetical criminal proceedings against the publishers, reporters and information sources involved, even though such questions had not been briefed, were dreadfully difficult, and were quite unnecessary to a ruling about the injunction.").

102. Snepp v. U.S., 444 U.S. 507, 515–16 (1980).

103. *See also* James A. Goldston et al., Comment, *A Nation Less Secure: Diminished Public Access to Information*, 21 HARV. C.R.-C.L. L. REV. 409, 441–42 (1986) (citing the case's unusual procedural posture and "cursory attention to first amendment questions" as an additional basis for caution in applying its holding).

104. *Snepp*, 444 U.S. at 524–25 (Stevens, J., dissenting); Goldston et al., *supra* note 103, at 442 n.165; Diane F. Orentlicher, Snepp v. U.S.: *The CIA Secrecy Agreement and the First Amendment*, 81 COLUM. L. REV. 662, 665 n.23 (1981).

105. *Snepp*, 444 U.S. at 524–25 (Stevens, J., dissenting).

106. Archibald Cox, *Foreword: Freedom of Expression in the Burger Court*, 94 HARV. L. REV. 1, 9–10 (1980); Orentlicher, *supra* note 104, at 665 n.23.

107. Cox, *supra* note 106, at 9–10.

108. U.S. v. Aguilar, 515 U.S. 593, 606 (1995).

109. *Id.* at 605–6.

110. In *Wilson v. CIA*, the Second Circuit correctly cited *Aguilar*'s limited statement about the relative protection accorded speakers who voluntarily take on nondisclosure obligations. 586 F.3d 171, 183 (2d Cir. 2009). It went on, however, to suggest the broader point that "once a government employee signs an agreement not to disclose information properly classified pursuant to executive order, that employee 'simply has no first amendment right to publish' such information." *Id.* at 183–84. For the latter point it relied on *Snepp* and other cases specific to the issue of prepublication review contractual enforcement. *Id.* at 183–86. Two years after *Wilson*, the D.C. Circuit framed *Aguilar*'s reasoning more broadly still. In *Boehner v. McDermott*, the D.C. Circuit wrote: "*Aguilar* stands for the principle that those

who accept positions of trust involving a duty not to disclose information they lawfully acquire while performing their responsibilities have no First Amendment right to disclose that information." 484 F.3d 573, 579 (D.C. Cir. 2007). The *Boehner* Court upheld a damages award against U.S. Representative McDermott for disclosing an illegally obtained recording of a conference call that took place among a group of other congresspersons. *Id.* at 575, 581. The court explained that Representative McDermott, as a member of the House Ethics Committee investigating a party to the phone call, had explicitly taken on special duties of confidentiality. *Id.* at 579–81. *Boehner* can and should, however, be limited to its facts, which are not incompatible with the notion that executive branch insiders who leak classified information merit a degree of First Amendment protection. *Boehner*'s characterization of the *Aguilar* Court's reasoning is dicta, and it misstates the *Aguilar* Court's limited position. *See id.* at 588–89 (Sentelle, J., dissenting) (criticizing the *Boehner* majority's reading of *Aguilar* on grounds similar to those advanced here). For its part, the District Court for the District of Columbia also erred in citing *Boehner*'s mischaracterization of *Aguilar* to support its own rejection of Stephen Kim's motion to dismiss his indictment for leaking classified information. U.S. v. Kim, 808 F. Supp. 2d 44, 56–57 (D.D.C. 2011).

111. Connick v. Myers, 461 U.S. 138, 140 (1983) (quoting Pickering v. Bd. of Educ., 391 U.S. 563, 568 (1968)).

112. Garcetti v. Ceballos, 547 U.S. 410, 421 (2006).

113. *Id.* at 420 (quoting *Connick*, 461 U.S. at 154).

114. The cases, in other words, are about "managerial prerogative." *See* Lawrence Rosenthal, *The Emerging First Amendment Law of Managerial Prerogative*, 77 FORDHAM L. REV. 33, 43 (2008) (deeming managerial prerogative "critical to the outcome in *Garcetti*").

115. *Garcetti*, 547 U.S. at 421–22; *See also* Vladeck, *supra* note 93, at 1540 (citing this language and interpreting it to preclude constitutional protection for leaking classified information).

116. *Garcetti*, 547 U.S. at 420 (quoting *Connick*, 461 U.S. at 154).

117. *Id.* at 419; *See also id.* at 419–20 (approvingly citing earlier cases to the effect that government employees are especially well qualified to comment on matters that pertain to their employment).

118. Wilson v. CIA, 586 F.3d 171, 185 n.15 (2d Cir. 2009); *See also* Rosenthal, *supra* note 114, at 63 n.99 (agreeing that *Garcetti* does not preclude protection for classified information leaks); Mika C. Morse, Note, *Honor or Betrayal? The Ethics of Government Lawyer-Whistleblowers*, 23 GEO. J. LEGAL ETHICS 421, 430 (2010) (same).

119. *See, e.g.*, Fairley v. Fermaint, 482 F.3d 897, 899, 902 (7th Cir. 2006) (noting that testimony by county jail guards as to knowledge of inmate abuse acquired on the job was not part of their employment duties and thus not within *Garcetti* exemption); Pattee v. Ga. Ports Auth., 477 F. Supp. 2d 1253, 1257–58, 1261 n.4 (S.D. Ga. 2006) (explaining that Georgia Port Police officer's whistleblowing e-mails

containing information acquired on the job were not covered by the *Garcetti* exemption because they were not sent in the course of his employment).

120. *See, e.g.*, N.Y. Times Co. v. Sullivan, 376 U.S. 254, 269–71, 273–76 (1964).

121. *See, e.g.*, Thornhill v. Alabama, 310 U.S. 88, 95, 101–2 (1940); Grossjean v. Am. Press Co., 297 U.S. 233, 243, 249–50 (1936).

122. *Thornhill*, 310 U.S. at 101–2.

123. *See, e.g.*, Heidi Kitrosser, *From Marshall McLuhan to Anthropomorphic Cows: Communicative Manner and the First Amendment*, 96 Nw. U. L. REV. 1339, 1339–42, 1345–49 (2002) (summarizing the rule and citing cases, though noting that the Supreme Court does not always treat communicative manner as content).

124. For discussions reflecting this consensus, see, for example, GEOFFREY R. STONE, PERILOUS TIMES: FREE SPEECH IN WARTIME 179–207, 403–11 (2004); Martin H. Redish, *Advocacy of Unlawful Conduct and the First Amendment: In Defense of Clear and Present Danger,* 70 CAL. L. REV. 1159, 1166–73 (1982).

125. For discussions of the doctrinal evolution from *Schenck* through *Brandenburg,* see, example, HARRY KALVEN JR., A WORTHY TRADITION: FREEDOM OF SPEECH IN AMERICA 227–36 (Jamie Kalven ed., 1988).

126. Brandenburg v. Ohio, 395 U.S. 444, 447 (1969).

127. *id.* at 447–49; *See also* Landmark Commc'ns, Inc. v. Va., 435 U.S. 829, 842–44 (1978).

128. N.Y. Times Co. v. Sullivan, 376 U.S. 254, 279 (1964).

129. Garcetti v. Ceballos, 547 U.S. 410, 419 (2006).

130. Pickering v. Bd. of Educ., 391 U.S. 563, 572 (1968).

131. For more on institutional approaches to the First Amendment generally and their relationship to classified information leak punishments, see Kitrosser, *supra* note 68, at 440–42, 444–45, 444 n.161 and accompanying text. *See also supra* notes 111–16 and accompanying text.

132. *See, e.g.*, ERWIN CHEMERINSKY, CONSTITUTIONAL LAW: PRINCIPLES AND POLICIES § 11.3.5.2, *Defamation*, 1008–18 (2d ed. 2002) (summarizing these distinctions in defamation and libel law). For more on this aspect of calibration as it relates to classified information leaks, see Kitrosser, *supra* note 68, at 445. For more on the notion of a "penalty sensitive First Amendment" more broadly, *See generally* Michael Coenen, *Of Speech and Sanctions: Toward a Penalty-Sensitive Approach to the First Amendment,* 112 COLUM. L. REV. 991 (2012).

Chapter Seven

1. Ilya Somin, *Distinguishing the Scope of Executive Power from Its Distribution,* VOLOKH CONSPIRACY (Aug. 14, 2007, 3:09 PM), http://www.volokh.com /2007/08/14/distinguishing-the-scope-of-executive-power-from-its-distribution/ (quoting Justice Alito at his confirmation hearings).

2. *See, e.g.,* Steven G. Calabresi & Saikrishna B. Prakash, *The President's*

Power to Execute the Laws, 104 YALE L.J. 541, 595 (1994); Steven G. Calabresi & Kevin H. Rhodes, *The Structural Constitution: Unitary Executive, Plural Judiciary*, 105 HARV. L. REV. 1153, 1158, 1166 (1992).

3. *See infra* chapter 8 at notes 29–33 and accompanying text.

4. U.S. CONST. art. II, § 1, cl. 1.

5. Saikrishna Prakash, *The Essential Meaning of Executive Power*, 2003 U. ILL. L. REV. 701, 704.

6. *Id.* at 716; *See also* Morrison v. Olson, 487 U.S. 654, 705 (1998) (Scalia, J., dissenting); Calabresi & Prakash, *supra* note 2, at 579–82, 594–95.

7. Prakash, *supra* note 5, at 716; *See also Morrison*, 487 U.S. at 709–10 (Scalia, J., dissenting); Calabresi & Rhodes, *supra* note 2, at 1175–81.

8. Prakash, *supra* note 5, at 721, 731; *See also* Calabresi & Rhodes, *supra* note 2, at 1167–68, 1184–85, 1206–8; Calabresi & Prakash, *supra* note 2, at 582–85.

9. In one representative discussion, for example, a pro-unity commentator writes:

> The Philadelphia Convention chose a unitary executive to secure vigorous, uniform, and responsible administration of the laws. Delegates understood that a plural executive might result in "uncontrolled, continued and violent animosities" in the executive branch. During the ratification struggles, many participants likewise understood the salutary consequences of a unitary executive. There would be no councils to hide behind; there would be no plural, divided executive that might lead to chaos. Instead, one responsible person would superintend the administration of federal law.

Prakash, *supra* note 5, at 783; *See also, e.g.,* Steven G. Calabresi, *Some Normative Arguments for the Unitary Executive*, 48 ARK. L. REV. 23, 42–45 (1995).

10. *See, e.g.,* Saikrishna B. Prakash, *New Light on the Decision of 1789*, 91 CORNELL L. REV. 1021, 1026 (2006).

11. Peter L. Strauss, *Overseer, or "The Decider"? The President in Administrative Law*, 75 GEO. WASH. L. REV. 696, 705 (2007); *See also* Peter L. Strauss, *The Place of Agencies in Government: Separation of Powers and the Fourth Branch*, 84 COLUM. L. REV. 573, 648 (1984).

12. *See, e.g.,* Strauss, *Place of Agencies, supra* note 11, at 597–99; Strauss, *Overseer or Decider, supra* note 11, at 702–5; David M. Driesen, *Toward a Duty-Based Theory of Executive Power*, 78 FORDHAM L. REV. 71, 83–94 (2009); Martin Flaherty, *The Most Dangerous Branch*, 105 YALE L.J. 1725, 1800–01 (1996); Peter M. Shane, *Independent Policymaking and Presidential Power*, 57 GEO. WASH. L. REV. 596, 611 (1988–89).

13. David Driesen makes this point about the passive nature of the Take Care Clause in Driesen, *supra* note 12, at 83–84.

14. *See, e.g.,* sources cited *supra* note 12.

15. U.S. CONST. art. I, § 8, cl. 18.

16. *Compare* M. J. C. VILE, CONSTITUTIONALISM AND THE SEPARATION OF POWERS 156–57, 171–72 (Liberty Fund 2d ed. 1998) (suggesting that the appointment power was a remnant of the royal prerogative with which states seeking "merely executive" governors dispensed), *and* GORDON S. WOOD, THE CREATION OF THE AMERICAN REPUBLIC 143–50 (1998 ed.) (same), *with* THE FEDERALIST NO. 47, at 134 (James Madison) (Kindle edition) (explaining that powers need not be fully separated, as exemplified in part by state constitutions granting legislatures the appointment power, which is "in its nature an executive function."). A statement by James Wilson at the Philadelphia Convention arguably fell somewhere in the middle. As Rakove recounts, Wilson stated "that the royal prerogative did not provide 'a proper guide in defining the Executive powers.' Some of those prerogatives were actually legislative.... 'The only powers he conceived strictly executive were those of executing the laws, and appointing officers' not otherwise 'appointed by the Legislature.'" JACK N. RAKOVE, ORIGINAL MEANINGS 257 (1997).

17. RAKOVE, *supra* note 16, at 274 (referring to Tench Coxe, *An Examination of the Constitution of the United States, Essay I, in* AN AMERICAN CITIZEN (Sept. 26, 1787)).

18. Coxe, *supra* note 17.

19. THE FEDERALIST NO. 77, at 208 (Alexander Hamilton) (Kindle edition). A recent article challenges the long-standing view that Hamilton's statement referred to the removal power. The article suggests that by "displace," Hamilton might have meant "replace," and thus might have been referring only to the Senate's role in confirming new appointees to replace those removed by the president. *See* Seth Barrett Tillman, *The Puzzle of Hamilton's Federalist No. 77*, 33 HARV. J.L. & PUB. POL'Y 149 (2010). While this is a provocative thesis, I believe that it is an unlikely one, largely for reasons captured in a response essay by Jeremy D. Bailey. Jeremy D. Bailey, *The Traditional View of Hamilton's Federalist No. 77 and an Unexpected Challenge: A Response to Seth Barrett Tillman*, 33 HARV. J.L. & PUB. POL'Y 169 (2010). Even if Tillman's thesis were accurate, the record is clear that at least some founders understood Hamilton to have been referring to the removal power, and that others, including Tench Coxe, publicly expressed the view that the president's removal power was not unlimited. *See* Tillman, *supra*, at 161–63; *See also infra* notes 17–18 and accompanying text.

20. *See infra* chapter 4 at text accompanying notes 38–43; *See also* Flaherty, *supra* note 12, at 1790–92 (connecting this uncertainty to the lack of a unity directive).

21. This was famously observed by Madison in *Federalist* No. 47, who cited the examples of the states to demonstrate that it was neither possible nor desirable to completely separate the three major powers. THE FEDERALIST NO. 47, at 134–35

(James Madison) (Kindle edition); *See also, e.g.,* WOOD, *supra* note 16, at 153–56; VILE, *supra* note 16, at 131–33, 146–49, 154–74; Flaherty, *supra* note 12, at 1765–71, 1776–77; Gerhard Casper, *An Essay in Separation of Powers: Some Early Versions and Practices,* 30 WM. & MARY L. REV. 211, 217–19 (1989); Edward S. Corwin, *The Progress of Constitutional Theory Between the Declaration of Independence and the Meeting of the Philadelphia Convention,* 30 AM. HIST. REV. 511, 514, 516 (1925).

22. Flaherty, *supra* note 12, at 1791; *See also* sources cited *supra* note 21.

23. *See, e.g.,* Michael P. Riccards, *The Presidency and the Ratification Controversy,* 7 PRESIDENTIAL STUDIES Q. 37, 38, 41, 44 (1977) (citing arguments made by Federalists during the ratification process to the effect that the president's powers were not meaningfully greater than those of state governors).

24. 9 THE DOCUMENTARY HISTORY OF THE RATIFICATION OF THE CONSTITUTION 1097–98 (John P. Kaminski & Gaspare J. Saladino eds., 1990) [hereinafter DOCUMENTARY HISTORY, vol. 9]; *See also* earlier reference to this quote, *infra* chapter 4 at text accompanying note 49.

25. Foreign Affairs Department Act § 1 (July 27, 1789); *See also* War Department Act § 1 (Aug. 7, 1789).

26. Treasury Department Act § 2 (Sept. 2, 1789).

27. DAVID P. CURRIE, THE CONSTITUTION IN CONGRESS: THE FEDERALIST PERIOD 41–42 (1997) (internal citations omitted); *See also, e.g.,* Jerry L. Mashaw, *Recovering American Administrative Law: Federalist Foundations, 1787–1801,* 115 YALE L.J. 1256, 1284–88 (2006); Casper, *supra* note 21, at 240–42.

28. Jerry Mashaw uses the term "mongrel administrators" toward the same end as I use it here in Mashaw, *supra* note 27, at 1289–92. He quotes the first attorney general, Edmund Randolph, who described his own role as that of a "mongrel," though Randolph used this term to convey a different point than that made by Mashaw. *Id.* at 1289.

29. Judiciary Act of 1789 § 35; *See also* Susan Low Bloch, *The Early Role of the Attorney General in Our Constitutional Scheme: In the Beginning There Was Pragmatism,* 1989 DUKE L.J. 561, 578–79.

30. Mashaw, *supra* note 27, at 1289–91; Bloch, *supra* note 29, at 581–82.

31. Bloch, *supra* note 29, at 581–82.

32. *Id.* at 585–89; *See also* Mashaw, *supra* note 27, at 1290–91.

33. *See, e.g.,* Mashaw, *supra* note 27, at 1291–92, 1296, 1301–2; Lawrence Lessig & Cass R. Sunstein, *The President and the Administration,* 94 COLUM. L. REV. 1, 16–21, 29–32 (1994).

34. Bloch, *supra* note 29, at 582.

35. *See, e.g.,* Calabresi, *supra* note 9, at 35–37, 59, 65–66; Prakash, *supra* note 5, at 701, 731–32, 751–52, 783–85.

36. THE FEDERALIST NO. 70, at 428–29 (Alexander Hamilton) (Clinton Rossiter ed., 2003).

37. *id.* at 426–27.

38. *Id.*

39. THE FEDERALIST NO. 76, at 456 (Alexander Hamilton) (Clinton Rossiter ed., 2003).

40. THE FEDERALIST NO. 77, at 460 (Alexander Hamilton) (Clinton Rossiter ed., 2003).

41. 2 DOCUMENTARY HISTORY OF THE RATIFICATION OF THE CONSTITUTION 635 (Merrill Jensen ed., 1990) [hereinafter DOCUMENTARY HISTORY, vol. 2].

42. 8 DOCUMENTARY HISTORY OF THE RATIFICATION OF THE CONSTITUTION 44 (John P. Kaminski & Gaspare J. Saladino eds., 1990).

43. DOCUMENTARY HISTORY, vol. 2, *supra* note 41, at 495.

44. DOCUMENTARY HISTORY, vol. 9, *supra* note 24, at 679–80.

45. DOCUMENTARY HISTORY, vol. 2, *supra* note 41, at 141.

46. 3 DOCUMENTARY HISTORY OF THE RATIFICATION OF THE CONSTITUTION 241 (Merrill Jensen ed., 1990).

47. 1 ANNALS OF CONG. 455–585, 590–591 (1789).

48. *See, e.g.*, Myers v. U.S., 272 U.S. 52, 112–14, 119 (1926); Prakash, *supra* note 10, at 1026, 1031–33, 1042.

49. See Prakash, *supra* note 10, at 1024–26, 1042–43 (summarizing arguments to this effect).

50. 1 ANNALS OF CONG. 495–97, 578–79 (Madison); 464–65, 585 (Vining); 469, 527–28, 583 (Boudinot); 538–40 (Ames); 489 (Clymer); 505–6 (Benson).

51. *Id.* at 520–21, 583–84 (Sedgwick); 484–86, 583 (Lawrence); 524–25 (Lee); 584 (Tucker).

52. *Id.* at 479–81, 585 (Hartley); 532–33 (Scott); 534 (Goodhue); 560 (Baldwin); 562–63 (Sylvester).

53. *Id.* at 455–56, 513–515 (White); 473, 502–4, 535–36, 574–75 (Gerry); 477–79, 543 (Livermore); 486–89, 530–32, 554–55 (Jackson); 490–91, 519–20, 548–51 (Page); 491–92, 538 (Sherman); 493–94, 564–65, 568–69 (Stone); *See also* Prakash, *supra* note 10, at 1036–38.

54. *See* Prakash, *supra* note 10, at 1035–36.

55. Morrison v. Olson, 487 U.S. 654, 685–86 (1988) (distinguishing the good cause limitation that the Court upheld in *Morrison* from earlier provisions that the Court had struck down because Congress had impermissibly "reserve[d] for itself the power of removal of an [executive] officer.").

56. *See, e.g.*, 1 ANNALS OF CONG. 461–62, 499 (Madison); 569 (Vining); 481 (Hartley); 485–86 (Lawrence); 506–07 (Benson); 533 (Scott); 557–58 (Baldwin); *See also* sources cited *infra* note 58 (to the effect that many in the 1789 debate voiced concerns that the Senate—whose members were not, at the time, elected directly by the people—would be less politically responsive than the nationally elected president).

57. 1 ANNALS OF CONG. 611, 615; *See also* Prakash, *supra* note 10, at 1071.

58. 1 ANNALS OF CONG. 462; *See also, e.g., id.* at 499 (Madison); 465 (Vining); 474, 477, 539–40 (Ames); 489 (Clymer); 522–23 (Sedgwick); 525 (Lee). Members of the majority also deemed the president intrinsically more responsible to the people than the Senate because of the respective modes by which each is elected. Given the national scope of the Electoral College through which the president is elected and reelected, some echoed Representative Lawrence's statement that "[t]he President is the representative of the people in a near and equal manner; he is the guardian of his country." *Id.* at 483; *See also, e.g., id.* at 581 (Hartley); 499 (Madison), 533 (Scott); 572 (Vining). In contrast, they emphasized that senators at the time (prior to the Seventeenth Amendment's passage in 1913) were elected not by the people but by state legislatures, and that each state has two senators regardless of population. *See, e.g., id.* at 483 (Lawrence), 533 (Scott), 572 (Vining). As James Madison asked rhetorically, "Shall we trust the Senate, responsible to individual Legislatures, rather than the person who is responsible to the whole community?" *Id.* at 499.

59. 1 ANNALS OF CONG. 519; *See also, e.g., id.* at 458, 472, 508–9 (Smith); 473, 502, 575 (Gerry); 487–89; 530–31 (Jackson); 568–69 (Stone).

60. *Id.* at 488 (Jackson). Representative Page, too, warned that "this clause of the bill contains in it the seeds of royal prerogative." *Id.* at 490. Members of the minority also harnessed these points to respond to the textual argument that removal power is implicit in executive power. They explained that the scope of executive power is context-dependent. Its meaning is informed by the type of government in which it exists. They emphasized that the United States is not a monarchy and that it accords Congress, not the president, the power to create and shape executive offices. In this context, they argued, the executive power cannot include an implicit, unalterable right on the president's part to remove executive officers at his pleasure. *See, e.g., id.* at 466, 513–15 (White); 477 (Livermore); 486–89 (Jackson); 494 (Stone); 504 (Gerry); 510, 545 (Smith); 548 (Page).

61. U.S. CONST. art. II, § 2, cl. 1.

62. Flaherty, *supra* note 12, at 1796–97.

63. Akhil Reed Amar, *Some Opinions on the Opinions Clause*, 82 VA. L. REV. 647, 671 (1996) (citing 4 DEBATES IN THE SEVERAL STATE CONVENTIONS ON THE ADOPTION OF THE FEDERAL CONSTITUTION 108–10 (Jonathan Elliot ed., 2d ed. 1968) (statement of James Iredell)).

64. U.S. CONST. art. I, § 8, cl. 18.

65. *See, e.g.,* Calabresi, *supra* note 9, at 35–37, 58–70; Lessig & Sunstein, *supra* note 33, at 97–99.

66. *See* Flaherty, *supra* note 12, at 1785 (cited in Heidi Kitrosser, *The Accountable Executive*, 93 U. MINN L. REV. 1741, 1748–49 (2009)); Peter M. Shane, *Political Accountability in a System of Checks and Balances: The Case of Presidential Review of Rulemaking*, 48 ARK. L. REV. 161, 197–209 (1995) (cited in Kitrosser, *Accountable Executive*, at 1749–50); *See also* Cynthia R. Farina, *The Consent of the Governed: Against Simple Rules for a Complex World*, 72 CHI.-KENT L. REV. 987,

992–1007, 1017–20 (1997) (cited in Kitrosser, *Accountable Executive*, at 1749 n.36); Jerry L. Mashaw, *Structuring a "Dense Complexity": Accountability and the Project of Administrative Law*, ISSUES IN LEGAL SCHOLARSHIP, Mar. 2005, 12–15, 35–38 (cited in Kitrosser, *Accountable Executive*, at 1749 n.36).

67. *See* Rebecca L. Brown, *Accountability, Liberty, and the Constitution*, 98 COLUM. L. REV. 531, 552–59, 564–65 (1998) (cited in Kitrosser, *Accountable Executive*, at 1750); Shane, *supra* note 12, at 613–14 (cited in Kitrosser, *Accountable Executive*, at 1750).

68. Kitrosser, *supra* note 66, at 1750 (citing Edward Rubin, *The Myth of Accountability and the Anti-Administrative Impulse*, 103 MICH. L. REV. 2073, 2076–83, 2119–22, 2134–35 (2005)); *See also* Jide Nzelibe, *The Fable of the Nationalist President and the Parochial Congress*, 53 UCLA L. REV. 1217, 1221–22, 1232–34, 1249 (2006) (deeming fallacious the notion that the president is the most nationally accountable figure (if accountability means politically responsive) in American politics); *cf.* Matthew C. Stephenson, *Optimal Political Control of the Bureaucracy*, 107 MICH. L. REV. 53, 55, 93–94 (2008) (casting doubt on the notion that maximizing political control—by either the president or other political actors—over the bureaucracy will maximize bureaucratic responsiveness to majoritarian preferences).

69. 272 U.S. 52 (1926).

70. *Id.* at 127 (citing U.S. v. Perkins, 116 U.S. 483, 485 (1886)); *See also id.* at 161–62, 173–74.

71. *Myers*, 272 U.S. at 135.

72. 295 U.S. 602 (1935).

73. *id.* at 619, 623–26.

74. *id.* at 629.

75. *Id.*

76. 487 U.S. 654, 686–93 (1988).

77. More precisely, the statute permitted termination only for "good cause, physical disability, mental incapacity, or any other condition that substantially impairs the performance of such independent counsel's duties." *Id.* at 663 (quoting 28 U.S.C. § 596(a)(1) (Supp. V 1982)).

78. *id.* at 685–686, 691–92.

79. 130 S. Ct. 3138 (2010).

80. *id.* at 3147–48.

81. *id.* at 3148. *But see* Peter L. Strauss, *On the Difficulties of Generalization—PCAOB in the Footsteps of Myers, Humphrey's Executor, Morrison, and Freytag*, 32 CARDOZO L. REV. 2255, 2276–78 (2011) (pointing out serious flaws in the majority's conclusion that SEC members can be removed only for cause).

82. 130 S. Ct. at 3157–61.

83. *id.* at 3151–52; *See also, e.g.,* Richard H. Pildes, *Free Enterprise Fund, Boundary-Enforcing Decisions, and the Unitary Executive Branch Theory of Government Administration*, 6 DUKE J. CONST. L. & PUB. POL'Y 1, 2, 7–8 (2010); *cf.*

Neomi Rao, *A Modest Proposal: Abolishing Agency Independence in Free Enterprise Fund v. PCAOB*, 79 FORDHAM L. REV. 2541 (2011) (arguing that *PCAOB* embraces far-reaching pro-unity principles).

84. Strauss, *supra* note 81, at 2281; *See also id.* at 2275–76 ("if one looks past the PCAOB to the enormous variety of statutory provisions respecting government employment, one easily finds hundreds if not thousands of government employees who can only be removed 'for cause' by superiors who themselves can only be removed 'for cause.'").

85. *Cf.* Pildes, *supra* note 83, at 4–5 (deeming it uncertain whether *PCAOB* will prove "substantively transformative" or merely a "boundary-enforcing decision").

86. 130 S. Ct. at 3154–57; *See also* Strauss, *supra* note 81, at 2275 ("Strikingly, every reference in the majority opinion to the President's constitutional authority invoked his necessary prerogative to oversee, not to decide, the actions of executive departments").

87. 130 S. Ct. at 3159–60.

88. *Id.* at 3160.

89. Strauss, *supra* note 81, at 2278.

90. *See, e.g.,* Mistretta v. U.S., 488 U.S. 361, 372 (1989).

91. *See* A. L. A. Schechter Poultry Corp. v. U.S., 295 U.S. 495, 521–22, 539–40 (1935); Panama Refining Co. v. Ryan, 293 U.S. 388, 406, 432–33 (1935).

92. 5 U.S.C. §§ 551–569 (2006).

93. *Schechter Poultry*, 295 U.S. at 521–22, 539–41.

94. *See Panama Refining Co.*, 293 U.S. at 431.

95. *Schechter Poultry*, 295 U.S. at 539–40; *Panama Refining Co.*, 293 U.S. at 432–33.

Chapter Eight

1. Terry M. Moe, *The Politicized Presidency, in* THE NEW DIRECTION IN AMERICAN POLITICS 235, 244 (John E. Chubb & Paul E. Peterson eds., 1985).

2. *id.* at 245.

3. FORREST MCDONALD, THE AMERICAN PRESIDENCY: AN INTELLECTUAL HISTORY 329 (1994).

4. *Id.* at 329–31; *See also* PERI E. ARNOLD, MAKING THE MANAGERIAL PRESIDENCY: COMPREHENSIVE REORGANIZATION PLANNING 1905–1996, at 11, 19–21, 27–51 (2d ed. 1998).

5. Budget and Accounting Act of 1921, Pub. L. No. 67-13, 42 Stat. 20.

6. *The Need for a National Budget*, 62d Cong. 1–8, 140 (1912) [hereinafter Taft Commission Report] (message from President William Howard Taft transmitting the Report of Commission on Economy & Efficiency on the subject of the need for a national budget); ARNOLD, *supra* note 4, at 26–51.

7. Taft Commission Report, *supra* note 6, at 1–8, 141–48, 204–6, 217–23.

8. Elena Kagan, *Presidential Administration*, 114 HARV. L. REV. 2245, 2275 (2001); *See also* ARNOLD, *supra* note 4, at 53–54; ADMINISTRATIVE MANAGEMENT IN THE GOVERNMENT OF THE UNITED STATES 15–16 (1937) [hereinafter Brownlow Commission Report].

9. *See* Brownlow Commission Report, *supra* note 8, at 1–3, 43, 47; ARNOLD, *supra* note 4, at 103–7, 116–17; McDonald, *supra* note 3, at 332–34.

10. ARNOLD, *supra* note 4, at 104 (citing Brownlow Commission Report, *supra* note 8, at 6–7).

11. ARNOLD, *supra* note 4, at 107–9; McDonald, *supra* note 3, at 333.

12. ARNOLD, *supra* note 4, at 114; *See also* Reorganization Act of 1939, Pub. L. No. 76–19, 53 Stat. 565.

13. *See, e.g.*, ARNOLD, *supra* note 4, at 85–87; McDONALD, *supra* note 3, at 332–34; Kagan, *supra* note 8, at 2275–82; Peter L. Strauss, *Overseer, or "The Decider"? The President in Administrative Law*, 75 GEO. WASH. L. REV. 696, 701–2, 719–20 (2007).

14. *See, e.g.*, McDONALD, *supra* note 3, at 338–39; Kagan, *supra* note 8, at 2275–76.

15. *See, e.g.*, Robert V. Percival, *Who's in Charge? Does the President Have Directive Authority Over Agency Regulatory Decisions?*, 79 FORDHAM L. REV. 2487, 2487, 2497–2505, 2511–15, 2529–30 (2011); Steven Croley, *White House Review of Agency Rulemaking: An Empirical Investigation*, 70 U. CHI. L. REV. 821, 824–30 (2003); Kagan, *supra* note 8, at 2275–82; Alan B. Morrison, *OMB Interference with Agency Rulemaking: The Wrong Way to Write a Regulation*, 99 HARV. L. REV. 1059, 1061–63 (1986); Strauss, *supra* note 13, at 701–2, 719–20.

16. Taft Commission Report, *supra* note 6, at 1 (message from President Taft).

17. *Id.* at 19–22, 143–44, 147–48, 203–5.

18. *Id.* at 139–42, 219–20.

19. *id.* at 214–23.

20. Brownlow Commission Report, *supra* note 8, at 5.

21. *Id.* at 43.

22. *Id.* at 19–20, 43–44.

23. *id.* at 15, 20–21.

24. *Id.* at 7.

25. *See, e.g.*, Steven G. Calabresi & Saikrishna B. Prakash, *The President's Power to Execute the Laws*, 104 YALE L.J. 541, 595 (1994); Steven G. Calabresi & Kevin H. Rhodes, *The Structural Constitution: Unitary Executive, Plural Judiciary*, 105 HARV. L. REV. 1153, 1158, 1166 (1992).

26. *See infra* notes 29–33 and accompanying text.

27. *See infra* notes 80–82 and accompanying text.

28. *See* Saikrishna B. Prakash, *Fragmented Features of the Constitution's Unitary Executive*, 45 WILLAMETTE L. REV. 701, 716 (2009). Aaron Saiger, too, argues that

a pro-unity reading of the Constitution does not encompass a presidential freedom to "deputize agents on his staff to wield executive power on his behalf just as he could wield it himself." Aaron J. Saiger, *Obama's "Czars" for Domestic Policy and the Law of the White House Staff*, 79 FORDHAM L. REV. 2577 (2011).

29. Statute Limiting the President's Authority to Supervise the Director of the Centers for Disease Control in the Distribution of an AIDS Pamphlet, 12 Op. O.L.C. 47, 57 (1988) (internal citations omitted).

30. *See* PAUL C. LIGHT, MONITORING GOVERNMENT: THE INSPECTORS GENERAL AND THE SEARCH FOR ACCOUNTABILITY 16–17 (1993).

31. Inspector General Legislation, 1 Op. O.L.C. 16, 17 (1977).

32. *See* Memorandum from Peter R. Orszag, Director, Office of Mgmt. & Budget, to the Heads of Dep'ts & Agencies (Jan. 27, 2009), *available at* http://www .whitehouse.gov/sites/default/files/omb/assets/memoranda_fy2009/m09-09.pdf (informing department and agency heads of the "[e]xecutive branch's formal legislative coordination and clearance process" detailed in *Circular No. A-19*, OFFICE MGMT. & BUDGET (1979), *available at* http://www.whitehouse.gov/omb/circulars_ a019 (detailing process by which agencies must submit testimony and reports to the OMB for "coordination and clearance")).

33. Statement on Signing the Omnibus Appropriations Act, 2009, GPO (Mar. 11, 2009), *available at* http://www.gpo.gov/fdsys/pkg/DCPD-200900145/pdf /DCPD-200900145.pdf.

34. *The Amount and Fate of the Oil* 1–8, 14–16 (Nat'l Comm'n on the BP Deepwater Horizon Oil Spill & Offshore Drilling, Working Paper No. 3, 2010).

35. *See, e.g.*, Ben Gemen, *OMB Denies Report It May Have Suppressed Data During BP Spill*, E2 WIRE, THE HILL'S ENERGY & ENVTL. BLOG (Oct. 6, 2010, 3:46 PM), http://thehill.com/blogs/e2-wire/677-e2-wire/123041-white-house -denies-it-suppressed-oil-flow-data.

36. NAT'L COMM'N ON THE BP DEEPWATER HORIZON OIL SPILL & OFFSHORE DRILLING, DEEP WATER: THE GULF OIL DISASTER AND THE FUTURE OF OFFSHORE OIL DRILLING 135 (2010).

37. *Id.* at 146; *See also id.* at 167 (breaking down the numbers a bit further).

38. MARK BOWEN, CENSORING SCIENCE 3, 227–28 (2008).

39. *See* 5 U.S.C. § 553(b)–(d) (2006).

40. *Id.* § 553(c).

41. *See id.* § 706.

42. *Id.* § 706(2)(A), (2)(C).

43. *See, e.g.*, Motor Vehicle Mfrs. Ass'n of the U.S., Inc. v. State Farm Mut. Auto. Ins. Co., 463 U.S. 29, 43 (1983).

44. *See* Sierra Club v. Costle, 657 F.2d 298, 401–2 (D.C. Cir. 1981) (explaining that the Clean Air Act must be based on the record compiled and made public by the EPA).

45. *Cf.* Cary Coglianese, *Presidential Control of Administrative Agencies: A Debate Over Law or Politics?*, 12 U. PA. J. CONST. L. 637, 647–48 (2010) (de-

scribing the many ways in which presidents can and do distance themselves from actions that they required or strongly influenced, "[a]s long as the ink on signed administrative rules or orders comes from pens controlled by the hands of administrators"). I suggest here that presidents can use the same means to distance themselves even from decisions that formally belong to them. For a general discussion of presidential incentives to maintain "plausible deniability" for agency actions and examples of presidents so doing, see, for example, Nina A. Mendelson, *Disclosing "Political" Oversight of Agency Decision Making*, 108 MICH. L. REV. 1127, 1161–63 (2010).

46. *Compare* Saikrishna B. Prakash, *A Critical Comment on the Constitutionality of Executive Privilege*, 83 MINN. L. REV. 1143 (1999) (arguing that executive privilege is not constitutionally required), *with* Saikrishna Prakash, *The Essential Meaning of Executive Power*, 2003 U. ILL. L. REV. 701 (supporting unitary executive theory).

47. *See, e.g.*, Heidi Kitrosser, *Accountability and Administrative Structure*, 45 WILLAMETTE L. REV. 607, 608–9 (2009) (citing use of executive privilege in greenhouse gas rulemaking controversy described below).

48. Franklin v. Mass., 505 U.S. 788 (1992). For discussions to the effect that OIRA's exemption from APA review fosters secrecy, see, for example, Thomas O. McGarity, *Administrative Law as Blood Sport: Policy Erosion in a Highly Partisan Age*, 61 DUKE L.J. 1671, 1735 (2012); Nicholas Bagley & Richard L. Revesz, *Centralized Oversight of the Regulatory State*, 106 COLUM. L. REV. 1260, 1281–82, 1309–10 (2006).

49. Bagley & Revesz, *supra* note 48, at 1311; *See also* Peter M. Shane, *Political Accountability in a System of Checks and Balances: The Case of Presidential Review of Rulemaking*, 48 ARK. L. REV. 161, 172–73 (1995).

50. Shane, *supra* note 49, at 172–73.

51. Mass. v. EPA, 549 U.S. 497, 528–30 (2007).

52. Linda Greenhouse, *Justices Say E.P.A. Has Power to Act on Harmful Gases*, N.Y. TIMES, Apr. 3, 2007, at A1.

53. *See, e.g.*, Darren Samuelsohn & Robin Bravender, *EPA Releases Bush-Era Endangerment Document*, N.Y. TIMES (Oct. 13, 2009), http://www.nytimes .com/gwire/2009/10/13/13greenwire-epa-releases-bush-era-endangerment -document-47439.html; Katherine Boyle, *EPA Docs Show Aborted Effort to Regulate Vehicle GHG Emissions — Waxman*, GREENWIRE (Mar. 12, 2008), http://www .eenews.net/greenwire/stories/62134/search?keyword=katherine+boyle.

54. Felicity Barringer, *White House Refused to Open Pollutants E-Mail*, N.Y. TIMES (June 25, 2008), http://www.nytimes.com/2008/06/25/washington/25epa .html; *See also* Darren Samuelsohn & Katherine Boyle, *Questions Remain About Two Withheld EPA Documents*, GREENWIRE (Aug. 22, 2008), http://www.eenews .net/greenwire/stories/68366/search?keyword=Darren+Samuelsohn+%26+ Katherine+Boyle.

55. *See, e.g.*, Samuelsohn & Boyle, *supra* note 54; Boyle, *supra* note 53.

56. For background on the review process and its history, see, for example, CUR-
TIS W. COPELAND, CONG. RESEARCH SERV., FEDERAL RULEMAKING: THE ROLE
OF THE OFFICE OF INFORMATION AND REGULATORY AFFAIRS 1–9, 18–19, 22–
23 (2009); U.S. GOV'T ACCOUNTABILITY OFFICE, GAO-03-929, RULEMAKING:
OMB'S ROLE IN REVIEWS OF AGENCIES' DRAFT RULES AND THE TRANSPAR-
ENCY OF THOSE REVIEWS 3–4 (2003).

57. *See* Samuelson & Boyle, *supra* note 54; Darren Samuelsohn, *Former EPA
Official Details White House Retreat on GHG Regs*, E&E DAILY (July 18, 2008),
http://www.eenews.net/eedaily/stories/67066/print.

58. *See* Mendelson, *supra* note 45, at 1154.

59. *See* Robin Bravender, *GOP Blasts Admin for Rushing to "Endangerment"
Conclusion*, E&E NEWS PM (Oct. 15, 2009), http://www.eenews.net/eenewspm
/stories/83461/search?keyword=Robin+Bravender; Samuelsohn & Bravender,
supra note 53; Darren Samuelsohn, *Bush Admin Rejects Bid to Unseal EPA Endangerment Finding*, GREENWIRE (Jan. 5, 2009), http://www.eenews.net/greenwire
/stories/72682/search?keyword=Darren+Samuelsohn; Katherine Boyle, *Citing
"Grave Concerns," EPA Misses Deadline to Hand Over Subpoenaed Documents*,
GREENWIRE (Apr. 17, 2008), http://www.eenews.net/greenwire/stories/63486
/search?keyword=Katherine+Boyle.

60. *See generally* Lisa Schultz Bressman & Michael P. Vandenbergh, *Inside the
Administrative State: A Critical Look at the Practice of Presidential Control*, 105
MICH. L. REV. 47 (2006).

61. *id.* at 49–50.

62. *id.* at 97.

63. *id.* at 81.

64. *See* Rena Steinzor, Michael Patoka & James Goodwin, *Behind Closed
Doors at the White House: How Politics Trumps Protection of Public Health,
Worker Safety, and the Environment* 7 (Ctr. for Progressive Reform, White Paper
No. 1111ES, 2011) (citing Exec. Order No. 12,866).

65. *Id.* at 53.

66. *Id.* at 54.

67. *Id.* at 10, 38–42, 45–48, 53.

68. *See* U.S. GOV'T ACCOUNTABILITY OFFICE, GAO-09-205, FEDERAL
RULEMAKING: IMPROVEMENTS NEEDED TO MONITORING AND EVALUATION OF
RULES DEVELOPMENT AS WELL AS TO THE TRANSPARENCY OF OMB REGULA-
TORY REVIEWS 29–38 (2009); U.S. GOV'T ACCOUNTABILITY OFFICE, GAO-03-
929, RULEMAKING: OMB'S ROLE IN REVIEWS OF AGENCIES' DRAFT RULES
AND THE TRANSPARENCY OF THOSE REVIEWS 13–16, 53–57, 94–102, 110–15
(2003).

69. Steinzor, Patoka & Goodwin, *supra* note 64, at 54.

70. *Id.* at 4.

71. Mendelson, *supra* note 45, at 1150–51.

72. *OIRA Letters*, OFF. INFO. & REG. AFF., http://www.reginfo.gov/public/jsp /EO/letters.jsp (last visited Oct. 28, 2013) (listing return, review, and prompt letters).

73. *See, e.g.*, Tuan Samahon, *The Czar's Place in Presidential Administration, and What the Excepting Clause Teaches Us About Delegation*, 2011 U. CHI. LEGAL F. 169, 197–98; Saiger, *supra* note 28, at 2598.

74. *See, e.g.*, *Examining the History and Legality of Executive Branch Czars, Hearing Before the Subcomm. on the Constitution and the S. Comm. on the Judiciary*, 111th Cong. 5–6 (statement of Bradley H. Patterson Jr.) [hereinafter Feingold Hearing Transcript]; *id.* at 30–33 (statement of Sen. Robert C. Byrd, Author, "To Serve the President: Continuity and Innovation in the White House Staff" (2008)); *id.* at 50–51 (statement of T. J. Halstead, Deputy Ass't Director, American Law Division, Congressional Research Service); *id.* at 83–85 (statement of Matthew Spalding, Director, B. Kenneth Simon Center for American Studies, The Heritage Foundation); *id.* at 91–93 (letter from Collins et al. to President Obama).

75. *See, e.g.*, Saiger, *supra* note 28, at 2586–95; Feingold Hearing Transcript, *supra* note 74, at 83 (statement of Matthew Spalding, Director, B. Kenneth Simon Center for American Studies, The Heritage Foundation); *id.* at 91–93 (letter from Collins et al. to President Obama).

76. Colin Sullivan, *Vow of Silence Key to White House-Calif. CAFE Talks*, GREENWIRE (May 20, 2009), http://www.eenews.net/greenwire/stories/78273 /search?keyword=Colin+Sullivan; *See also, e.g.*, Feingold Hearing Transcript *supra* note 74, at 16 (comment by Matthew Spalding expressing some concern over Browner's role in the negotiations).

77. Moe, *supra* note 1, at 244–45.

78. *See, e.g.*, Christopher S. Yoo, Steven G. Calabresi & Anthony J. Colangelo, *The Unitary Executive in the Modern Era*, 90 IOWA L. REV. 601, 660 (2005) (arguing that early civil service laws were consistent with unity as they did not hinder the president's removal power and lamenting that modern civil service laws limit this power and thus are inconsistent with unity); Christopher S. Yoo, Steven G. Calabresi, & Laurence D. Nee, *The Unitary Executive During the Third Half-Century, 1889–1945*, 80 NOTRE DAME L. REV. 1, 11–12, 22–23, 36–37, 108–9 (2004) (arguing that early civil service laws were consistent with unity because they "left the President's removal power largely unfettered"); *id.* at 23 (referring approvingly to Grover Cleveland's refusal to issue an executive order requiring statements of reasons for removing civil servants).

79. *See, e.g.*, Inspector General Legislation, *supra* note 31, at 18; Yoo, Calabresi & Colangelo, *supra* note 78, at 681, 693, 723.

80. *William J. Clinton: Statement on Signing the Lobbying Disclosure Act of 1995*, AM. PRESIDENCY PROJECT (Dec. 19, 1995), http://www.presidency.ucsb.edu /ws/?pid=50917.

81. *William J. Clinton: Statement on Signing the Coast Guard Authorization Act*

of 1996, Am. Presidency Project (Oct. 19, 1996), http://www.presidency.ucsb
.edu/ws/?pid=52132.

82. *See* Strauss, *supra* note 13, at 721 (and sources cited therein); *See also, e.g.*,
Richard J. Pierce Jr., *Saving the Unitary Executive Theory from Those Who Would
Distort and Abuse It: A Review of* The Unitary Executive *by Steven G. Calabresi
and Christopher S. Yoo*, 12 U. Pa. J. Const. L. 593, 612 (2010) (expressing the view
that "statutory limits on the appointment power contained in all of the statutes
that create independent agencies are unconstitutional").

83. *See, e.g.*, Paul C. Light, Thickening Government 46–47, 54, 57, 88–93
(1995); Moe, *supra* note 1, at 259–61; David E. Lewis, *Staffing Alone: Unilateral
Action and the Politicization of the Executive Office of the President, 1988–2004*,
35 Presidential Stud. Q. 496, 497, 499–501 (2005); Patricia Wallace Ingraham,
"You Talking to Me?" Accountability and the Modern Public Service, 38 Pol. Sci. &
Pol. 17, 17–18 (2005); Patricia W. Ingraham, James R. Thompson & Elliot F. Eisenberg, *Political Management Strategies and Political/Career Relationships: Where
Are We Now in the Federal Government?*, 55 Pub. Admin. Rev. 263, 264–66, 270
(1995); Patricia W. Ingraham, *Building Bridges or Burning Them? The President,
the Appointees, and the Bureaucracy*, 47 Pub. Admin. Rev. 425, 426–28 (1987);
See also David J. Barron, *From Takeover to Merger: Reforming Administrative Law
in an Age of Agency Politicization*, 76 Geo. Wash. L. Rev. 1095, 1123–28 (2008)
(citing political science literature to this effect).

84. *See, e.g.*, Moe, *supra* note 1, at 255–61; Barron, *supra* note 83, at 1128–32.

85. *See, e.g.*, Light, *supra* note 83, at 50–53, 57–58; Ingraham, Thompson &
Eisenberg, *supra* note 83, at 265–66; Lewis, *supra* note 83, at 499–501; Ingraham,
supra note 83, at 425–26, 430–32.

86. *See, e.g.*, Nick Gallo & David E. Lewis, *The Consequences of Presidential Patronage for Federal Agency Performance*, 22 J. Pub. Admin. Res. & Theory 219,
222, 238 (2011); David E. Lewis, *Testing Pendleton's Premise: Do Political Appointees Make Worse Bureaucrats?*, 69 J. Pol. 1073, 1074–75, 1083, 1086 (2007); George
A. Krause, David E. Lewis & James W. Douglas, *Political Appointments, Civil Service Systems, and Bureaucratic Competence: Organizational Balancing and Executive Branch Revenue Forecasts in the American States*, 50 Am. J. Pol. Sci. 770,
771–76, 779–85 (2006); Lewis, *supra* note 83, at 501.

87. *See, e.g.*, Gallo & Lewis, *supra* note 86, at 221–23, 230–33, 236–38; Lewis,
supra note 86, at 1081–86; Lewis, *supra* note 83, at 501, 510–11; Ingraham, *supra*
note 83, at 426, 428–32.

88. Krause et al., *supra* note 86, at 779–782, 785.

89. *Id.*

90. For an excellent discussion in the legal literature of the role that nonpoliticals play in facilitating the flow of accurate information within and outside of the
executive branch, see Seth F. Kreimer, *The Freedom of Information Act and the
Ecology of Transparency*, 10 U. Pa. J. Const. L. 1011, 1017–19, 1037–49 (2008).

91. *See, e.g.*, Bowen, *supra* note 38, at 16–17, 66–68, 93–94, 116, 134; Andrew C.

Revkin, Bush vs. the Laureates: *How Science Became a Partisan Issue*, N.Y. TIMES, Oct. 19, 2004, at F9.

92. BOWEN, *supra* note 38, at 93–94; *See also id.* at 116 ("[I]t is unusual for the two highest positions in public affairs [at NASA] to be filled by 'politicals.'").

93. *Id.* at 16–17, 49–50, 67–68, 81, 116–17, 119, 123–28, 136, 140–41.

94. *Id.* at 15–16, 34, 36, 49–50, 56, 124.

95. *Id.* at 117.

96. In 2013, the Supreme Court invalidated § 4 of the act, which determined the jurisdictions to which § 5 applied. Shelby Cnty. v. Holder, 133 S. Ct. 2612 (2013).

97. Joseph D. Rich, Mark Posner & Robert Kengle, *The Voting Section, in* THE EROSION OF RIGHTS: DECLINING CIVIL RIGHTS ENFORCEMENT UNDER THE BUSH ADMINISTRATION 32–34 (William L. Taylor et al. eds., 2007), *available at* http://www.americanprogress.org/issues/2007/03/pdf/civil_rights_report.pdf.

98. *See id.* Joseph Rich served in the Civil Rights Division from 1968–2005 and was Voting Section chief from 1999–2005; Mark Posner served in the Civil Rights Division from 1980–2003 and was in the Voting Section from 1980–1995; Robert Kengle served in the Civil Rights Division Voting Section from 1984–2005, was special counsel and acting deputy chief from 1996–1999, and was deputy chief from 1999–2005.

99. *id.* at 38.

100. *id.* at 36–38.

101. *Id.*

102. *Id.*

103. *See, e.g.*, Steven G. Calabresi, *Some Normative Arguments for the Unitary Executive*, 48 ARK. L. REV. 23, 50–55, 59–70, 81–86 (1995).

104. *See, e.g.*, WALTER J. OLESZEK, CONG. RESEARCH SERV., R42108, CONGRESSIONAL LAWMAKING: A PERSPECTIVE ON SECRECY AND TRANSPARENCY 8–12 (2011); Jason A. MacDonald, *Agency Design and Postlegislative Influence over the Bureaucracy*, 60 POL. RES. Q. 683, 683–84 (2007); Barbara S. Romzek, *Accountability of Congressional Staff*, 10 J. PUB. ADMIN. RES. & THEORY 413, 413–14 (2000).

Chapter Nine

1. JOHN ADAMS, NOVANGLUS ESSAYS, NO. 7 (1775).

2. MICKEY EDWARDS, RECLAIMING CONSERVATISM 10–11 (Kindle edition).

3. *id.* at 10.

4. *id.* at 81.

5. George F. Will, *No Checks, Many Imbalances*, WASH. POST, Feb. 16, 2006, at A27.

6. Bruce Fein, *Restrain This White House*, WASH. MONTHLY, June 10, 2006, at 38–39.

7. *Id.*

8. Ben Smith, *GOP Lawyer Drafts Obama Impeachment*, POLITICO (Apr. 6, 2011), http://www.politico.com/blogs/bensmith/0411/GOP_lawyer_circulates_Obama_impeachment_articles.html.

9. Glenn Greenwald, *Obama the Pioneer*, SALON (Aug. 4, 2012), http://www.salon.com/2012/08/04/obama_the_pioneer/.

10. *See* chapter 4, note 10 and accompanying text.

11. *About the National Security Archive: 25 Years of Opening Governments at Home and Abroad*, NAT'L SECURITY ARCHIVE, http://www.gwu.edu/~nsarchiv/nsa/the_archive.html (last visited Oct. 30, 2013).

12. Seth F. Kreimer, *The Freedom of Information Act and the Ecology of Transparency*, 10 U. PA. J. CONST. L. 1011, 1024 (2008).

13. *id.* at 1011.

14. *Id.* at 1025.

15. *id.* at 1036–45.

16. *id.* at 1047.

17. *Id.* at 1056.

18. *id.* at 1024–25.

19. Brief for Professor Erwin Chemerinsky et al. as Amici Curiae in Support of Hepting and Urging Affirmance at 5–21, Hepting v. AT&T Corp., 539 F.3d 1157 (9th Cir. 2008) (Nos. 06-17132 and 06-17137).

20. Heidi Kitrosser, *What if Daniel Ellsberg Hadn't Bothered?*, 45 IND. L. REV. 89, 91–92, 98–101, 111–20 (2011).

21. *See, e.g.,* Stephen I. Vladeck, *The Espionage Act and National Security Whistleblowing After Garcetti*, 57 AM. U. L. REV. 1531, 1533–37, 1542–46 (2006); Mary Rose Papandrea, *Lapdogs, Watchdogs, and Scapegoats: The Press and National Security Information,* 83 IND. L.J. 233, 245–48 (2008); Mika C. Morse, *Honor or Betrayal? The Ethics of Government Lawyer-Whistleblowers*, 23 GEO. J. LEGAL ETHICS 421, 439–42 (2010); Richard Moberly, *Whistleblowers and the Obama Presidency: The National Security Dilemma*, 16 EMPL. RTS. & EMPLOY. POL'Y J. 51, 81–86 (2012).

22. *See* REPORTERS COMMITTEE FOR FREEDOM OF THE PRESS, http://www.rcfp.org/ (last visited Oct. 30, 2013); *History,* REPORTERS COMMITTEE FOR FREEDOM OF THE PRESS, http://www.rcfp.org/about-us/history (last visited Oct. 30, 2013).

23. *See* REPORTERS COMMITTEE FOR FREEDOM OF THE PRESS, http://www.rcfp.org/about-us/history (last visited Oct. 30, 2013); *See also, e.g., Digital Journalist's Legal Guide,* REPORTERS COMMITTEE FOR FREEDOM OF THE PRESS, http://www.rcfp.org/browse-media-law-resources/digital-journalists-legal-guide (last visited Oct. 30, 2013); *Guides,* REPORTERS COMMITTEE FOR FREEDOM OF THE PRESS, http://www.rcfp.org/browse-legal-resources/guides (last visited Oct. 30, 2013).

24. *See, e.g.,* Press Release, Reporters Committee for Freedom of the Press, Reporters Committee Urges Defense Department to Improve Record Access During Manning Court Martial (Mar. 12, 2012), *available at* http://www.rcfp.org/reporters

-committee-urges-defense-department-improve-record-access-during-manning
-court-martial; David Saleh Rauf, *Shield Law Showdown*, AM. JOURNALISM
REV. (Sept. 2010), *available at* http://www.ajr.org/article.asp?id=4959; Lucy Dal-
glish, *Protecting Reporters Who Protect Their Sources*, NIEMAN REPORTS (Summer 2005), *available at* http://www.nieman.harvard.edu/reports/article/101100
/Protecting-Reporters-Who-Protect-Sources.aspx.

25. *See Litigation,* GOV'T ACCOUNTABILITY PROJ., http://www.whistleblower
.org/program-areas/litigation (last visited Oct. 30, 2013); *Legislation,* GOV'T AC-
COUNTABILITY PROJ., http://www.whistleblower.org/program-areas/legislation
(last visited Oct. 30, 2013).

26. *See, e.g., In the Courts,* AM. CIVIL LIB. UNION, http://www.aclu.org/courts
(last visited Oct. 30, 2013); *Legislative Update,* AM. CIVIL LIB. UNION, http://www
.aclu.org/legiupdate (last visited Oct. 30, 2013).

27. *See* chapter 8, note 28 and accompanying text.

28. STEVEN G. CALABRESI & CHRISTOPHER S. YOO, THE UNITARY EXECU-
TIVE 19 (2008).

29. *id.* at 20.

30. *See* chapter 4, note 10.

31. This slipperiness follows from the weight that unitarians attach to the fact
that the term "executive power" has substantive content, combined with their imprecision in leaping from this point to the conclusion that every aspect and instance of the executive power belongs personally to the president, and their vagueness in defining the executive power. *See infra* chapter 7 for discussion on these
points. Victoria F. Nourse and John P. Figura make a similar point in their review
of Calabresi and Yoo's book:

> Calabresi and Yoo argue that the unitary theory in no way
> "compels" an absolutist model; the theory does not define execu-
> tive power, but asserts only that whatever is an executive power
> must be under presidential control. But this is precisely the prob-
> lem. Even Supreme Court Justices find it difficult to define "exec-
> utive" power. Absent a strong, general limiting principle to coun-
> ter power creep, there appears little reason why Calabresi's and
> Yoo's textualist theory does not provide the opportunity for Pres-
> idents to aggrandize their power by simple assertion that an exer-
> cise of power is "executive." The authors provide no distinguish-
> ing principle; they criticize the George W. Bush presidency for
> taking an "unduly vigorous view of presidential power" and for
> transgressing "the logical boundaries of the unitary executive,"
> but they do not state where the limits of due vigor and logic lie.

Victoria F. Nourse & John P. Figura, *Toward a Representational Theory of the Executive,* 91 B.U. L. REV. 273, 287–88 (2011).

32. *See generally* David J. Barron & Martin S. Lederman, *The Commander in*

Chief at the Lowest Ebb — A Constitutional History, 121 HARV. L. REV. 941 (2008); David J. Barron & Martin S. Lederman, *The Commander-in-Chief at the Lowest Ebb — Framing the Problem, Doctrine, and Original Understanding*, 121 HARV. L. REV. 689 (2008).

33. *See* Heidi Kitrosser, *National Security and the Article II Shell Game*, 26 CONST. COMMENT. 483, 500–21 (2010).

34. *See* Bowsher v. Synar, 487 U.S. 714 (1986). The Court in *Bowsher* deemed congressional control over the comptroller general's removal unconstitutional in light of the job's executive character. In explaining that the job is executive in nature, the Court noted that the comptroller general calculates and prepares a report on required budget cuts. The Court emphasized that the report is not advisory. Rather, it binds the president, who must carry out the specified cuts. It was significant to the Court, in other words, that the comptroller general does not merely report facts or views, but decides what budget cuts are to be made. *id.* at 726–28, 732–33.

35. *See* Saikrishna B. Prakash, *The Essential Meaning of Executive Power*, 2003 U. ILL. L. REV. 701, 793 n.530. Prakash identifies a "possible difference between law execution and information submission." He adds that "[a]s a matter of constitutional policy, perhaps it is problematic when the chief executive's instruments are made to provide information and opinions to Congress that might hinder the chief executive's agenda. . . . As a matter of constitutional law, however, perhaps Congress may seek the independent opinions of the executive branch." *id.* Lessig and Sunstein, who embrace unity for functional reasons, seem more definitively to take the view that "people who perform merely investigatory and reportorial functions" do not execute the law. Lawrence Lessig & Cass R. Sunstein, *The President and the Administration*, 94 COLUM. L. REV. 1, 114 (1994).

36. *See, e.g.,* CALABRESI & YOO, *supra* note 28, at 366–68.

37. *See* chapter 8 at notes 39–44 and accompanying text.

38. I allude, of course, to the well-known phrase "eternal vigilance is the price of liberty." For a discussion of the phrase's origins, see, e.g., Thomas L. Jipping, 2 LIBERTY U. L. REV. 419, 419–20 (2008).

Index

tion Act requests and, 104–5; journalists subpoenaed under, 110–12; leakers and, 4, 110, 111–12, 125; Office of Information and Regulatory Affairs and, 188; Office of Management and Budget and, 175; presidentialism and, 9, 201; prosecutions for classified speech and, 107–8; screening of congressional testimony by, 181; secret law and, 104–5; state secrets privilege and, 4, 98, 100; Terrorist Surveillance Program and, 125; Bob Woodward and classified information from, 64

Office of Information and Regulatory Affairs (OIRA), 186–88, 263n48

Office of Legal Counsel (OLC), 5–6, 92–93, 102–6, 180, 241n90

Office of Management and Budget (OMB): climate change research and, 182–83, 187; Deepwater Horizon oil spill and, 182; delegation of power to, 198; information clearance requirements and, 180–83; naming of, 175; presidential control and, 179; presidential enhancements of power and, 173; review of agency rulemakings by, 175, 185–86, 187, 188; screening of congressional testimony by, 181, 262n32; unitary executive theory and, 180

OIRA. *See* Office of Information and Regulatory Affairs (OIRA)

OLC. *See* Office of Legal Counsel (OLC)

OMB. *See* Office of Management and Budget (OMB)

Opinions Clause, 148, 152, 158–61

originalism: appointment and removal powers and, 149; conservative ideology and, 28; core premises of, 37; determinism and, 25–29, 32–33, 35; discretion vs., 25–26, 28, 215n18; First Amendment and, 59; framers' intent vs. original public meaning and, 26, 33, 37–39, 75–76, 80, 215–16n24, 219n70, 220n83; Free Press Clause and, 227n69; hypothetical readers and, 32–33; vs. judicial activism, 27, 29, 215n13; judicial restraint and, 28; limitations on, 26–27; neutrality and, 25–26, 27, 29, 215n18; old vs. new, 26–27, 32–33, 38; origins of, 24–25, 215n16; overreach in, 32–33, 75–76; predictive traits of, 28; presidential control and, 149–51;

presidential supremacy and, 31–32, 71–72, 218n61; public discourse vs. conventional academic wisdom on, 27–28, 216n28; text and principle of Constitution and, 40; thick vs. thin directives and, 39, 221n89; traditional moral beliefs and, 28, 216n34; Vesting Clause and, 70

Pacificus. *See* Hamilton, Alexander
Panama Refining Co. v. Ryan, 170
Pattee v. Ga. Ports Auth., 252–53n119
Paulsen, Michael, 33, 81, 219n68, 220n83, 231–32n17, 241n88
PCAOB case. See Free Enterprise Fund v. Public Company Accounting Oversight Board
Pentagon Papers, 131, 203
Persily, Nathanial, 28
Peterson, Todd David, 225n55
Pickering v. Board of Education, 134, 138–40, 141–42, 250–51n95
Pierce, Richard J., Jr., 266n82
Pike Committee investigations, 30
Pildes, Richard, 55, 260n85
Pinckney, Charles, 78, 159
Poindexter, John, 4
Posner, Eric, 13–14, 218n62
Posner, Mark, 267n98
Pozen, David E., 224n44
Prakash, Saikrishna: on broad powers of Congress, 222n4; on Commander-in-Chief Clause, 82–83; on early claims of executive privilege, 90; on law execution vs. information submission, 270n35; on limits of president's powers, 204; on presidential primacy in foreign affairs, 230–31n9; on unitary executive theory, 254n9
presidency: Congress's power to punish the president and, 46–47; council-less, 152–55, 159–60, 162; Electoral College and, 258n58; fettered vs. unfettered, 71, 74; impeachment and, 46–47; information flow and, 176–77; overseer vs. decider role and, 147–48, 150, 178, 260n86; political responsiveness and, 257n56, 258n58, 259n68; power of bully pulpit and, 55; power of veto and, 55; secrecy as energetic trait of, 91; structure of, 152; substantive accountability